# 这样地活着
Living like this.

齐帆齐 著

BILLSON International Ltd.

Published by
**Billson International Ltd**
27 Old Gloucester Street
London
WC1N 3AX
Tel:(852)95619525

Website:www.billson.cn
E-mail address:cs@billson.cn

First published 2024

Produced by Billson International Ltd
CDPF/01

ISBN 978-1-80377-113-7

©Hebei Zhongban Culture Development Co.,Ltd All rights reserved.

The original content within this product remains the property of Hebei Zhongban Culture Development Co.,Ltd, and cannot be reproduced without prior permission. Updates and derivative works of the original content remain the property of Hebei Zhongban. and are provided by Hebei Zhongban Culture Development Co.,Ltd.

The authors and publisher have made every attempt to ensure that the information contained in this book is complete, accurate and true at the time of printing. You are invited to provide feedback of any errors, omissions and suggestions for improvement.

Every attempt has been made to acknowledge copyright. However, should any infringement have occurred, the publisher invites copyright owners to contact the address below.

Hebei Zhongban Culture Development Co.,Ltd
Wanda Office Building B, 215 Jianhua South Street, Yuhua District, Shijiazhuang City, Hebei province, 2207

## 这样地活着

只有相对，没有绝对 / 003

初中学历的宝妈到成为月入 1.3 万 + 的小城斜杠青年 / 008

农村女子从 0 学写作到出书多本，月入 3 万 + 成长之路 / 014

我的闺蜜 / 017

李娟的《我的阿勒泰》再次点燃了我对写作的热情 / 025

往事如烟，卖菜的往事 / 029

那年，我家四处借钱买来的缝纫机 / 035

只和别人学，只同自己比 / 038

陪母亲交公粮的陈年往事 / 041

我曾无比渴望远离家乡 / 044

我们都不知天高地厚过 / 046

我曾住过的城中村印象 / 050

从砍柴工到搞工程的小舅 / 054

开花甲米粉店的温州人 / 058

关于泥土 / 061

记录生活，就是在记录历史 / 065

难忘的童年趣事 / 071

记忆里的门前小路 / 075

我们都是年味变淡的"稀释者" / 078

因为没有学历，我用了18年才活成一个体面的普通人 / 081

本来无一物，每进一寸都是欢喜 / 086

写作最终是思想洞见和心智模式的比拼 / 090

从来不用想起，永远也不会忘记 / 092

我用7年时间从底层生活爬了起来，成为内容创业者 / 097

中年后常恨过去的自己 / 099

文学是世道人心最后的温暖 / 102

时常感到彷徨 / 106

我的村庄，我的梦 / 110

自我疗愈之路 / 113

每个人都在自己的命运里沉浮 / 116

无常才是人生，好心态最重要 / 121

你有这样的房东阿姨吗？ / 125

关于门前的那条火车路 / 128

奶奶陪伴的童年时光 / 130

记忆里的粉蒸肉 / 132

阅读与智者对谈，与灵魂共舞 / 134

岁月如歌，每个人的人生都是一部书 / 136

那些远去的手艺人 / 144

老屋和土灶台 / 147

所有的一切都有它的局限性 / 149

抓住一次风口能少奋斗10年？ / 154

人强得过命吗？在命运面前，休论公道…… / 159

命运之神的力量 / 164

那一年在镇上学裁缝的时光 / 171

往事如烟——继父篇 / 174

我就是矛盾的人 / 178

她先天残疾，出身农村，在网络创业第3年时就实现年入百万 / 180

# Living like this.

Only relative, no absolute / 187

A treasure mother with a junior high school education has become a small town slash youth with a monthly income of 13000 +. / 192

Rural women learn writing from 0 to more than one book, and enter the of 30000 + growth path every month. / 198

My best friend / 201

Li Juan's "My Altay" once again ignited my enthusiasm for writing / 210

The past is like smoke, the past of selling vegetables / 214

That year, my family borrowed money to buy sewing machine / 220

Only learn from others, only compare with yourself / 224

The Old Past of Accompanying Mother to Hand in Public Grain / 227

I was so eager to be away from home   / 231

We all don't know how high the sky is.   / 234

Impression of the village in the city where I once lived   / 238

From a firewood cutter to a little uncle in engineering.   / 242

Wenzhou people in the shop of flowering rice noodles   / 247

About the soil   / 250

To record life is to record history.   / 254

Unforgettable childhood fun   / 260

The path in front of the memory   / 265

We are all "diluters" of the fading taste of the year"   / 268

Because I had no academic qualifications, it took me 18 years to live as a decent ordinary person.   / 271

Originally there was nothing, every inch was joy.   / 277

Writing is ultimately a contest between insight and mental models.   / 282

Never remember, never forget   / 285

It took me 7 years to get up from the bottom of my life and become a content entrepreneur.   / 290

After middle age often hate past self   / 292

Literature is the last warmth of the world   / 295

Often feel loss   / 300

My village, my dream   / 304

The path of self-healing   / 307

Everyone is in their own fate.   / 310

impermanence is life, good attitude is the most important   / 316

Do you have such a landlord aunt? / 320

About the train road in front of the door / 323

Childhood with Grandma / 325

In the memory of steamed pork / 327

Reading and Wise Men Talk about to, Dance with Soul / 329

The years are like songs, and everyone's life is a book. / 331

Those far away craftsmen / 340

Old house and earth hearth / 344

Everything has its limitations / 347

Can you seize a tuyere and fight for 10 years less? / 353

Are people strong enough to live? In the face of fate, stop talking about justice... / 358

The power of the fate god / 364

That year in the town school tailor time / 371

The past is like smoke–stepfather / 374

I am a contradictory person. / 378

She was born with a disability and was born in the countryside. In her third year of online entrepreneurship, she achieved an annual income of one million. / 380

这样地活着

## 只有相对,没有绝对

### 01

城中村,顾名思义,既是城市也是农村,是一个尴尬的存在。对于城市的管理者来说,他们恨不得将其迅速铲平,换成统一的高楼大厦,这样市容和政绩都会显得更好。但对于我们这些外来打工者来说,我们希望有更多的城中村,因为那里有更便宜的房子可以租住。

我曾在城中村居住了七年。2008年和2009年,我在温州鹿城区黎明工业区附近的一个城中村里,我们在一排活动铁板房下卖早点。那时,我住的房子每月租金是250元。

2007年,我在温州茶山区大学城附近的一家女装厂工作。每周末有一天休息,我就会坐公交车回到城中村的店里改善伙食。我们组的一位湖北大姐总是羡慕地说,我周末回家有青菜吃,家里还开着店。

我们组组长的妻子专门负责上袖子,这是工价最高的一道工序,大家都暗暗羡慕她,因为她每月的工资高达三四千元人民币。2007年时,我最高的一次工资是2000多元,通常在一千四五左右,这比我之前在福建做外贸服装的待遇要好很多,每周还有单休,晚上工作到十点半就结束了。

我所在的温州服装厂是生产品牌服装的,衣服在国内外的专卖店都有销售，工艺要求特别高，工作压力也很大，稍有不慎就可能需要返工。

为什么能吃到青菜会让人羡慕呢？因为那个女装厂每天下班铃一响，我们就争先恐后地冲向食堂，像一群刚从饥饿中释放出来的人。只有这样，我们才能在食堂里打到更好的菜，新鲜青菜非常有限，来得晚的人就没有了。

食堂里放着一桶汤，里面是细碎的鸡蛋和西红柿，有时候是紫菜。我们为了能捞到稍微大块一点的鸡蛋和西红柿，常常要争抢。放汤的铁桶周围常常围着八九个人，只是为了能捞到稍微大块一点的西红柿和鸡蛋。

厂里的伙食费每月150元，从工资中扣除。老板想从饭钱中赚取利润，所以伙食非常简陋。所谓的两荤一素一汤，两条一寸长的小鱼就算是一个荤菜；两三个小辣椒蘸一点鸡蛋沫子，就算是辣椒炒鸡蛋。青菜通常只有来得早的人才能吃到。所谓的汤就是我之前描述的那种清汤。

也许有人会问，为什么不去饭店吃？因为出去吃饭要走很多路，耽误时间，而且外面的饭菜更贵。在食堂吃饭，一个月150元就足够了，如果在外面吃，这点钱远远不够。

我们同样生活在这片蓝天下，同在这片辽阔的土地上，我们生而为人，但我们的人生却各不相同。每个人的人生都像一部厚厚的书。

我的一些读者和文友，他们几代人都生活在城市里，看到我写的这些经历，可能会觉得不可思议，但这确实是真实发生的事情。

当我读到丁燕的《工厂女孩》系列时，我也感到震惊和心痛。书中描述的很多是95后的生活，他们在地下啤酒厂、模具厂工作，双手长年都是破的，每天都要贴创可贴。还有地下黑工厂，工人们工作半年后身体就会受到伤害，然后换一批新人。还有注塑厂工人断脚趾的事故……

我是 80 后，也许还能理解这样的生活。但难道现在还有工厂是这样的吗？社会上还有这么多人过着这样的生活吗？

2008 年和 2009 年，我住在工业区的城中村里，我的邻居是一个河南的女子，她和我同龄，长得非常漂亮，瓜子脸，皮肤白皙透红。每天早上，我都要在天还没亮的时候起床做事，心里总是羡慕那些还在睡觉的朋友。我堂嫂有假期，工作体面，早上九点才上班。

然而，我所厌恶的生活却是别人所羡慕的。我的邻居总是羡慕我，她带着两个儿子，一个三岁，一个一岁多，肚子里还有一个。她的丈夫在温州车站做搬运工，每月收入 1300 元，又特别爱打牌。她几乎没有什么闲钱，有时候还要捡垃圾瓶子卖。

她经常傍晚去超市买打折的西红柿和其他处理的菜品。她的一些老乡羡慕她，因为她和我们关系好，常常能吃到免费的花卷和馒头。我们家还卖鲜奶，如果剩下了，也会半卖半送给她家。

现在回想起来，即使是在工厂和城中村，每个人的生活也各不相同。你习以为常的事情，可能是别人所羡慕的。

每次想起我在温州住过的城中村，我都会想起那位漂亮的邻居，想起那个住房楼，还有店铺房子一大排的铁板房。后来，那个工业区要拆迁，我们就搬走了。她可能也回老家生了第三个孩子。当时有温州本地人想收养她的第三个孩子，但她没有同意。

那时候通讯不发达，我和那位邻居没有留下联系方式，就这样消失在了各自的人生里。

人生漫长，过客匆匆。

## 02

我们合肥有一位 60 后的 S 老师，她也曾出版过书籍。她过去曾在合肥某知名国企工作，也曾担任过本科院校的老师。

S 老师阅读了我的作品《追梦路上，让灵魂发光》后，在微信上给我发来了长篇留言："帆齐，读完你的书，我久久不能平静。你和你书中的人物让我看到了一个全新的世界。我难以想象你们比我年轻许多，却有着如此多的艰难经历。你们如此坚韧，就像巨石下的小草。如果换成其他人，可能早已被压垮，沉入泥潭，难以再爬起来。我对你们深感感动，也非常佩服……"

在与她聊天的过程中，我了解到，她18岁来到省城上学后便定居在合肥。她家祖上四代都是教师，她的曾祖父是位私塾先生，在地方上享有很高的声望。

她的丈夫曾是博士生导师，由于参与了某个重要项目，在2019年时曾被我们国家的最高领导人接见。

与 S 老师相比，我感到无比感慨。我比她年轻约 20 岁，但她家祖上四五代的学识和起点，已经远远超出了我目前的成就。我的奋斗目标可能还不及她的起点。

这让我深刻体会到，人与人之间没有可比性，只有相对而言，没有绝对的标准。

如果不是因为在合肥参加线下会议，不是因为写作和出版书籍，如果我还在工厂工作，我与 S 老师可能永远不会有交集，我们不在同一个社交圈，也没有机会认识。

然而，结识之后，我们互相赠送了各自签名的书籍，并约定在其他学习活动中再次相聚。有一次，我去她家附近的小区办事，S老师热情地邀请了我们姐妹和其他文友一起共进晚餐，进行了一次愉快的小聚。

我们都是热爱学习和成长的人，经常参加读书会、演讲比赛等活动，很快就能打成一片。

尽管她早已实现了财务自由，但她依然不断挑战自我，积极融入年轻人群体，学习了解新事物。

我们都在自己的生命轨迹上，修炼着各自的人生课题，体验着各自的悲欢离合。

# 初中学历的宝妈到成为月入 1.3 万 + 的小城斜杠青年

我的二妹齐梅齐，是这个世界上长得和我最为相似的人。无数人都说看我们简直分不清。她是 85 后的初中学历宝妈，目前居住在 18 线小县城，月收入超过 1.3 万元，享有五险一金，工作时间为朝九晚五，周末双休。（她正在自考大专学历，来自安徽舒城县）

二妹今年才正式进入职场的第三年。在刚刚过去的 2 月份，她的主业保底工资为 2200 元，标书提成 4010 元，副业剪辑视频收入 4575 元，企业人力资源管理师补贴 900 元，再加上快团团购佣金和朋友圈分销佣金等，累计月收入超过 1.3 万元，并且享有五险一金。对于别人来说，这样的月收入可能并不稀奇，但对于我妹来说，这却是值得记录的成就。

回忆起年少时的二妹齐梅齐：

小时候，周围的人都说她是我们姐妹三人中长得最齐整的，也是亲戚们喜欢夸赞的对象，嘴甜且特别勤快，相比之下，我们显得黯然无光，毫无亮点。在年少无知的岁月里，我对她充满了不屑和反感，总觉得她是在刻意卖乖讨喜。而我则是最调皮捣蛋的那一个，总是爱和大人对着干。

她总是全力以赴地扮演好每一个角色，不管有多疲惫或琐碎，她都享受其中，乐在其中。我妹从小就是一个非常细致的人，这或许是天性，也或许是她处女座追求完美的心态所致。

当年我们一起在福建的服装厂工作时，厂领导经常拿着我二妹做的衣服，指着让老师傅们看："都来看看，这是刚来学徒做的衣服，这么平整，一点线头都没有……"

我二妹手背上有一个小小的疤痕，她说那是当年和我在一起学做衣服时，因为我发脾气用剪线头的小剪刀戳到她的手背。我自己都忘记了，原来在青春时期我是如此的暴戾，对最亲近的人也能如此粗暴。我甚至不记得用小剪刀戳她手的事。可能是在生气时不小心戳到了她，她没有及时缩回手，真的伤到了手背。

随着年岁的增长，我反而变得越来越平和了。

更早一些，当我们还是学生时，周末和假期，我们会在村庄堂哥的厂里打工，暑假也会去隔壁小队厂里烘啤酒套。二妹烘出来的啤酒套总是比其他人的质量更好，她也是老板娘夸赞的对象，做出来的东西平整、整洁、看着舒服。

同样的一双白鞋，我二妹穿上三个月，看起来还是白白净净的。

二妹先后做过好几年的服装厂工人，也曾经担任过导购员、服务员、营业员等工作。

她是如何在人到中年成为一名斜杠青年，在18线小城还能月入过万的呢？虽然二妹起点低，没有进过高中校门，但她一边做宝妈，一边坚持学习。她照顾孩子、做家务，同时接摄影业务、做标书、剪辑视频、做自媒体人等，累计月收入至少一万元，未来大概率会更多。

作为旁观者，也是她姐姐，回顾她这几年的成长之路，历历在目。

## 1. 首先是浸泡在网络好学积极的圈子里

我是在2016年接触自媒体，从零开始尝试写作，后来签约简书和百度平台，做社群出书等，成为自由工作者至今。写作大半年后，我搭建了一些微信社群。二妹也在我的几个群里，尽管她一个人带两个孩子，每天忙得头昏脑胀，但还是每天抽空看看群里的动态，阅读一些好文章。加上看到我的一路成长，无形中都看到了互联网的机遇，对网络运营知识也能稍微懂一点。

那些年，老家人对她的评价是："多少家庭两个人带一个小孩都叫苦不迭，齐梅齐一个人带两个孩子，还搞得这么整洁精致，从不抱怨，抽空还会看看书，真是了不起。"

2. 自身的内驱力

虽然她家人从没有像有的农村人说儿媳在家多年，花了家里钱之类的话语，但二妹想还是得做点自己喜欢的事，实现自我价值，不想过手心朝上的日子。她也尝试写过好几万字，出了本电子书，她说没有我对文字那种天生的热爱，她认为自己更喜欢摄影。于是她从各种网站上每天看美图，提升美感，后来又攒钱买了部相机，自学捣鼓，如何构图，如何找合适的拍摄角度等。

她拍摄了孩子的老爷爷，拍摄山上的树木，自己做的各种美食。她所拍摄的鸡蛋照片登上了某摄影杂志，她又上传图片到视觉中国网站和图虫网站，成为这两个平台的签约作者。这些都是她业余自学的小确幸，也给她带来了信心和动力。

那几年，她有时在研究自媒体或捣鼓照片时，闹钟一响就得立马起身接娃烧饭等，一天闹钟响起多次，周末孩子要上一些特长班，每天接送就是八趟。她无怨无悔，乐在其中。哪怕是在一地鸡毛、兵荒马乱的生活里，二妹依然争分夺秒地学习探索自己的热爱，想为自己的未来找到更多可能性。

3. 不断探索认知边界

大前年，两孩子稍大些了，二妹的时间宽裕起来，她自考二建，接摄影约拍，接视频剪辑，做标书等。那家做标书的公司就在她的本小区，比较自由，标书是按提成结算。

现在，二妹在小县城月入也可破万元，不差于大学生了。曾经我们都无比羡慕上了大学的人，觉得他们是高不可攀的存在，都是天之骄子。现在也有很多重点大学出身的人，反而很佩服我们，觉得我们身上的学习力很强，韧劲十足，能量满满。

果然学习力比学历更重要，成长比成功更重要。二妹齐梅齐成为斜杠中年，在家也能接到这么多工作业务，离不开她前期的积累铺垫。由于摄影的练习，学剪辑上手也比较顺手，又由于这些综合能力，使她做网络相关的工作入门都很快。

她和几个朋友一起应聘县城的兼职直播工作，她很顺利地就被通过了。下午下班，她骑电瓶车去小区附近的直播基地，兼职直播两小时，卖家纺产品，30元一小时加上提成，两小时也有七八十到一百多元收入。

后来老板家看她朋友圈会摄影又会剪辑，就把抖音账号的几个视频外包给我二妹做，拍摄加剪辑，每天发布6个视频，每个抖音视频10秒左右。我二妹每天花费3小时多，副业视频剪辑月入四五千元。（因上月是过年边上，平常会更多点）

二妹后来就没有兼职直播了，拍摄和剪辑视频至今，时间自由度更高了。她还参加过好几次安徽合肥格桑花公益摄影工作，助力留守儿童和公益事业，结识一些摄影界的老乡们。她还是我们当地的摄影协会会员。

现在，她时常也会接一些县城里面的静物拍摄，电商产品拍摄。卖家快递来产品，让她拍摄再发原图过去，再结算佣金，产品均是赠送。她还接过老家面条厂、养鸡场拍摄照片和视频制作等全套业务。

二妹第一次承接老家那个养鸡场的视频制作时，压根自己没做过视频，完全是靠网络搜索流程步骤，一步一步地摸索去剪辑成功的。一个人成事与否，和他的行动力和决心是息息相关的。

她还做美食博主。二妹会做日式鳗鱼饭、鲍鱼红烧肉、泰式菠萝饭、珍珠肉丸等，中餐西餐都有喜欢研究，其实也是在各个自媒体平台观摩自学的。她把自己亲手做的美食发布在某厨房APP，很快也有几万粉丝，小红书也有几千粉。有时也能接到一些商家合作，她靠自学几年拥有了多维度能力，即便不依靠某个公司组织，在家自由办公，可做着自己喜欢的工作，也能生活得丰盛优雅，且未来有更多想象空间。

从我二妹的成长故事中可以看出，哪怕身在偏远小城，哪怕是起点极低的人，哪怕是人到中年有两个娃的牵绊，只要学会拥抱网络，拥有自学能力，找到内心热爱，也可借助网络的杠杆传播，让自己活得充实丰盈。

他们公司标书按提成，人际简单，没有标书时就研究自媒体和一些软件学习。没有职场的内耗，没有人际关系的繁杂，只是一心研究所喜爱之事，还能拥有高于当地的平均工资待遇，已经是锦上添花了。

现在的自媒体足以承载任何一种形式的才华，在这个时代不存在有怀才不遇这回事。现在的网络提供了无数种学习途径，只要你愿意，只要你想学。即便你真没有一点专长和热爱，你也可以边学边分享，一边提升能力，扩大人脉圈，再去接单赚钱，或者注册自媒体账号，持续输出内容，积累粉丝读者用户，形成滚雪球效应，打造出个人品牌，这些都是无价财富。

人生不设限，未来才无限！世界以痛吻我，也要报之以歌。即便是再疲惫琐碎的生活里，也有人仍在追求英雄梦想！一个人的成长上行归根结底，最终是通过提升自我客观条件，丰富自己的精神世界，从而让自己拥有更多的生命自由度，并实现人生价值。

# 农村女子从0学写作到出书多本，月入3万+成长之路

光阴似箭，日月如梭，转眼间我从0开始写作已经第9个年头了。我是从0粉丝、0点赞、0关注开始，手上没有任何存稿。那时，我特别羡慕那些手上有存稿的人，感觉那就像是丰厚的"家底"。我完全依靠临时"挤牙膏"似的去写文章，常常是公众号没有内容可发。

我从开始一周写800字都非常困难，到现在能够持续输出，轻松日更三千字，也是非常容易的事。只要我能写得出来，就能随时出版。多年前我就幻想过，未来书架上有一格全部放自己的书。现在，梦想仿佛近在眼前。

写着写着，一晃这么多年过去了，时间是一堵高墙，你跨过艰难险阻翻过它，你就可以打败很多同行者。当年和我一起写作的文友，坚持到现在的寥寥无几。而我，成为坚持到最后并吃到一些红利的幸运儿。

我是凭着一种死磕到底的精神，只要写不死，就往死里写。没有纠结，没有内耗，不怕嘲笑，不怕打击。别人说我没读几年书，是不是有很多字不认识？我沉默不语。当时我每周都在床头贴很多成语、生僻字，每天早晚反复看并背诵。过一周再换一批，如此循环。

我就要做个打不死的小强，岩石下面的小草，相信上天终究会厚待我。曾经做梦都想成为一个自由工作者，命运终究让我实现了，不用通勤打卡，不用坐班，不用被区域空间束缚。我常笑说，我每天的工作就是读书、写书、卖书、玩手机。

那是因为我持续在写作，身处自媒体的大好时代。写作一年多，我

终于实现了签约两家平台。一年半过后，我已经成为全职自由工作者，并且签了出书合同。

于是，我的第一本书《追梦路上，让灵魂发光》出版了，并且加印了，还有幸在美国新泽西州图书馆展示。再到后来，我注册了文化传媒公司，经营多平台，文章先后上稿人民网、《哲思》《青年文学家》《作家文苑》《女友》、学习强国等杂志报纸和网络平台。

我出版了《人人都能学会的写作变现指南》，因为这本书全部是实操经验分享，干货非常多，写的都是我所做到的。我不是学院派出身，我是野路子江湖派作者，完全一路摸索实践成长。这本书在各个平台搜索关键词都是在榜首。几乎每天都有读者因为这本书联系我。看到有这么多人因这本书得到启发，开启了梦想之路，我觉得这是无上的荣耀，甚至超越了金钱。

还有一本书《只做唯一的我，不做第二个谁》也多次参加了北京线下大型书展活动。《左手月亮，右手六便士》这本书主要写到一些数字游民在这个互联网时代的生存状态。在内卷和躺平之间，应该还有怎样的一种生活？这本书的很多内容会给我们一些启发和思考。

这个世界上只有一种成功，那就是以自己喜欢的方式过一生。于我而言，最喜欢的当然就是写作了。因为写作，我摆脱了在工厂里日复一日、单调枯燥的缝纫工生活；也跳出了在城中村起早贪黑地出摊卖早点的摊主生活。

如今，只需要在家里拿着手机、笔记本，每天读读书，写写文，接商稿，做社群等，就可以实现月入5万+。每个人都有一项能力是超过1万个人的，挖掘找到自身的优势所在。爱好加坚持就等于天赋所在。无用即大用，你所热爱的事物终会在某一天给予你丰厚的回报。

沉下心好好打磨自己的写作技能，再加上一些商业思维，充分利用互联网的优势。互联网可以把一个普通人的能力放大100倍、1000倍。

比如，我身边就有这样一群人，他们出身普通，却有着一颗不甘平庸的进取心。

她们有的喜欢追星，去横店待了一个多月，后来写了一本书，一上市就卖了 30 多万册，靠这本书实现了人生的第一桶金。还有放弃了令人羡慕的体制内工作，却通过互联网自媒体实现年入 50 万+。有的喜欢收藏崖柏，靠着自己深入研究钻研，成为该领域的行家。崖柏资产大 9 位数，教人鉴赏，售卖手作，还出了专业书籍。

这些人不分年龄、性别、职业，完全凭着自己对某个领域的兴趣，脚踏实地地精进提升，加上一定的商业认知，在互联网上积极勇敢地展示自己，打造了个人品牌，实现了个体崛起，从而实现了一手白月光，一手面包香，过上了自由自在的生活。

互联网让很多底层普通人实现了突破式成长，多记录，多展示，积极借助自媒体的力量，打造个人品牌。勇敢地做自己，以自己喜欢的方式过生活，可以参考《左手月亮，右手六便士》。

# 我的闺蜜

我的闺蜜云儿生得瘦小，皮肤白皙，天资聪明，反应敏捷，对人非常实在和热情。

截至今年，她去世已经6年了，她的生命永远定格在36岁那年的生日那天。

## 01

在美好的青春岁月里，我们在同一个车间做服装。做衣服的车位是面对面，我们住在同一个宿舍，一起搭伙烧饭，一起择菜收拾刷碗。可以说我们24小时形影不离，一起度过了快乐的几年时光。

有空时，云儿能把胡萝卜切成花瓣状，能把洋葱雕刻成玫瑰花模样。她做事既好又快。同样是买碗，她会选择非常精致的。我没有概念，在我内心，实惠是第一，但她说这样每天快到吃饭时就会心生喜悦。那对碗我们一直用到离开那家工厂，的确让人心情很好。

云儿总能在有限的条件下，尽可能地收拾得很精致，很有自己的生活品位，也很会享受生活的点点滴滴。每每想到她如此热爱生活，热情大气，总把快乐微笑挂在脸上，这般美好的人就这样早早没有了，心痛感觉萦绕心头。

在我这半生里数次经历身边人过早地死亡，常觉得自己身上是否有自带某种前世罪孽和不祥的神秘力量，还是上帝对我的另一种残忍方

Living like this.

式？命运的地图里是否暗藏着深不可测的威力？我想问上苍这是为什么？谁能帮我解答？

还记得2018年7月的某天，我收到云儿先生的微信，说云儿在合肥住院，医生们估计很不乐观，大概率是肺癌晚期。还发了张她睡在病床上的照片。我顿时脑子一懵，心头一酸，患肺癌晚期？不久前我们不是还见过面，还聚会了吗？怎么和癌症扯上关系了？我觉得不可思议，眼泪忍不住地流下来。

这病不是爱抽烟的老头才可能得的吗？是不是搞错了？云儿还这么年轻，又从不抽烟，没有任何不良嗜好。命运是不是在开玩笑？肯定搞错了？

第二天，我从老家去合肥肿瘤医院看闺蜜云儿。她骨瘦如柴，面色蜡黄，真的是皮包着骨头。她看到我打了声招呼，示意让我坐下，讲了几句话后，她往床上一躺马上就睡着了，好像特别累，没有了能量。仅仅两个月没见面，怎么突然成这样了？那天在等穿刺检查的最终确定结果。

## 02

云儿，和我不是一个村庄的人，她家在我家稻田下面的河对面的生产队。她比我大一点，高一届，但我从小就知道下面村庄里有这样的一个人，有时在上下学路上也会常看到她。大家都知道她学习很好，非常聪明，学校校长和老师都很喜欢她，每次别人还在埋头考试，她总能第一个做完卷子出来。她和老师们在操场上打羽毛球玩，试卷还都是满分。

自从我在隔壁堂哥厂里打临工，便和云儿接触多起来，她那年中考完，也来到我们村庄这边上班。还记得她收到了高中录取通知书，但是她家里没钱供她读书，她就把通知书放到水里漂走了。

她家姐妹五个，她是最小的一个，她大姐姐的儿子（云儿的外甥）比她还大。她二姐在家里招亲，有两个孩子，都是老实巴交的农民，在那时生活条件也都比较艰难。她有位三姐，还在小姑娘的年纪就和我们村里另外两位女生一起去了尼姑庵。据说她们的理念是今生没有好命，为了好好修行来世。

在我读小学的时候就听到这个村庄新闻，三个女生一起相约去尼姑庵。有一位是我们小学附近开鞭炮加工厂家的女儿，还是特别漂亮的大美女，我还见过她；剩下两位其中有一个是云儿的三姐。貌似最后一次云儿跟我聊到她三姐的时候，她三姐正在五台山，还跟我说过她三姐的法号，现在我也记不清了。

虽然我的闺蜜云儿是家里最小的一个，但是她却不能享受到任何更好的照顾，因为她父母年迈体弱，姐姐们各自忙于自己的生活，无暇顾及她，家庭没有任何资源和生产资料惠及她这位老小。初中的时候，她知道自己家里没钱读书，每次要零花钱和学费都是七拼八凑，很痛苦，所以对读书也就无所谓了，主要也是当时没人引导、强调读书的重要性。

可是即便在这样无所谓的心态下上学，她也收到了高中录取通知书，如果生在稍微好的家庭，凭她的天资完全是另一番景象。我当年就读的初中学校里，初三班上一共有72个同学，后来据说只有三位同学考得最好，考进了普高，其他要么复读，要么读职校，要么像我这样早早辍学回来……

## 03

少女时代，在我们村庄门口的厂里，我们相处了两个多月。暑假期间，厂里都是和我们年龄相近的学生在干，那是一个做啤酒套的厂，下半年都不开，所以云儿后来就去了外地，听说是到广东。

2001年腊月，云儿突然来到我家，还带了水果和零食，妹妹们吃得很开心。看到我进门后，她说希望和我一起去学做衣服，还是学门手艺踏实点。我当时刚开始自己独立做服装，还是第一年，没有底气自己带她，也怪自己胆小，就把她介绍给带我的师傅当学徒。

她很聪明，学做衣服时上手很快。她跟师傅后干了8个月学徒后，就自己领衣服开始独立做。我们一起搭伙做饭，偶尔忙里偷闲，一起去海边逛逛。同事们喜欢八卦一些事，我们俩都是属于不爱掺和的人，比较特立独行。

她也爱读书，爱写写画画，其实她各方面功底都是很不错的，只是缺少了一个好的土壤环境。记得她曾经和我聊天时说过一句话，小时候，她父亲就给她算过命，那算命先生讲云儿"原本是一个小姐，可惜生了个丫鬟的命"。

她有那么好的读书天赋，却没有走读书这条路，这是命运对她的第一次捉弄。她那么年轻，就生了可怕的重病逝世，这是命运的极度无情。

她人善良，对人大方，宁可自己吃亏，也不让别人吃一点亏。她曾经和我开玩笑说，我宁可被天下人负，也不可负任何人。她真是这么做的，自己省吃俭用都要对人大方热心。

如果真有上苍，为什么上苍如此无眼，为何要如此对待她？

## 04

2018年，云儿在合肥检查病时，所有的费用都是临时凑的。那时，她的生意一直在亏损，根本没有多余的资金，连挂号费都是借的。刚开始进合肥肿瘤医院时，她只能住在走廊上。由于医院人满为患，要想住进正规病房，还得再找人花钱。

在她陷入昏迷后，她的家人发起了水滴筹捐款。我和几个当年的同事朋友捐了很多。同事们纷纷慷慨解囊，400、600、800元地捐，我们还转发给了许多熟人和朋友圈。记得当时一天多就筹到了8万多元。

另一个同事告诉我，如果云儿醒着，她绝对不会让我们这样做。的确，她那种性格肯定是不愿意的。即使再苦再难，她也不会开口求人，她把尊严和面子看得比生命更重要。

我到合肥肿瘤医院的第一天看过她之后，第三天，另一位同事去看云儿，同事发信息告诉我，估计云儿情况不太好，她开始喊我的名字，一会儿又问我是谁，记忆力下降得厉害。

那同事看后的第二天，云儿头部出血，已转进重症室。那天我们再次去医院，几个好朋友以及她的姐姐和家人都在。进重症监护室的第三天，刚好是云儿36周岁生日，她的生命就定格在这一天，从此与我们天人永隔。

从进合肥肿瘤医院到她去世，仅仅一周的时间。一周时间！命运是何其残忍！

我常感到困惑，人的生命为何会如此脆弱，一个大活人说没就没了。不久前，我们还在一起商量着以后要住在一起，一起做什么什么。死神在无情地逼近她，我们却浑然不知，人生就是这般无常。

在她来合肥医院的两个月前，我们还一起短暂相聚过。那时候她说自己腰不好，以为是妇科毛病，后来又说是坐骨神经，找偏方一直在家里喝中药。谁也没想到这竟然跟癌症扯上关系。

或许是她性格好强，或许是她自我屏蔽，没往太不好的方面去想，也没有去省医院好好检查。直到某一天，她早上起来，发现脖子上突然长了一块大疙瘩，才去我们桐城市医院检查，检查了血样和心电图。结果出来后，医生说情况非常不好，不确定是肺结核还是肺癌，让她赶快再去合肥医院检查一下。

她后面几天在重症监护病房，预约医生申请才能穿防护衣服排队去看。我站在她的面前和她说话，看到她的眼泪在流，泪水中还带着一点血丝，但是她不能动，也不能说话，比我第一天来看时，又瘦了很多，嘴唇没有一丝血色……

我和几位老同事轮流看过后，在走廊上就哭了起来，还没讲几句话，大家又接着哭。大家都说云儿已不像人样了，这才几天时间。

其中两位同事前不久刚和云儿聚会，在一起吃饭拍照。凤儿说当时她们三个人在一起吃饭，大家有说有笑，云儿大笑的时候，本能地把手扶着腰，说腰有点痛。（去合肥肿瘤医院前一天早上，脖子上突然有个大疙瘩，那已经是癌细胞转移了）

后来那天，在医院里看云儿时，我碰见她几个姐姐，她小姐姐说云儿是舍不得钱，所以没有早点去检查。她为什么都不跟我和几位好友说呢？检查看病的大事多少也会尽力去凑呀！我们一直都有微信、QQ，可她都没有说过。

她姐姐还说了云儿老公那几个月的一些事情，可能也促成了患病的主要原因之一，情绪真的很重要。经济的压力，情感的不顺，而她内心一直又那么好强，或许她真的是太累太累了。

云儿有个姐姐说，女性在生病时候就怕过生日，生日是一个很大的节点，是一道坎儿。没想到，正好是云儿36岁生日，彻底停止了呼吸，难道这都是既定的命数？

## 05

2015年下半年，我去了上海小妹那个公司，那是一家大型互联网公司。我住在浦东新区东方路。那是妹妹同人合租的房子，小区外面环境非常好，只是里面是简装，但非常宽敞，110平米以上，价格比市场价便宜一大半，同事们都羡慕坏了，因为我们离公司很近。

房东大姐每次来，反而带东西给我们吃。在我离开上海之前，她还送了我一本《圣经》。记得我刚写作的时候，还把房东大姐写在文章里。

我小妹曾吐槽说，大姐到哪里，什么都是现成的。她说自己那么多年每去一个地方全部靠自己折腾，还说我们姐妹三个，如果她要是老大，可能早就改变命运了。

好吧！每个人的性格认知都有他与生俱来的局限。

2015年，没想到云儿也去上海了，更巧合的是，她住在离我公交车站只需要几站路的地方。她是比我早几月到上海的。

她住的那个地方只能放一张窄床，桌子紧挨着床，都是二手房东搞的那种隔断间，人站着转个身都很难，房租还要1500多元。

云儿刚开始是在一家快递公司打码，一个月4000多元。她老公送快递，后来她又到一家连锁超市上班，超市里也给她买五险一金，其实挺好的。

我周末就去她那边，她和我发小一样，都非常会照顾人，也非常擅长做美食家务之类。

我曾劝说她也去我们公司做销售吧！如果业绩做得好，工资还是挺高的，你在超市上班工资太死板了。

我们公司接触的都是大学生，接触网络知识，也可以锻炼咱们，以后回家也可以做轻松点的工作。如果熟人内部介绍，你肯定是可以直接应聘上的。

2016年年中，我已经在网络写作了，我也劝过她，我说你当年是学霸，文采也好，你也来写作吧！可惜不管是哪样建议，她都不干。我不知道她是因为自卑，担心自己干不好，还是因为怕麻烦我。

2016年的暑假，我们两家还把孩子带到一块儿，在上海好多地方游玩。她在早上出发前卤了鸡爪、鸡蛋和豆干等，亲手做了好多吃的带上，搞得像是家庭野餐，而我只是在超市买的一包东西带着。那天大家都玩得非常开心。

她比我提前一步回到老家。他们当时的想法是回家自己开一个加工厂，但是现实很残酷，一切都不如想象，甚至不如给别人打工简单开心。这也是造成她后来生病的一个原因。

我有段时间经常想起她，如果她晚点离开上海，可能还好一点；如果他们不是回去搞加工厂创业，单纯地上上班，也许身体也会好一点；如果她早一点剥离家庭，也许也会好点，就算发病也可能晚10年以上。

上帝的无形大手，是如何在操纵着人世间的一切？

在云儿去世后，我翻看她朋友圈很久，原来她也在简书写作过，却不曾和我说过哪个账号是她。

## 李娟的《我的阿勒泰》再次点燃了我对写作的热情

写作是一项极其耗费脑力的工作，它在无形中消耗着大量的脑细胞。尽管表面上看起来并不劳累，但实际上，它如同软刀子般伤人，尤其是对长期写作的人来说，每天锻炼身体显得尤为重要。

写作不仅考验着脑力，也考验着体力。世上没有一件事是容易的，不是体力上的辛苦，就是精力、脑力上的付出，而后者往往更为伤人。有时，我真想只是每天看看书，发发呆就足够了。谁不渴望能够退休，享受宁静的生活呢？

但我们大多数人处于既不能全心投入竞争，又不能安心躺平的尴尬状态。我原本答应编辑要交几篇稿件，可惜我陷入了僵局，时间就这样在不经意间流逝。我真心不喜欢命题作文，更偏爱随心所欲地写作，想到什么就写什么。

在写作这条路上，我始终坚持自由书写，不拘泥于技巧。虽然我了解一些写作方法和框架，但我依然任性地写作。

回想起当初，我零基础开始写作，仅用了一年多的时间就实现了月入五位数。这多亏了自媒体时代的到来。我自己注册账号，自己发布、运营，有了一种"我的地盘我做主"的感觉。如果在纸媒时代，像我这样任性地只按照自己的心意去写，恐怕很难脱颖而出。

此刻，我戴着防噪音耳机，在阳台上的书房里敲打着文字。耳机里循环播放着李翊君的《诺言》，让我想起第一次听这首歌时，我正在一家店里做营业员，那时的工资只有300元一个月。那是2004年，我从福建的服装厂回老家休养几个月后，在桐城的街上做了几个月的营业员。

店里的两位同事都很会唱歌，让我这个五音不全的人羡慕不已。她们一个喜欢唱李翊君的《诺言》，另一个则偏爱张惠妹的《原来你什么都不想要》。正是因为她们，我熟悉了这两首歌，甚至能倒背如流。

《诺言》原唱版早在1995年就已发布，并在当年就广受欢迎。《还珠格格》的主题曲《雨蝶》，以及早年流行的《萍聚》，都是李翊君的作品。我是在2004年才了解到《诺言》这首歌的。多年后的今天，因为一位1999年出生的歌手在抖音上的翻唱，这首歌再次爆火，一周内粉丝增长了1000多万。

这就是音乐艺术的力量，加上网络流量的惊人传播速度。在浩瀚的互联网世界中，总会有人被平台和流量选中，他们仿佛是天选之子。

想想我和我身边的无数写作者，埋头写作七八年甚至更久，全网的粉丝也不过几十万，这在写作界已经算是不错的成绩了。但与视频、直播和抖音算法相比，还是显得稍逊一筹。

近年来，网络数字媒体的崛起，尤其是抖音的汹涌流量和网红的巨大影响力，让许多优秀作品再次走红。例如，迟子建的《额尔古纳河右岸》，因董宇辉的推荐，很快就卖出了一两百万册，而在过去的十几年里，销量仅为5万册。

实际上，这是迟子建早在2005年所写的长篇小说，首发于《收获》杂志2005年第6期，并于2005年12月出版。

最近，央视推出的《我的阿勒泰》是少数由散文改编而成的电视剧。央视平台的品牌影响力，加上各大自媒体的报道和转发，使得全网再次掀起了一股追捧李娟作品的热潮。现在，无论是朋友圈、公众号还是各大视频平台，随处可见李娟及其作品的介绍和推荐。

《我的阿勒泰》是作家李娟于2010年7月首次出版的散文集，主要描绘了她在阿勒泰的乡居生活。这部散文集成功地再现了新疆北部的风土人情，充满了清新的气息，是李娟的成名作和代表作之一。

李娟，1979年出生，从1999年开始写作。2003年1月，她出版了首部作品《九篇雪》。2004年，李娟凭借其卓越的写作能力，被破格录取进入体制内。如今，她再次成为全国的焦点，这无疑是天时地利人和的结晶。机会总是留给有准备的人。

她的作品具有明显的非虚构性、地域化和日常化特征，吃到了地域红利。她的文字非常治愈且耐看，也满足了人们对新疆这片神秘土地的好奇心。

2010年出版《我的阿勒泰》时，李娟在新疆乃至全国已有一定的知名度。今天，我们群里还有学员聊到，李娟刚开始写作时，有人嘲笑她连高中都没读完，还想成为作家。甚至有人当众读出她的文字来嘲笑她。这和我当初的写作经历何其相似。

写着写着，我们就成为了自己喜欢的模样。虽然我无法与李娟相提并论，但我在她身上看到了继续写作的无限可能性，并再次激发了我写作的热情。

当年，许多人对我说："你是不是有很多字都不认识？你怎么敢有这么大的梦想？你太天真了，还想成为作家？你知道我们学校中文系一年毕业多少人吗？"甚至还有服装厂的前同事对我说："你下班后不早点睡觉，还看书？看书又不能当饭吃，也不能当菜吃。几年后，大家不都还是村妇吗？"

我心里默默地想，即使是村妇，我也要做有思想的村妇。（她们这样说也是出于好意）

无论何时，无论男女老少，只要有闲暇时间，就应该多读书。书籍能够滋养你的灵魂，丰富你的精神，让你受益终生。

（附言：2004年冬天，我还是选择在一家门店做衣服，为顾客定制羽绒服。毕竟，技术活比做营业员的待遇要好一些。老板娘负责裁剪，我负责制作，还有人负责称绒、装绒，我再套里布、上领子等工序。)

## 往事如烟，卖菜的往事

记得著名作家铁凝曾说过，她最喜欢逛菜市场，这里有着浓浓的烟火气，是真正的人间烟火味，是最接地气的地方，可以看到人间百态。

在我很小的时候，菜市场对我而言是一个陌生的概念，家里只吃菜园地里自种的菜或咸菜，从不买外面的菜。长大一些后，我了解到菜市场是可以赚钱的地方。

当我会骑自行车时，常常和妈妈一起去桐城街上卖菜，把一个菜篮子绑在车后，妈妈跟在后面走，因为她不会骑自行车。我曾尝试让妈妈坐在车后座上，提着菜篮，但她总担心我会累坏，坐一下就不肯再坐。

印象最深的是，在一场雨后，家里地里的豇豆长得很多。妈妈得意地说，地里的豇豆像扯挂面，明天我们一早去街上卖，听说最近可以卖到一块钱一斤。那天早上三点多，妈妈就喊我起来，我们摸黑推车到街上，天刚蒙蒙亮。但一到市场，就听说豇豆跌价到三毛了。原来，一场雨水之后，菜农的菜都长出来了，菜价很快就下跌了。我看到了妈妈眼中掩饰不住的失望。

我们刚把菜篮摆好，市场管理员就来收费，交了三毛钱的摊位费。由于我们只带了几个旧食品袋，没有新食品袋，我又去边上买了几个，花了五毛钱。等了半天也没有人买，我和妈妈只得沿街推车叫卖。那筐豇豆最后以每斤两毛五的价格卖给了一家饭店。我还吵着肚子饿，花一元钱买了四个包子，妈妈一个都舍不得吃。那天到家，只赚了四五块钱。

妈妈不识字，很多时候办事都喜欢带着我，依赖我，比如去卖菜、去交公粮，需要记账的地方等，她心里好像没有安全感似的。而少不更事的我，因此常常在妈妈面前顶嘴，甚至蛮不讲理，压根不听她的话，总觉得自己有这样一个无用的妈妈而自卑、生闷气。

之前妈妈一个人卖菜时，有几个人东问西问就容易晕，还被别人骗过，白忙一场。每斤菜都耗费很多精力和心血，奶奶因此劝说妈妈，不要一个人去卖东西。

妈妈讲话时有些口齿不清，我读书时特别不希望她去学校，不希望任何同学知道她。其他孩子受欺负了，总喜欢回家跟妈妈讲，而我从来不讲，因为即便讲了也没用，妈妈只会劝我让着他们，而且那些大孩子也不怕我妈妈。

1998年金融危机，所有农作物都不值钱，鸡蛋、黄豆、菜都大幅跌价，100斤的稻谷只能卖35元，交公粮就得交走一半。那一年真的很艰难，大年三十前一天，我和妈妈在街上卖米、卖菜，寒风吹得人瑟瑟发抖，家里却等着那钱过年。那一年还发大水，很多地方受灾，村里发了救济衣服到我家，我们姐妹很开心地试穿，妈妈却让我们留着开学或走亲戚时穿。

我初三下学那年，流行南下打工，都说南方打工可以赚很多钱。但那时出门的路子很少，远不比现在网络发达，有很多机会可以选择，而我们那时得四处求人带。我的发小和我同一年出远门打工，她爸爸腊月里就找好人选，请他们带她去打工。为此，她父母那年帮别人干了很多农活，把那家当恩人似的对待，只想女儿在外面能稍微好点。那些年打工的行情就是这样。

当发小确定出门日期时，我还在家里，不知道跟谁出去，非常着急。直到正月去亲戚家拜年时，亲戚给我介绍了一位师傅。那是一位比我大12岁的女子，她看到我时貌似很满意。那些年，沿海的工厂，很多人都是专门带徒弟的，自己干活得到一份收入，再带几个徒弟干杂活，一年可以赚到两三万（1999—2000年时），有的更多。有个老乡夫妻带12个徒弟，相当于12个徒弟都帮他们赚钱。

当师傅的自然喜欢徒弟能吃苦，看起来越老实、越穷苦出身的，师傅越喜欢。因为你想赚钱，不会受不了苦，不会半途而废，不会闹着跑回家。我提前一天住在师傅家，因为她家离火车站不太远，同去的还有另一个女徒弟。第二天一大早，我妈妈突然出现在师傅家门口，我感到很惊讶。妈妈是给我送身份证来的，头天晚上她才收到身份证，之前一直没有办下来。妈妈说她四点多就从家里出门了。就这样，我开始了人生里的服装厂女工生涯，路费是师傅垫的。我兜里揣着妈妈前几天卖头发的20元钱，妈妈心爱的长发养了好几年，为了我，无可奈何地剪了。还有奶奶，也给了我五元钱。奶奶的零花钱全是大伯给她的，大伯是吃商品粮的，因为大伯年轻时当过两年兵，后来分配在安庆化肥厂工作，大伯把该补贴的柴米油盐直接折合成现金给了奶奶。我家当时穷得连一个月三四块钱的电费有时都拿不出来。奶奶知道我家穷得可怜，她把自己手上那点零花钱抠着用，大多贴给我家了，自己常常好几个月都不买肉吃。记得她曾唠叨说，你妈跑了一个村庄，都没能借到五块钱电费钱，想想都寒心。最后还是奶奶知道了这事，把仅有的零花钱全掏给我妈交了电费。

小时候，我家的电费是全村最少的，用的是20瓦带钨丝的那种灯泡，昏黄昏黄的弱光。为了节省电费，两间屋子用一个灯泡，挂在两间屋子之间的门框边。

出门第一年的腊月回家，带发小打工的师傅给了她2000元，她父母非常满足，甚至想要退500元回去。其实我们都在家学过缝纫机，只是为了有人带，找个靠谱的工厂，学几天平车就可以。我的师傅给了我1000元，我们都是在福建，只是不在一个镇，他们厂做的是夹克衫，

Living like this. 031

我们厂做的是非洲人穿的沙滩短裤，价格不同，师傅收入不同，工作时间每天都是十六七个小时以上，赶货时还不止。在我所在的那个厂，我师傅对我算很好的了，从不大声说我，更不会像别的师傅那么凶，甚至打人。我干活速度很快，她也很知足。师傅每个月会给我45元，那1000元工资是到年底回家才有。45元是我每月买早餐和日用品的费用，早餐我常常不吃，洗衣粉也是省着用。我把45元零花钱再省一半多出来，写信时夹在信里寄回家。

在福建打工时，休息日特别少，除非是端午和中秋，或者偶尔的停电。难得有休息日，我会和老乡去菜市场逛逛。那里有卖各种海鲜、服装、小吃的，音响里唱着流行歌曲，大街上都是操着各种方言的打工仔、打工妹们，统称为"农民工"。那些年在福建打工的，主要是安徽、江西、四川、贵州的人。

每次路过菜市场，我就会想起妈妈，不知道她一个人还会去卖菜吗？会不会有人因为她不识字趁乱再欺骗她？还是她和妹妹一道去？即便是现在我去菜市场，也不知道为什么，脑子里总会出现妈妈的模样。

世事无常，命运弄人，妈妈在2002年不幸永远离开了我们。那年，家里盖了三上三下的楼房，小妹就快初中毕业，我第二年开始独自做衣服，一年下来可以赚6000多元，二妹也已出来打工。家里的生活逐渐有了好转，再不用像过去那样，把"人死得，穷不得"挂在嘴边，再不用外面下大雨家里下小雨。家中用上了亮堂堂的日光灯，土地也变成了水泥地，过年杀猪时也可多腌点腊肉了，不用再像过去那样：过了正月十五，家里没有一点肉，全都卖了留作学费。

这些都是我妈妈的心愿。当妈妈的全部心愿差不多可以实现时，她却突然间因急性脑膜炎永远地离开了我们。命运真是要多无情就有多无情……那些天，我都是恍惚的，分不清是梦还是现实，大悲无言，我竟然没怎么哭。只是这些年，一想起妈妈，我甚至会在黑夜里泪流满面。

妈妈短短的一生，难道就是为了把我们姐妹带到人间，抚养长大？2003年后，我们那种田地再不用交公粮，不用交农业税、水费，再后来，土地流转，家家不用再辛苦种田了。过去每年交公粮是我家最辛苦的头号大事。如此好的时代红利，母亲没有来得及看到。

更重要的是，我们都长大了，不需要再低声下气，卑微地到处借钱度日。尤其是为人母后，我更体会到母亲的种种不易。如果母亲还在，我肯定再不会和她顶嘴，再不会说她为什么没有别人母亲有本事，再不会学她讲话，笑她话都说不好。但是，人生没有如果了。

当我们懂得这些时，母亲已永远离开了我们，离开了这个她还没看明白的世界。人间最悲痛的事，莫过于此，子欲养而亲不待。心痛、心痛、心痛……

无比羡慕那些五六十岁，父母都依然健在，子孙满堂，享受着天伦之乐的人。

每一头白发何尝不是命运的恩赐？

我这一生，因为失去了苦难中坚强生活的妈妈，即便是未来发展得再好，我的幸福都从一开始就大打折扣，我的人生再无圆满。

祝福天下所有母亲，天天都能幸福快乐！

妈妈，如果可以选择来生，我一定要再做您的女儿，报答今生没有来得及报答的养育之恩。

妈妈，如果有来生，我一定做一个让你自豪的女儿。妈妈，您听见了吗？

夜夜想起妈妈的话

闪闪的泪光鲁冰花

天上的星星不说话

地上的娃娃想妈妈

天上的眼睛眨呀眨

妈妈的心呀鲁冰花
家乡的茶园开满花
妈妈的心肝在天涯
夜夜想起妈妈的话
闪闪的泪光鲁冰花
啊～啊～
夜夜想起妈妈的话
闪闪的泪光鲁冰花

# 那年，我家四处借钱买来的缝纫机

每次看到家里那台缝纫机，就会让我想起许多往事，如同电影镜头一样，一幕幕浮现在眼前。

在二十世纪七八十年代，缝纫机、手表和自行车被称为"三大件"，拥有其中一样，就会觉得十分荣耀和体面。那时的人们，结婚时以三大件为标准，就像现在结婚要有房有车一样。

我接触缝纫机是在15岁那年。初三预选前，我辍学回家，在堂哥的工厂里做啤酒套。那时候，一天能挣8元钱左右，我感到非常开心和满足。但好景不长，后来堂哥的厂停办了，小姐妹们都去街上拜师学缝纫技术。

那些年，小姑娘流行学缝纫、理发，男孩子流行学油漆、木匠装潢技术，老人们都说"大荒年饿不死手艺人"。

看到小伙伴们都去学缝纫，大家都谈论着去外面做服装是如何赚钱，而我从堂哥的工厂回来后，不知道要做什么，因为家里没有钱买缝纫机，找师父还要交押金。

听小伙伴们说，一台蝴蝶牌缝纫机要420元，还得配一把大剪刀，要22元，一共近450元，加上押金，对于我家来说是一笔很大的开销。看着小伙伴们每天骑自行车早出晚归学手艺，我心里无比羡慕。那时候也不怎么懂事，天天吵着让妈妈去买缝纫机。妈妈说家里没有钱，我就让她去借。我说某某家很有钱，你去帮我借嘛，一直吵，一直哭个不停。妈妈其实不想去，谁愿意低声下气地去借钱呢？被我吵得实在没有办法，妈妈那晚才出去借钱，找屋后的人家，他们家没有上学的，都已在打工，结果还是没借到钱。第二天晚上又换了一家借钱，还是没借到……后来妈妈决定坐车去我小姨家借钱，小姨家在另一个县城。我小姨父一直在山区小学当老师，在当时的环境里，相对来说收入比较稳定。小姨看到我妈大老远来借钱，也知道周边肯定是借不到了，她拿出自己积攒很久的500元钱给我妈，还给了几个小板凳，并买好车票送我妈上车。

小姨还嘱咐我妈说不要着急，这个钱就让帆儿打工赚钱后再还。妈妈回来可开心了，一个劲儿地唠叨还是自己家亲妹妹好，跑了那么多家，一分钱都借不到，小时候没有白带她。

还记得那天去桐城街上买缝纫机，我们挑了一台蝴蝶牌缝纫机和一把张小泉牌的21号大剪刀，还价下来，一共420元。那是我们家很象样的大物件了。我每天小心地擦拭它，如同心头宝贝，还用布小心地盖起来，唯恐弄脏了它。

经人介绍到镇上一家裁缝店学习，那天，妈妈挑着缝纫机，走着送我到裁缝店去。店里还卖布匹、床单、窗帘等，店里已有六个师姐妹。师傅30岁左右，风姿绰约，被称为镇上四大美女之一。她主要负责裁剪，接待顾客，做衣服及其他杂事都由几个大师姐做。

刚到裁缝店，我就是挑挑裤子的脚口边，锁锁扣子眼，或者哪里有需要拆的就拆拆，每天还得帮忙照顾师傅家的小孩，给她家洗衣、拖地，这些都是我那时的主要工作。那一年，我并没有做过任何整件衣服，最多只是上了几条裤腰头。后来师傅热衷做窗帘生意，因为接一家单位的窗帘，就能赚七八千元。当时我们都佩服师傅，她不但长得漂亮，还非常有头脑。她是我们镇上第一家代卖布匹的裁缝，也是第一家把窗帘生意做起来的裁缝店。

我吵着买了缝纫机，感觉并没有学到什么，听到南方打工的人说，南方工厂用的是电机，叫"平车"，去工厂后还是要学习。一年后，好不容易找到师傅肯带我出去，在家说好，车费她出，跟她干一年给我1000元，等于她给我带条出路，学会电机和厂里的服装工艺。

一天除了睡觉的五六个小时，其他时间都在干活，人似机器，枯燥麻木。厂里另一对老乡夫妻，徒弟就有12人，一年能给他们赚好几万元。师傅们之间互相羡慕谁的徒弟手脚快。讽刺的是，当年我们那些学缝纫机又外出学平车的姐妹们，花了那么多时间代价，如今却都没有再干做衣服这一行，或许都是做怕了。

若知道后来家里发生那么多变故，我离开学校后，应该直接去镇上刷子厂或猪鬃厂工作，而不是浪费两年多的时间学所谓的缝纫技术。仔细算起来，在外面打工的工资，按工作时间算起来，也并不比在家乡工作高多少。只是后来大家为了可怜的面子，都不想再回老家工作。传言中的别人在外赚了多少多少，毕竟是极少数。正月出门到过年才回家一次，错过多少家人之间的陪伴，平添多少挽不回的疼痛。

我怎么就没有自己的主意呢！总是人云亦云，怎么开窍懂事那么晚呢！

家里的那台蝴蝶牌缝纫机已搁置多年，每每看到它，就想起15岁那年的青涩和无奈，想起那时做梦都渴望拥有的这台缝纫机。那时候，天真的我以为拥有了这台缝纫机，就会变得非常厉害。以为出门打工三年，就可以给家里盖一栋宽敞气派的楼房，这就是我年少时光里的全部梦想。

后来这些梦想的确是实现了，但时间不止三年，而我失去的更多更多……

## 只和别人学，只同自己比

人世间，有很多人爱计较、爱攀比，他们喜欢盯着身边的人，和他人比来比去，似乎看不到更广阔的星辰大海。适当的比较有利于自己的进步，但过分的攀比只会让自己身心俱疲。

镇上有几位做生意的老板娘，她们喜欢一起去做美容、逛商场、去健身房。表面上是一片祥和，其实暗地里互相较着劲。背后谁也不认同谁好看，都觉得自己比对方有优势，自己的孩子更可爱、更聪明，自己穿的衣服更显身材。每个人甚至都会觉得自己比较年轻。

其实，人都会有一种幻觉，同是40岁的两个人，隔几年遇见，总感觉对方比自己老。犹如每对父母，就是觉得自己的孩子最优秀、最可爱，谁也不会认为自己的孩子比别人的孩子差，即便自己孩子的智商并不高，也一样认为自家孩子小脑更发达，更有前途。

人们喜欢不自觉地放大自己以及和自己有关的人、事的优点，扩大对方的缺点。这是人类的共性。

有的女子喜欢比老公、比孩子，看对方的老公收入如何，是否比自己老公更疼爱自己。一旦发现对方样样都比自己好时，心里就会不平衡，开始抱怨生活、抱怨老公、抱怨命运。她们不曾去想，有很多事是无法比较的，每个人表达爱的方式也都不同。既然两个人能够走在一起，总归是有共性之处的。

而且，别人所描述的，也未必就是她真正的感受。家家都有一本难念的经，生活都是喜忧参半，如鱼饮水，冷暖自知。

许多妯娌间喜欢暗暗较劲，你买了银耳环，我得去买个银镯子；你买了新上衣，我去买条新裤子。有人说，女人和女人之间大多只有同情和嫉妒两种感情。这句话当然是言过其实的，但也说出了一些现象。电视剧《芈月传》中的芈月和芈姝开始是一对好姐妹，芈姝对芈月照顾有加，彼此掏心掏肺。却随着芈月的一步步得宠，好姐妹最后竟反目成仇，令人唏嘘。

攀比和嫉妒，让芈姝一步步走向万丈深渊。

写文字的人，有的也很喜欢同别人比较，比较刊载了多少，刊载在什么报刊，比出版的书发行了多少万册，甚至比粉丝比人气等，所谓文人相轻。这有啥好比的呢！

每个人写作风格不同，写作动机不同，有的人纯粹是写我心所想。写作这条漫长道路，未来会如何都是未知的，谁也无法看到终点。乐观坦然地写自己的作品才是正确的做法。现在没写出名堂的，未必将来不会；现在在业内红透了、在某个平台红火了，未必就能一直火下去。在A平台默默无闻的，或许会在B平台风生水起。写作这条路有无限想象的空间。

比来比去，最终比的是谁身体更健康，这才是硬道理。

"爱攀比，爱嫉妒"在生活中无处不在。它能给人压力，也能给人动力，但如何把握那个度，需要我们去正确把握。人生太短暂，少把焦点放在别人身上，多关照自己的灵魂，多注重自己的成长，只和别人学，只同自己比。

多锻炼身体，早睡早起，保持好心态，开心工作，快乐生活，这是最正确的人生态度。

沃兹基硕德说：不论你是谁，少说都有三分野心。没什么好遮掩的，野心本身就是一种追求更好生活的意愿。但太过好胜，也是一种病态，是把一切快乐都建立在输赢之上。要强的人生不争强，抗争和妥协，一样都不能少。生活就是这样，一半要争，一半要退。缺了哪一半，都难顺心。

生活中，有人喜欢评价和对别人指指点点，喜欢揪住别人的缺点来满足自己的虚荣，喜欢用攀比心来掩盖内心的空虚和底气不足。但我们要区别攀比和良性竞争。良性竞争促进发展，出发点不一样，满足的需求也不一样。

良性竞争，是带着欣赏的心态学习他人的亮点，最终成为更好的自己。

芸芸众生，茫茫人海，比来比去何时了？少一点攀比心，多一点自我提升心。提高格局，扩大眼界，多花心思修炼自我，专心做好自己。

## 陪母亲交公粮的陈年往事

过去，粮食都要上交国库。在封建社会，这被称为上交皇粮；新中国成立后，改称为公粮和购粮。这是每户农民按照要求的比例上交给国家用于粮食储备的制度，已延续了数千年。直到2003年，公粮、购粮以及农业税、水费等才被正式取消。公粮通常是每亩50斤，必须无杂质、干燥、饱满，一半用于抵消农业税，另一半无偿上交国家。

还有一种购粮，每亩需上交140斤，我家总共要上交600多斤。购粮有一定的报酬，100斤约17块钱。随着物价波动，报酬有所变动，但通常都低于市场价，大约是市场价的一半。

当队长通知要交公粮时，每家每户都会用蛇皮袋或麻袋装上自己认为最好、最饱满、晒得最干燥的稻谷。每家有大大小小的十几到二十袋，天刚蒙蒙亮，大家就用板车、三轮车或拖拉机，将粮食拉到离家8公里的镇上粮站。

我母亲不会拉板车，家里也没有任何车，而且她不识字。每次交公粮，她都得说好话，央求同村的人让我们搭车过去，这和交学费一样，对母亲和我们整个家庭来说，都是一次巨大的挑战。那时，农民们积极交粮，排着长长的队伍。粮食能否被接收，还得看粮站工作人员的脸色。质检员说好就好，说差就差。所谓好，就是粒粒饱满，成色好，晒得干燥，无其他杂质。

交公粮时，各村各小队陆陆续续、浩浩荡荡地赶往镇粮食站。到达粮站后，我们需要登记排号。我们到粮站时，大院里挤满了各村汇集来的板车、拖拉机和人流，正是炎炎夏日，个个都汗流浃背。至今还记得，粮站的工作人员中有一个体形特别胖的女子，据说体重有200多斤，她负责登记和称重。其他工作人员有的负责算账，算盘打得啪啪响；还有的负责开票记账。

工作人员都是吃商品粮的人，个别人显得高高在上，享受着大家的端茶递水和敬仰的目光。庄稼人同他们说话都是小心翼翼的，我母亲更是如此。

那年，我还是个小学生，懵懂无知，跟着母亲去镇上交公粮。烈日当空，我们汗流浃背，人人都想早点办完回家。本分老实的母亲，虽然起得很早，排队也在前面，却总是被后面来的人插队，母亲却无可奈何。同村的人陆陆续续地交完粮食，拿着空袋回家了，有些比我们来得晚的也交完了。

眼看前面还有那么多人，我们焦急地等待，直到快天黑才轮到我们。母亲和我艰难地一袋一袋地将粮食往前挪，偶尔也有好心人上来帮我们扛一袋。我们焦急地看着质检员用一根空心铁棍往装粮食的袋子里一戳，然后听他熟练地往嘴里磕得吱吱响，再把剩下的往稻床上一扔，漠然地说："这稻谷不行，再翻晒一天。"我和母亲只得把稻谷一袋袋地往一边搬，又是满头大汗。心里恨透了那个质检员，准备第二天再晒。那晚我们就在粮站的临时小屋里过夜。

晚上，几家还没交掉公粮的人唉声叹气。他们说，许多一次性顺利交掉的，并不见得他们的粮食好，有的是给检验员塞了烟，有的是会说话巴结、会变通。我们几家没能交掉粮食的，肯定是各个村里的老实人。工作人员总要做点样子给领导看。某某稻谷明明比我们的还少晒一天，都过秤交掉了。我们明天下午能顺利交掉就算好了。这大热天的，家里还有那么多活等着干呢！

母亲也说，她特意挑了家里最好、最饱满的稻谷，而且比庄子里谁家晒的都干。那又能怎样呢？他们早都交掉了，估计这会儿都到家了。塞烟？家里连买一包盐的钱都要攒好久。幸好第二天是个大晴天，母亲又把一袋袋稻谷拖到粮站院子里摊开晒，直到下午五点多，我们再拿去检验，这次总算顺利地交掉了，遗憾的是被其他人偷了一袋稻谷。

走在回家的路上，母亲说："带你来，就是因为你能识字。你东张西望的，肯定是我抱稻谷时，后边或边上的人顺手偷走了一袋，那可有70多斤啊，能换多少包盐。"随后妈妈又自我安慰道："偷掉了就偷掉了，当破财免灾吧！下次得看紧些。好在总算没让我们再留下来晒一天稻谷，稻谷也带得够量，今天下午插队的人也比昨天少了很多……"

后来我长大了些，曾无数次在心里想，外婆为啥七个子女中唯独没让母亲读书？还有为啥要把母亲从舒城嫁这么远？如果在当地本镇本村，有舅舅、姨们的照顾，总会少受很多委屈。像这样被插队、被偷稻谷、被欺负的事，在我的记忆里是不胜枚举的。有时我更恨自己懂事那么晚，又不够强悍，只知道玩、好奇，不曾盯着自己家的稻谷，更恨自己没有生成男儿身，不能保护妈妈。

那时候的庄稼人，尤其是我所在的皖中地带，每年的农村"双抢"时节，收割早稻、播种晚稻，能把人累得虚脱，还得乖乖地上交公粮，亲自送到粮站，似乎得乞求那些吃皇粮的，看他们脸色，生怕他们不要。

如今的庄稼人，不但不用交公粮，不用交水费、农业税，国家还反倒补贴农民，而且现在老家人个个拿着田租，都不用再下田了，真是赶上了一个好时代啊！

# 我曾无比渴望远离家乡

我猜想,每个人在年少的时候,都曾想远离家乡,这是源于骨子里的叛逆,或者说是成长必经的过程。

自从我知道女孩子可以通过远嫁来摆脱自己的家乡,我就一心盼着长大。17岁那年,我到了离家3000里的福建晋江打工,这是被生活所迫。当时,我只认识在晋江打工的师傅,找不到其他人带我出去,所以晋江成了我打工生涯中的第一站。那时,懵懂的我十分高兴,因为可以到离家如此之远的地方打工。

打工几年才回一次老家,每次回老家,就陆续有邻居介绍相亲对象。由于年少时对家乡的厌恶,我觉得家乡的许多人太势利,瞧不起我家,因此就不愿意在家乡找对象,连见都不想见。这都是从小种下的"厌恶种子",那时觉得全国任何地方都会比自己的家乡好。

现在我们姐妹三人都没在家乡定居。我离开安庆到了池州,小妹定居在省会合肥,二妹跟随小姨和男友,在六安的舒城县城安家,都实现了小时候的"愿望",离开了家乡所在的县。

其实桐城真的不好吗?安徽桐城,是安庆市下辖的县级市,自古有"文都"之称。清朝乾隆皇帝曾说"天下文章皆出桐城","桐城派"文化曾雄霸文坛200多年,"桐城三杰"更是写进了高中历史课本……

真正长大后才明白,嫌贫爱富是人的劣根性,也是本性。一个小村庄就像一个小王国,地方恶霸更可怕,天高皇帝远,弱小贫穷的人自然少不了被欺负。

而如今，我常以出生于"文都"桐城而骄傲。每次回桐城，都难掩激动之情。我给女儿讲桐城的历史，带她逛那条闻名遐迩的"六尺巷"，给她讲解这同名诗背后的故事，以及"一门两宰相，五里三进士，隔河两状元"这些桐城历史和著名人物。

甚至偷偷地想，如果有一天，我的子女或外甥女们中有人取得了一点成绩，我一定要让他们多讲讲曾受"桐城派"文化熏陶的经历。这些年，看过听过其他许多农村老家的人和事，觉得自己家乡人的整体素质已很不错了，生活条件也算比较好。而且家乡民企、私企发达，小镇上到处都是刷子厂，被称为"中国制刷之乡"。家乡还有"塑料袋之乡"之称，全国70%的塑料袋都是我们那儿出产的。地理位置在安庆与合肥中间，交通发达，人杰地灵，物华天宝。真不明白自己为啥会那么讨厌家乡。

曾听一个年长的姐姐说，她15岁就立志长大后要离家远远的：越远越好。总觉得父母太唠叨，也觉得家乡有些人的嘴脸看不惯。青春年华刚开始的19岁，她就远赴外省，每两年才回来一趟。多年后她和我说，她人生最后悔的事，就是结婚太早，还嫁得那么远……

我明白，她是用这种叛逆的方式来脱离家乡，其实心智并没有真正成熟。像她这样想法的人应该还有很多。对于家乡，从热爱到想逃离，再到更深入骨髓地热爱，这是我们不断成长的过程，也是心态不断趋于成熟的结果。

不管走过多少个城市，踏遍多少足迹，最后定居在哪一隅，但在我们的梦里，最常出现的地方一定是家乡，一定是自己的出生、成长的地方。

关于家乡，你也曾有过逃离的想法吗？

## 我们都不知天高地厚过

想起一位同事分享的亲身经历。他说上学时的一个暑假,学校介绍同学们到上海实习,工作地点在上海嘉定。到了以后才发现,那是一个骗子工厂,不包吃住,工资还低得可怜,租房又十分贵,算起来还不如不干。

他和几个同学打算在东方明珠转一圈看看,就离开上海回家乡。离开的前一天,他们想在附近找宾馆,家家都贵得吓人,几个人身上所有钱加起来都不够住一宿。几个刚尝试步入社会的男孩,无奈之下只得在外滩那儿露天睡了一夜。他们一起指着东方明珠说:"10年后,我们每个人都要在那儿买间房子当厕所用!"真是豪言壮语啊!把我们所有同事笑得前仰后合。是不是每个人年轻时都曾这样?

记得张小娴书中有段话:"20岁的男人,总以为世界都可以踩在脚底下,觉得自己未来会无所不能。到35岁后,再也不敢这样说,生活给了他残酷的现实,哪里还有底气去如此自信张扬。"

在年少时,谁都有一张没被生活欺负过的脸,棱角还没被磨平,拥有对前途胜券在握的自信自恋。那年在温州打工时,流水线对面的两个85后男孩,一说起未来的梦想,都是豪情万丈。有个男孩说:"宝马车我迟早会有的,女友和我分手,她妈就是嫌我家太穷,我以后要开着宝马车到她家门口转悠转悠,让她们后悔,让她气死。"另一个男孩说:"我肯定要买就买路虎车。"两个人击掌欢呼,觉得以后年入百万不是梦。

他们说这话的语气,就像宝马、路虎车已付过定金在等他们似的。

其实那时候在工厂流水线上工作，工人每月也就一两千元工资，男孩子只够自己花，个别人甚至每月还要借钱度日。因为年轻，所以无畏，任何狂话都敢说。一个农村出来的孩子，在没有任何人帮助的情况下，凭个人能力买宝马、路虎的概率是极低的。家里若有很厚的家底，也不会让儿子不读书老早去工厂做流水线工人。男孩子在工厂打几年工，绝大多数人都不会有啥积蓄，上升空间也有限，还要面对买房结婚成家的巨大压力，实现年入百万谈何容易。所有对未来的过高期许，只是因为他们太年轻。

去年我被拉入曾经的温州同事群，当年对面的两个男孩也在群里。一个已经结婚，夫妻俩一起在做服装。另一个还没结婚，开过服装加工厂，失败后再去打工。加工厂本来就利润极其微薄，得很会安排算计，每一环都非常考验人，即便成功也只能比做流水线工人好一点点，总附加值在那里，不会有太高暴利。他年迈的父母为他的婚事操碎了心，四处托人给儿子介绍对象，省吃俭用地帮儿子还债。近十年过去了，发现他们说话再也没有当年的自信。我想，他们已经看清了生活的本来面目。

在这样一个人才饱和的时代，农村出身、没学历、在工厂打工的人，再怎么努力也难以倒腾出多大浪花。能结婚成家，不让父母为自己操心，过着安稳的小康生活就已经很好了。这不是在改革开放之初，没有读书的人，只要胆大有想法都会有所成就。

而今，放眼看去，没学历的成功人士毕竟是极少数的。国内一些富豪大佬基本上都来自名校：雷军来自武汉大学；刘强东毕业于中国人民大学，曾是高考状元；马云12岁英语就说得好，能和外国友人轻松自如地交谈，上大学时就办杂志，做五份工作；百度的李彦宏更是北大骄子，又留美深造，是计算机天才……

社会基本已定型，你所处的环境、你的学识、你的家庭、你的眼界早已经决定了你未来可能到达的发展空间，你最多只能在小范围内折腾，上限的天花板已局限在那里。

再说前面那几个说十年后要买一间东方明珠房子做厕所的学生，之后大多没有踏上上海的土地，更不要说在上海买房子了。说这样豪气冲天话语的人应该还有很多很多，只不过是年少轻狂时的胡言、男人间的吹牛皮，过个嘴瘾。抑或当时满怀希望地来到上海，落得在外面打地铺睡觉，说点豪言来安慰受伤的心。

那个带头说买东方明珠一间房的男孩后来倒是来到了上海，如今他在上海做销售工作，工资忽高忽低。现在各个行业竞争越来越大，有好做的职业和好赚的钱。未来，也许他能实现曾经的梦想，也许永远只是梦想。我在十几岁时也曾暗暗想以后一定要站在高高的台上，光芒万丈地对很多人发言讲话，那一定很风光很拽。还曾幻想过，以后要成为我们村庄的前十名有钱人，让谁都不敢瞧不起我，现在想想觉得自己真是幼稚得可笑。

有人会说，可以从工厂出来创业或许就能实现年少时的梦想。创业？本钱没别人多，自然底气没别人足，好的项目或者黄金地段店铺会等着我们吗？我们手上有多少资源优势？有好信息能比别人早一步获取到？还是有高人一等的经商天赋？

成功者和时代机遇、自身努力、生活层次、学识眼界都是息息相关的，所谓天时地利人和。昨天，有位学员找我聊天，她说自己很想改变命运，本来是做平面设计工作，一月也有6000元工资，但她不甘心，想去自己做点什么，选择开淘宝店创业。我给她说，出发点是好的，只是现实太残酷，还是从一步步朝前走更靠谱。眼下的工作开始，和她交谈中，感觉她充满着哀怨，我担心她会抑郁，一遍遍地开导她，希望她能调整好状态。淘宝平台已发展十几年了，2010年前做淘宝的人应该都可以。现在才开始起步自然较难，好在投入并不算多，如果的确看不到希望，可以及时止损。我说，你还是做你的老本行设计吧，做得好还可以接接私活，算起来收入也不少，空时再写写文字，总比贸然换一个行业好。咱们都是80后，生命的有效劳动时间过了1/2，已折腾不起。

看吧：这就是生活的真相，年少时做过的梦有几人能够实现？

我们都曾不知天高地厚过，我们都不想碌碌无为过一生。

## 我曾住过的城中村印象

2008年,我们带着一岁多的女儿,在浙江温州鹿城区经营小吃生意。我们的店面位于黎明工业园门口,是一家活动板房,那一排几乎都是小吃店,有卖煎饼的、煮面条的、做麻辣烫的,还有卖奶茶的,偶尔也有经营电话亭的。

做小生意的人,住宿条件通常不太好,大多选择住一楼,因为店面放不下的东西可以暂时存放,而且存货和取货都很方便,还能节省时间。我们住房附近有许多私人小加工厂,生产圆珠笔和发夹。那些温州本地人仅靠收房租就能过上宽裕的生活。我们住的是两间一楼的老式楼房,由于本地人想多收房租,房屋盖得非常密集,采光非常差,大白天进门都必须开灯。当时的租金是280元一间。温州本地人确实很有商业头脑,思想活跃,生活富裕,有"中国的犹太人"之称。但在温州,做小生意的外地人占绝大多数,主要是安徽、河南、江西、四川、湖北等地的人。温州属于浙江的边缘地带,有时被称为"三不管"地区,自然会有各色人等,治安较乱。小偷小摸、抢劫事件时有发生。有一天中午,我回到出租房时,发现门开着,电视机不见了。原来大白天就有小偷,小偷竟敢明目张胆地把电视机搬走,真是让人气愤又无奈。还有一次,我们准备下季度进货用的几千元钱也被偷了,连皮夹都被扔在租房门口。更恐怖的是,我婆婆的一副金耳环,走在路上被人活生生拽走。还有的行人在路上用手机通话,抢劫者骑着摩托车直接把手机抢走……

那时的城中村,这样的情况比比皆是。一年丢5辆自行车、3辆电瓶车都是常态。小偷无论是破门而入还是偷车，动作之麻利，比电影里的特务还专业。

城中村的居民大多是底层各色人士，有做小生意的、拾荒的、开摩的的，还有三轮车夫、清洁工、搬运工等，治安状况特别差。

那年，我的隔壁住户是一对在温州汽车站打扫卫生的老夫妻，他们每月有900元的收入。他们每天带回许多瓶瓶罐罐。由于东西多，他们的儿媳妇每天都要带着两个孩子去路口接他们。那家人的儿子太懒，像个不懂事的孩子，贪玩不好好工作，爱打牌赌博。他的妻子和我同岁，非常漂亮贤惠。当时，她又怀上了第三个孩子，有温州本地人想预定抱养，但她舍不得，没有答应。

所有开支都依赖老两口帮衬。每天傍晚，总能看到那位妻子拖着两个孩子去接公公婆婆。老人也不会让他们失望，会买些打折的水果蔬菜，还会捡一些别人丢弃但还能用的衣物。

当我写下这些文字的时候，脑海里想起那位有着漂亮容颜的邻居，不知道她后来怎么样了。这么好的女子为什么就嫁给了不负责任的男人呢？美丽和幸福往往不一定是成正比的。

我的住房门口，常常聚集着一些在家带娃的主妇。她们有时会从工厂领些手工活儿回家做。我收摊回来时，常看到她们坐在一起做手工，虽然她们收入极少，却也很开心，似乎没有什么烦恼。她们围在一起做手工，有说有笑。她们常吃西红柿面，买菜常常都是等到傍晚超市打折时购买，但这并不影响她们的幸福指数。

我们住的房屋对面是一家四川人开的小诊所，老板是位40岁左右的女子。她的丈夫有自己的工作，偶尔来帮忙。城中村里的头痛脑热都去这家小诊所，里面屋里有几张床铺，输液常常还得排队。

那年正值金融危机，下半年很多人都搬走了，有的回老家，有的去外地。那座工业园也传言要迁移到别处。我们在2009年也离开了那个城中村。

2011年，我们又到了西安雁塔区，住在一个叫曹家庙的村子里。那时到处在拆迁改造。我们去找店铺时，大家都说这里绝不会拆迁，都喊好几年了，哪有那么容易拆，放心吧！

我们租下了门口一个大通道，人住在楼上，共有五层楼。在通道的一侧，我们自己用木板盖了间4平方米的小木屋，就在那里压面做包子、做馒头。做好后端出楼梯口，在楼梯坡下卖，放上两张桌子、蒸汽炉摆放蒸笼，打豆浆。

因为是城中村，租金倒还便宜。楼梯道每月600元，楼上住房每月300元。每月除去所有开销，能存上8000元。那时非常满足。下午切好菜准备好第二天的食材后，我就去附近旧书店淘很多书看，日子倒也是安稳静好。

只是好景不长，有一天早上起床后看到，全街道上都挂着红条幅，上面写着"为改善居住环境，要配合拆迁，为建设美好家园，三天之内全部搬走"。这消息突如其来，连房东也大感意外。

我们把冰箱里剩余的馅儿做了一点包子。八点多一点，穿着制服的人就来了，那阵势挺吓人……配有喇叭在喊，就是劝我们赶快撤离。那些人对我们的台面桌子敲打、脚踹，对我们大声呵斥。我说把这点卖完就收走，他们也不肯，只好浪费了好多食材。

又得搬家，出去找店。那些年赚点钱就这样倒腾掉了。市中心繁华好的位置不会拆迁，但又没底气、没资本去租，转让费就让人望而却步。在西安我才知道，仅面条就能做出那么多品种，如担担面、菠菜面、裤带面、蘸水面等。

我特意去点了份裤带面，一个大瓷盆里只放一根宽面条，放点芹菜叶，配个放有调料的小碗蘸着吃，吃起来倒也是筋道美味。

在西安四年，我知道了陕西是教育大省，知道了柳青、路遥、贾平凹、陈忠实等文学大咖。在十三朝古都几年的谋生，对我人生影响很大。也就是那时，我才看了《平凡的世界》《人生》《白鹿原》《我与地坛》《长恨歌》等文学书籍，得感谢旁边有个旧书店。

城中村各家店每天不知接待多少顾客，吆喝声、锅碗瓢盆碰撞声、三轮车从门口过响铃声，倒也是一片欣欣向荣。几多繁华，几多沧桑，人间烟火，市井气息，百态人生尽在这小小的村落！

再后来，听说我当年所住过的城中村都早已被改造得焕然一新，与过去已是天壤之别。曾经的不堪模样也是城市化进程中的必然，一切都是这个时代的故事。

# 从砍柴工到搞工程的小舅

我的小舅只比我大 9 岁,是 70 后,与我大表姐同岁。那个年代,类似这样的情况很多:母亲和女儿一起坐月子,谁也没空照顾谁。外婆共生育了 9 个孩子,长大成人的有 7 个。小舅是最小的一个,却没有得到更多的家庭照顾,反而承担得更多。到现在我都不懂那个年代是怎么分家的,老小似乎还吃亏更多。

小舅十几岁时,大舅、三舅他们都早已成家分出去了。80 年代的农村生活条件普遍艰苦,尤其是我外婆所在的大山区。年迈体弱的外公外婆同小舅一起过,住在山坳里三间空心砖搭建的房子里。年长的舅舅、姨们各自家里日子都忙不过来,也无暇顾及太多。那年,外公因病去世,13 岁的小舅读完小学,就退学了,开始了打临工独自谋生的日子。在没有更多人脉资源的情况下,小舅也只能和村子里的人一起上山去砍柴,挑到山外卖。靠山吃山,在当时也只能这样,剩下的劳动力不是砍柴就是烧炭卖。

就这样,年少瘦小的小舅开始了苦力谋生,干着大人们干的活:每天从天麻麻亮忙碌到傍晚才到家,往返穿梭于三十多里的山间小道。隔三岔五不忘买点山外的新鲜零食给外婆品尝。外婆看到年纪小小、肩膀被压得红肿的小舅,又担心他以后个子长不高,心疼得时常偷偷掉眼泪。(小舅身高现在就 1.65 米,估计真是被扁担压的 。)

就这样过了一年多,小舅也认识了几个关系比较好、很有想法的朋友。他们聊起外面的世界，聊起各种生意，心潮澎湃，觉得靠卖柴火实在是太低端，不是长久之计。他们打算一起批发服装来卖。

90年代初，做小生意的远没有现在多。小舅和朋友们就是批发服装、帽子，拖着大包上门买卖。但因小舅年纪太小，又缺少算计，所以赚的钱比其他人少很多。

但相比于砍柴卖柴，这已经有了质的飞跃，至少打开了眼界，接触到了很多信息资源。后来，小舅带上我小姨一起卖过衣服。

随后，小舅觉得背着包上门卖衣服，风里来雨里去，发展还是受限。也可能是年轻，心思无限大，觉得自己能把世界踩在脚下。

小舅又决定去承包一处百亩山头的茶园，交订金签合同。小舅让小姨、大姨帮他找几十个女工去采茶，按斤数来称。那时候在农村请人做工非常容易。也就在那一年，小舅认识了在茶场采茶的舅妈。现在小舅还常吹牛，他当年承包茶园时，一群姑娘为他献殷勤，每次换下的衣服都不知被谁洗得好好的，那是他的得意时光。舅妈比小舅小五岁，生得娇小玲珑，人很精灵。她当时也是小舅的膜拜者，小舅走到哪她跟到哪，慢慢他们就走到了一起。

正当小舅意气风发，爱情事业双丰收时，谁知请来的三位女工闲暇时去摘别人家田里的黄瓜吃，不幸农药中毒，两个抢救过来，一个身亡。年轻的小舅哪见过这阵势，吓坏了。

他是老板，人都是他招来的，自然脱不了干系。之前卖衣服的积蓄、承包茶园的所得，全赔进去还不够，还欠了很多钱。这件事情对他打击很大。屋漏偏逢连夜雨，外婆在那一年因心脏衰竭去世。小舅跪在灵堂，连给外婆的安葬费都拿不出来。是小姨借来八百元，才把外婆的丧事办好了。当时还是花季少女的舅妈，不管小舅怎样落魄，她都一直陪在他身边。她家没有兄弟，唯一的姐姐已出嫁。外婆走后，小舅就在她家住。舅妈只有爸爸，是个耳聋的老实人，靠收板栗茶叶维持生计，住的还是木结构房，条件也不好。那年，因小舅在外欠钱太多，腊月年关，天天都有债务人找小舅要钱。舅妈的爸爸把家里的两头大肥猪卖了，帮小舅还了债，那是舅妈家最大的家产。

当时他们都还没订婚，那些人看到一个花甲老人家如此仁至义尽，也不好再继续纠缠，各人拿了一点钱回去，小舅家总算顺利过了个太平年。此后，小舅和舅妈一起去了浙江温州，他想的是去发达地方寻找更多的机会。可他们都只有小学学历，也无法找到光鲜体面的工作，只好和本镇老乡一起在工地上挖土方，就是建房前的地基，那是十分辛苦的活儿，按平方米计算收入，每天黄汗淌黑汗流，只为攒钱还债。第一年去温州，他们过年都没回老家，想省点来回开销，再帮忙看工地，为多赚份收入。只是天不遂人愿，工地电缆线被偷，小舅又赔不少钱进去，半年工资白干。在那些艰辛不顺的时光里，好在还有舅妈不离不弃。

小舅在工地上挖了一两年的土方后，当上小组长，管理十几个人，自己慢慢不用再干重活儿，领导指挥工人干活儿就行。不久，他还把我两个表哥也都送去温州发展。

小舅当了两年组长后，已还清了老家所欠的全部债务，开始自己承包工地，带了三四十个工人。舅妈则在工地帮工人做饭记账。

2004年时，小舅接了浙江丽水的几栋别墅框架工程，那一年净赚了八万元，买了辆面包车开回老家，和舅妈热闹地办理了婚礼。小舅终于扬眉吐气！大姨、小姨、大家都为他高兴，遗憾的是疼爱小舅的外婆没看到这一天。

这些年，小舅一直在温州打拼，跟着一家大型建筑公司接活干。小舅为人真诚良善，哪怕是自己没及时接到工程款，他都想尽办法垫资给工人先发部分工资。他后面的工人都已跟随他多年，主要是安徽老家人和四川人。

小舅有次同我说，他遗憾自己文化水平太低，图纸看得很吃力，不敢肆意扩大规模。其实接工程外框架，没有室内装修利润高，他赚的都是辛苦操心钱，内心压力很大，常常失眠，尤其担心工人安全情况。上天厚待坚韧努力的人，温州这块神奇的土地给了小舅想要的一切，跟着他去温州打工的俩表哥在那边发展得都不错。

如今小舅虽然算不上大富大贵，但是2009年在舒城老家盖了栋小洋楼，花费55万元，去年又在合肥中心地段买了套大房子，车子也由第一部面包车换到第三部别克君威。

两个小表弟，一个11岁，一个8岁，懂事可爱，学习优秀。舅妈现在全职带娃，岁月静好。

小舅是非常顾家恋家的人，尤其重视俩表弟的教育。常有人夸舅妈命好，舅妈总笑着说，那些年讨债的跟身后一堆，大家都说我舅是个泡货（指不踏实的意思），是众人嘲笑的对象，现在稍微好点，都是慢慢走过来的，她自始至终相信能把日子过好。

在我心里，小舅已经非常了不起。从小学毕业后就靠自己一人谋生，从砍柴到卖衣服、包茶园，再到打苦工，又逆袭成包工头，一路风风雨雨，历经坎坷。

不经历风雨，怎能见彩虹，没有人能随随便便成功。

## 开花甲米粉店的温州人

每天中午去吃饭的那条街，新开了家花甲米粉店，主要是各种大小花甲之类，很是新奇。看着门口的大广告牌介绍，说花甲如何鲜美，高蛋白、低脂肪，对人体是如何有益，看得我就不由自主地走进店内。

花甲可加米线，加鱼丸，加牛肉丸。两口子在经营，店面约15平方米，桌椅都选的是那种小而精致类型的，比较节省空间。听女主人招呼我的口音，我猜测他们不是福建人就是温州人。那天晚上刚好顾客不多。女主人约30多岁，她一边熟练地把花甲放在锡纸里，一边问我是不是在沿海待过，我如实回答，在福建和温州都待过。

她说自己是温州瓯海人。看着她把花甲用锡纸包好放在电磁炉上，觉得这方式看起来蛮新鲜的，或许是我之前没有注意过这类店的原因。问他们生意如何，她说才开几天，这巴掌大的地，房租是每月五千多，转让费花了10万，惊得我张大嘴巴。这类店属细分专业，竞争应该小点。

我说，温州人就是聪明，有"中国的犹太人"之称。据说在非洲一些国家，温州的知名度比北京要高得多。

男店主黑瘦精明的模样，听到我俩的聊天，也主动加入我们的行列中。他说温州人最不怕的就是吃苦，很早就有"宁可睡地板，也要当老板"的古训。温州人是不甘心给别人打工的，哪怕是摆个地摊，开个小店，吃再多苦，遭再多罪，风里来雨里去，他们都情愿自己当老板，宁可做鸡头也不愿做凤尾。这来源于他们骨子里的创业基因。我曾在温州待过三年（茶山镇和鹿城区），那里有很多服装厂、鞋厂、打火机厂，还有剃须刀、发夹、圆珠笔厂等。像美特斯邦威、森马等许多服装知名品牌都在温州。

中国四大知名皮鞋中，奥康、康奈这两大品牌都是在温州诞生成长并走向世界的，也是中国人的骄傲。

我2007年在茶山大学城边一家女装厂做流水工（负责上袖口），那个名叫"雪歌"的女装，当时已在世界100多个国家有自己的专卖店，而老板只是个30岁左右的娇小美丽女子。听说她17岁学做服装和设计，后又自己注册商标，不断宣传推广，做成自己的品牌。她出嫁时，厂房机器都没要，留给她弟弟，只带走商标两个字，却依然能在几年内快速发展壮大，温州的很多中心路口都有她的服装广告。她本人也成了一个传奇神话，多家电台媒体报道过。

像这样起点很低的创业成功者，在温州还有很多很多。2008年我家早餐店对面是家"大虎"打火机厂，员工近千人，产品出口世界各地。最了不起的是，他们的打火机在墨西哥高原缺氧地区能打出火，而其他打火机却都无法点火，因此他们能在金融危机中安然无恙。

他们那一代创业者的文化水平并不高，凭借沿海地理优势，加上创业的氛围浓厚，肯吃苦钻研，绝大多数温州人都取得了不俗的成绩，为国家的经济发展、带动就业发挥了不可估量的作用。

那时候，我们安徽老乡一起聚会时常说，温州各个企业里面的中高层管理者大多都是安徽人。当时我的表哥和其他亲戚的确都是在厂里管理层。但又有老人说，温州在五六十年代还不如安徽条件好呢！既是山区又是盐碱地，还没有什么特产。温州人那时候背着大包去我们安徽经营打被絮、补锅等小生意。改革开放后，温州迅速发展崛起，我们都到他们这打工谋生，这叫三十年河东三十年河西啊！

吃着鲜美可口的花甲，想起往昔的时光。尽管实体经济竞争越来越激烈，一些传统企业经营每况愈下，但我相信，上面提到的温州企业一定会排除万难，立于不败之地。

温州人曾创造了奇迹和神话，未来，他们仍将创造各种传奇，为国家 GDP 的增长做出不可估量的贡献。

不管是摆地摊、开小店还是做企业的温州人，他们身上敢于拼搏吃苦耐劳的精神，永远值得我们学习，向他们致敬！

# 关于泥土

## 01

对于我们这些出身农村的人来说,泥土总是倍感亲切。那种泥土的芳香和记忆,深埋在我们的心灵深处。我们生来就与泥土为伴,从小到大,我所住的房屋都是用土坯建造的,门口的稻场、家边的菜地、田地,一切都离不开土地的滋养。

而今,许多人居住在大城市的高楼中,仿佛生活在高空,即便脚踏实地,四周也尽是水泥铺就的地面。想要养些花草,还得特地去偏远的乡村寻找泥土。时代的发展,让我们与泥土的距离越来越远。

## 02

回想起小时候,父亲曾用一个砖形的木模子,将和好的泥巴放入其中,制成一个个土坯,然后放在阳光下晾晒。晒干后,这些土坯便用来加盖家中的厨房、猪圈,甚至砌墙。那时,泥土在我们的生活中扮演着极其重要的角色,几乎是我们生活的必需品。

随着时间的推移,土坯房逐渐消失,取而代之的是空心砖。还记得我家曾买过一批砖,每块三毛钱,用来翻新猪圈。此外,还有一种略带黑色的青砖。再后来,个头小一些的红砖开始流行,建楼房都是用这种砖，而这种红砖至今仍在使用。但红砖的来源，依然是泥土，只是经过窑厂的高温烧制而成。

对于在农村长大的我们来说，泥土与我们的生活息息相关。

## 03

童年时光里，我们一群小伙伴喜欢用泥土搭建锅台，模仿大人的样子做菜烧饭。我们会用小石子当作菜肴，用泥土捏成各种形状的小块，作为锅台和灶具。

每当我们闹矛盾，就会用泥巴和小伙伴们打闹，你扔我身上，我甩你背上，不一会儿，大家又和好如初，继续在一起玩泥巴。我们还喜欢用泥巴做成收音机的模样，插上竹丝作为开关按钮，仿佛人手一个真正的收音机。有时，我们还用泥巴做成发报机的形状，互相喊着"喂，喂，你能听到吗？"然后相视一笑，仿佛那是真的一样。

如今回想起来，在那个物质贫乏的时代，泥土给我们带来了多少欢乐啊！

大人们更是每天与泥土亲密接触，去菜园地里翻土施肥，种植小白菜、豆角、大蒜，搭建黄瓜架子等。母亲常常裤脚上带着泥土回家，那种泥土的气息让人感到踏实和安心，这是我永不磨灭的记忆。

尤其是在农忙时节，我们小孩子也得下田，割稻、拔秧、插秧、除草，衣服上、脸上都是泥土，整个人像个大花猫。农忙时的干活衣服在池塘里一泡，浑水便浸染了一大片。那时，妈妈对我的要求就是把衣服上的泥土洗净就行。

## 04

对于世代以农为生的我们来说，泥土是我们生存的根本，是不可忽视的存在。

著名作家林清玄老师曾回忆起，他的老父亲从台南老家特意带上红薯苗送给他。当看到林清玄住在高楼之上，连一块泥土的地方都找不到时，他父亲无比失望地喊："儿呀！你怎么住在这无土的地方呀！"

这是老一辈人对泥土的深切热爱之情。另一位名人，在美国留学时，怀念祖国，思乡心切，托人辗转捎去北京的一小包泥土。每当思念家乡时，就拿出那包泥土来闻一闻，以解乡愁。

## 05

《圣经》里说，上帝用泥土造出了人类的始祖亚当："上帝用地上的泥土造人，将生气吹在他的鼻孔里，他就成了有灵的活人，名叫亚当。"上帝还对亚当说："你本是泥土，仍要归于泥土。"

在中国神话传说中，女娲也是用泥土造人的："女娲抟黄土做人。"这些相似的传说说明了一个深刻的道理：土地是人类的生命之源。

人类的生命、精神文明、物质追求都离不开大地的怀抱。在大地的怀抱里，我们才能看到辽阔的天空。是大地和天空赋予了我们宽阔的胸襟，让我们得以欣赏大自然的一切美好。

我们中国是农业大国，土地是人民立身之本。但现在种田的人越来越少，甚至有田地被荒废，这不免让人唏嘘、叹息。

现在的孩子也不会捏泥巴玩，而是有塑料做的假沙子和泥巴代替。

我们人类始终是依托大地而存在，那是我们灵魂的栖息地。怀念那玩泥巴的童年，怀念那些远去的岁月。

# 记录生活，就是在记录历史

### 01

许多人梦想撰写一部宏大的著作来反映时代的发展和进步，但这样宏伟的梦想往往容易让人畏缩不前，不敢轻易下笔。昨天我在学员群里说，实际上，我们记录自己的生活，就是在记录这个时代。后人将能从我们的记录中窥见我们现在的生活状况。

### 02

最近，我在读作家丁燕的《工厂女孩》，她还有一本《工厂男孩》。她所记录的，不也是这个时代的故事吗？她写了电子厂、注塑厂、焊接厂、音箱盒厂的工人等。这本书是丁燕在 2010 年亲历东莞电子厂和音响盒厂，历时 200 天的记录。她每天在厕所里快速记录，晚上下班或周末拖着疲惫的身躯写文章。

我也曾经是工厂的一分子，读这样的故事感到特别亲切。尽管她的笔下生活工作环境似乎比我经历过的更为严酷，工作时间虽然只有 11 个小时，比我们那时短了好几个小时，但他们有主管监督，精神必须高度集中。

我们那时候是多劳多得，没有人管束，大家都自觉地勤奋工作。想休息时，偶尔会在走廊上休息，喝喝水，聊聊天，相对自由。

我在厂里的第二年，已经有了六层的新宿舍楼，干净宽敞。我们那时没有单休，也不接触厂外的人，只和老乡相处，生活除了吃饭就是干活，虽然枯燥乏味，但环境单纯安全。

## 03

在她的书中，有的女孩做焊工，双手粗糙，指甲甚至脱落，不忍细看，骨节粗大，与脸蛋极不相符。而做服装工作的人手部保养得很好。如果说手是女人的第二张脸，我觉得我的第二张脸比第一张脸要好看。

很多年前，小姨曾戏称我有一双"艺术家"的手，适合弹钢琴，可惜投错了胎。

或许是因为我离开厂里已经有些年，过去的劳累困苦都已淡忘。在看《工厂女孩》时，我总觉得自己比书中的打工妹要幸运得多。我童年和少年时期的自卑是在工厂逐渐好转的。

我以前在微博上看到过这本书的介绍，在没有看这本书之前，我曾浅薄地认为，一位诗人作家，一位名校毕业生，再怎么深入一线，也是旁观者。但当我打开这本书，顿时失去了那份底气，佩服作者文笔的深度。尽管我在工厂待了更长的时间，却写不出她那样细腻深刻的文字。

她写了打工一代、打工二代，还有打工妹选择香港台湾人做二奶的故事，以及广东本地偏远山区的打工妹。她们虽比外省人有点优势，但总是被外来打工仔骗财骗色。

## 04

　　作者以不同的打工妹的故事串联成整本书。有的姑娘身体不好，做不了工厂的活；有的想走捷径。但这些姑娘虽然一时享受了福气，最后却把自己余生的全部幸福连本带利地还给了命运，有的甚至更惨。

　　书中还有注塑厂工人断脚趾残废的真实故事。这位工人家里有三个孩子要抚养，他整天想用啤酒瓶和老板干一架。在别人的劝说下，他最终还得和命运妥协，只是获得了少量的赔偿金。靠力气为生的人，双脚却不行了。作者的语言表达得极为克制，那家厂里没有一位工人不曾受过伤。

　　还有的工厂容易得肺病，每隔三四个月就重新换一批工人。还有地下黑工厂，拖欠克扣工资等。一个个活生生的故事触目惊心，而他们却真实地存在着。通常去沿海工厂的工人都是初中学历、小学学历，有的只有三四年级文化，以四川、湖南、湖北、贵州等地为主。

　　有一个四川女孩叫清荷，她是高中毕业，属于打工二代，高挑漂亮。她独自应聘了两千多人的日资电子厂。暑假曾在母亲厂干过暑期工，她看不上父母工作的小厂。

　　她的父母也在东莞打工多年，最大的梦想就是存钱回老家盖栋三层楼房。清荷从小是留守儿童，情感缺失，与父母有隔阂。在电子厂，每个周末可以和父母聚餐，比其他打工族稍微有一点优越感。

　　清荷在电子厂做电子元件三个月后转到文员工作，这是厂里自成立20年来的首个现象。但她面临着组长经理的不怀好意，聪明的她很有自己的主见，最后选择继续去读书精修日语。当时周边电子厂会日语的人择业很有优势。

　　无疑，清荷这个姑娘是在打工妹中最幸运的人。她的父母那年在家里盖了三层楼，借了7万债，准备继续来东莞打工还债。听说女儿要辞职学习，依然再为女儿筹借3万日语学费。

## 05

作家丁燕记录的是最底层最平凡人的故事，难道不是这个时代的故事吗？《工厂女孩》出版于2013年，《工厂男孩》出版于2016年，离我们并不遥远。

这些工厂女孩、工厂男孩，他们是生产线上的一颗颗螺丝钉。他们也是中国工业化现代化进程中的无数颗螺丝钉，他们更是中国乡镇经济发展史上的中流砥柱。

这本书也裹挟了无数人对现代化工业洪流的追问。全国数百万乡村女孩奔赴那里，他们的青春、他们的血汗、他们的梦想、他们的爱情……

## 06

我喜欢张爱玲说过的一句话，凡人比英雄更能代表这个时代的总量。曾经有人讽刺张爱玲的小说只会写一些小情小爱，不关心政治，不关心战争，没有家国情怀。

张爱玲的笔下写尽了旧上海的浮华掠影、市井百态、痴男怨女、升斗小民。她用文字记录了一代人的悲欢离合、爱恨情仇。她擅长刻画人性，而人性和爱情都是永恒的主题，永不过时。

香港的亦舒、张小娴，难道她们的小情小爱小说就不是时代的故事吗？还有写边缘情感的安妮宝贝，她主观独特却能洞见灵魂的文字照样受到无数人的欢迎。

任何一个创作者，他的创作载体或多或少都会有反映时代的故事，因为他无法脱离自己生活的时代。一名写作者首先是从小我写起，先从个人主观感受写起，不可能一开始就能驾驭宏大叙事结构。再说文学是百花齐放的，难不成所有作者都写同一个类型？

随着科技的日新月异，再过20年，人工智能普及，后人再看到《工厂女孩》这本书，他们不是在看历史故事吗？或许会感叹唏嘘，或许会觉得不可思议。

## 07

我曾写小时候稻田里搞双抢，陪母亲交公粮，父亲在稻田里用泥巴做土坯，用来盖猪圈，我和发小用泥巴做灶具玩。写当年春运为了赶火车的艰辛，为了买票排队两天，为家里寄钱得去邮电局汇款，用过插卡的打电话机，提前写好稿子，长话短说，为了减少电话费……

那些真实而遥远的故事，难道我们写在文章中，这不也是一个时代的缩影吗？虽然我们只是小小的写作者，只是这个时代的沧海一粟，但我们也是在记录属于自己的"历史"。我们的后代从文字中能窥见曾经的生活。

我认识多年的文友甘肃姑娘王托弟，她的文章喜欢写她家乡的黄土高原、甘肃的秦腔、浆水面、掐麦秸，一些特色非物质文化遗产……这些对于我来说都非常新鲜好奇，让我充满着向往。

她只是在记录自己和身边人的故事，但这也是在传播家乡文化啊！我曾经在文章中写道，有生之年如果有机会去甘肃，我一定要看看托弟笔下的天水秦安。

她在书写她家乡的故事，也是整个甘肃黄土高原的故事。她以出生于黄土高原而骄傲，如同我以出生于安徽"文都"桐城而骄傲。

去年有微信好友路过我的家乡,她停留游玩了一天,还给我发来照片。她说:"齐老师,我来到了你的家乡。"

这是作为一名写作者的最大意义所在吧!

## 08

2014年,87岁的马尔克斯去世,哥伦比亚总统桑托斯在致悼词中说:"对于我们哥伦比亚人来说,马尔克斯是这个国家最好的讲述者……哥伦比亚很感激马尔克斯。"

马尔克斯自己也说,他活着就是为了讲述。他还有句名言:"生活不是我们活过的日子,而是我们记录的日子。"

马尔克斯因为作品伟大,传播面够广,所以他的讲述和记录能被全世界知晓。我们写作者去记录、去传播、去写正能量的文字,我们的文字也都是有意义的字符。

茅盾文学奖获得者莫言,他当初走上写作之路是听说作家每天可以吃上饺子。在那贫瘠的岁月,能吃上饺子对莫言来说是最大的诱惑和动力。他不可能一开始是冲着诺贝尔文学奖去写作的。

## 难忘的童年趣事

小时候，我喜欢趿着妈妈做的手工布鞋，跑一步跳一步，一步一跳，还拍着小手，唱着小调，快乐得像只鸟儿。老远就朝发小燕子招手喊她，她走过来，我们小手牵着小手，一起去屋后玩泥巴。我们把泥巴捏成方的、圆的、长的，做成小车或房屋。不高兴时再将它们切成碎块，又重新揉起来。小小的我们凭着想象，自由控制泥巴的模样，任意发挥，也能从这单调的生活里寻到快乐的源泉。

有时，我们还将泥巴做成电影中看到的发报机、传呼机、收音机的形状，插上竹丝作为天线按钮，再学着大人的样子，各拿一个，边走边对着上面"喂喂喂"，再拍几下，相视大笑起来，笑声传出很远很远……

上学的路上，我每天用报纸包几块妈妈炒好的腌萝卜干，揣在口袋里。在路上，小伙伴们你拿一块，他拿一块，放到嘴边，先咝咝地吸掉萝卜干外边的辣椒面，再将腌萝卜一口塞进嘴里，咬得嘎嘣嘎嘣脆响。伴着小伙伴们的欢笑打闹声，吃着美味，不知不觉就到了离家两公里的学校。那时候没有大人接送一说，即便是读学前班，也一样走着，踢踢石子，扯扯野草，想跑就跑，想歇就歇，丝毫不影响我们的快乐感。

春天，上学路边不远处的大片桃园里，粉粉嫩嫩的桃花开得纷纷扬扬，像一片绯红的云彩，又像一幅美丽的山水画。人若站在桃树下，人花相映，便成画中人，看着都能让人沉醉。没几天，花谢了，桃树上长出了密密麻麻的小桃子，我们的心便急迫起来。在我们日复一日的期待中，桃子由青变红，越来越大，把桃树都压弯了腰。满园的桃子长得粉嘟嘟，散发着沁人的香气，远远望着，我们不停地咽口水。

一个假日的中午，估计主人正在吃饭，我们五个孩子偷偷商量好，结伴打算去偷桃子。一路上，既兴奋又紧张，见着熟人也不敢打招呼。没想到，我们刚到桃园地冒出头，一位五十多岁的奶奶就迎过来说："你们小孩不要乱摘呀，有的正在长个，别浪费了，我来摘些熟好的送些给你们吃……"

记得那天我的连衣裙下摆兜了一大兜桃子，屁颠屁颠地回来，真是乐坏了。我们个个吃得嘴唇都被染红了，还把桃核外面吮吃得干干净净，总算吃得肚儿圆。我的那件裙子，妈妈洗了好久，浇了好几次，才将上面的毛和颜色洗净。

大人们都说，那桃园一家人真好，没骂没吵闹，还白给你们送这么多，这样的人真是少见。人家是靠那些桃子卖钱生存的啊！以后我们都不好意思再去那家偷桃子了，走到那儿，脸都会红一下。有些条件好的小伙伴，就让父母去那家买了很多回来，当时好像是五毛钱一斤。

如今想来，那位桃园奶奶不经意间，在我们年少的心中播下了良善温暖的种子，让我们懂得给予。

实在没什么东西吃的，等到菜园有黄瓜时，管它长得粗或细，一把掐下，两手掌把黄瓜外的毛刺抹一抹，就当作洗过，往嘴里送，嘎嘣嘎嘣地大口嚼。

搭锅，这是许多成年人的共同记忆吧！我们那时会把家里的腊肉偷偷割一小块，包上一捧大米，带上小铁锅，咸菜，油盐调料，再带包火柴。一群孩子奔跑到山上，靠土岸边掏个小锅洞，然后各自分工，人人劳动。有的去淘米，有的去洗菜，有的负责生火，有的将腊肉切成小方块，在锅里就着调料烤着吃，虽然有着烟熏味，却也感觉特别香。

待到饭熟后，我们奔腾欢呼，激动的你一铲我一勺，甚至用手抓抢着吃，满满的一种成就感。如今想起来，那种暖暖的幸福立刻将我包围。

夏天，树上的知了叫得欢。我们顶着烈日、不畏酷暑，将小脸儿晒得通红，四处奔跑、爬树、追寻。一旦抓到，便如获至宝。将知了的翅膀掐短，伙伴们一起分享，或者将它装在火柴盒里，不时拍打一下，听它吱吱地叫。一个知了往往能玩上一天，到了傍晚，再将它放到某棵树上。

上学的路边，长着些野树野草。我们常寻找野果子吃。有一种生长在刺藤上的野果子（方言：小麦果子），小小的、红红的，有田野的清香，吃起来酸酸甜甜，很带劲。还有山坡边有一种外面带刺的果子，我们就叫刺果，也会小心地摘下来吃。以及草地上的一种草根，一节一节的，白白细嫩，咬一口，甜丝丝的。这都是孩童时的我们，最美味的天然零食。

记忆里，老家的田埂边，大人们从舍不得浪费。仅尺来宽的田埂，靠边沿上，春天种上黄豆，秋天种上萝卜。我们在田埂上来回奔跑，裤脚撩得那些植物叶子沙沙响。

冬天，我们一群孩子去田埂拔萝卜，扯掉萝卜缨子，三下五除二地把萝卜皮扒掉，像兔子一样，就美滋滋地开吃。脆生生的，甜甜的，吃得满嘴角都是萝卜沫子。

寒冬腊月，数九寒天，上学途中的几个池塘，都结了厚厚的冰。我们都要从冰上走，颤颤巍巍的，还嬉笑着喊"滑冰、滑冰啊！"有次我不小心摔倒在冰上，一下将冰砸出个大窟窿。一旁大点的小伙伴眼疾手快，赶紧把我拉起来。好在冬天的棉袄很厚，水没浸过。不过，那时候真不知道一个"冷"字，只要快乐，什么都可以放在一边。

那些年的冬天，感觉比现在冷多了，冬天也漫无边际。雪下得经常没过膝盖，但我们孩子却觉得特快活，最喜欢在那白茫茫的世界堆雪人、打雪仗，拿着竹竿敲屋檐下的冰凌。

雪，它是上天送给大地最美的情书，它是人间的精灵，它曾装饰过我们美丽的童年，带给我们纯白无邪的回忆。

那个时候的孩子，没什么多的玩具，都有收集的爱好，收集的宝贝有香烟盒、糖纸之类的。我们经常将烟盒里的锡纸刮一刮，与白纸分离出来，再折得整整齐齐，压平收藏。

印象里有种叫"小龙人"的糖果，大家都非常喜欢外面漂亮的包装纸，每个人都会收藏几张，有时候我们还会用不同的牌子互相交换，一日一日丰富自己的宝藏。那时有个叫"小龙人"的电视，我在隔壁大娘家曾看过，里面主要讲小龙人找妈妈的故事，一直到现在，我还记得里面的许多情节。而糖果纸的封面就是同电视里的小龙人一样装扮，每每看到糖纸，我就会想起那部电视剧。

大人们的世界与小孩子们无关，童年的我们只关心野花野草、蜜蜂蝴蝶，只关心所有能吃的一切，所有好玩的一切，所有我们感兴趣的东西。

童年的记忆，影响着我们一生的习惯、性格，以及情感。我们虽然在老去，但那些记忆永远不会老去。

愿我们永葆童心，永远纯洁而快乐！

# 记忆里的门前小路

提到家乡，我脑海中首先浮现的是家里门前的那条小路。它紧挨着我家的稻场，在最早的记忆里，小路仅有扁担宽，坑坑洼洼，雨天泥泞不堪。

孩提时代，我和小伙伴们喜欢在小路边玩耍，捡石子、捡糖果纸，视若珍宝地收藏。闲暇时，我们把小石子分类装在瓶子里，摇得叮当响；把糖果纸洗净、整理，再折成星星或宝塔形，连起来还能做成手镯，别提多开心了。那是属于我们的童年时光，单调却不乏快乐。

也曾在一个傍晚时分，我在路边等田间劳作的母亲，边等边幻想：这条路的尽头究竟是哪里？是通往遥远的天际，还是通往天堂，连接着天上的云朵？

随着时代的不断发展，门前的小路也拓宽了。为了防止雨天泥泞，路上逐步铺上了石子。有骑自行车的人路过时，老远就能听到咯噔咯噔的响声，像一阵风掠过。

记得我读四年级时，摩托车在农村还是稀罕物。我和小伙伴们喜欢蹲在路边数过往的摩托车。印象最深的是，有一天经过了八辆摩托车，我们拍着手高声欢呼，仿佛那些摩托车都是自家的。

五年级暑假，我和发小开始学习骑自行车。先学用一只脚踩踏板让自行车滑行，熟练后，再练习骑三角叉。每天骑得大汗淋漓，却乐此不疲。小路上，只留下叮叮当当的铃声和我们清脆的欢笑。

那个暑假，我们都学会了骑自行车，那条小路也更深地留在了我们的记忆中。

时间飞逝，我们也渐渐长大。几年后，已不再是喜欢数摩托车的花季少女，也过了那个充满好奇的年龄。

那年，发小家买了摩托车，她让我陪着一起学。从学习加速、刹车、转弯、掉头开始，一天一点进步。摩托车虽不用踩，但开始很难把握速度，尤其是在小路上掉头，比自行车重得多。每当这时，就喊大人过来帮忙。几天后，我们终于能轻松驾驭摩托车了。

我们像两条自由的鱼，在小路上穿梭。那是纯真的快乐时光，无忧无虑的美好岁月。

后来，门前的路再度拓宽，铺成了水泥路。而我们都开始外出打工。但在梦中，门前的小路却出现了无数次。

随着桐潜公路的通车，主干道迁移到了村委会后面，那是一条宽达20米的柏油大马路，两旁种着樟树，像卫士守护。相比之下，家门前这条路显得冷清，除了附近居民，已极少有其他村民。

门前的这条路，没有了往日的人气，路边杂草丛生，水泥路面破损也无人问津，仿佛已被人遗忘。

我出生的村庄如今也显得寂寞萧条。城镇化的加速，许多村民已搬到镇上或县城，有的搬到了安庆或省会合肥，留下的多是老弱妇孺和旧屋。

不管是门前的小路，还是家乡的村庄，如今都像一个迟暮的老人，守着一段旧时光，少有人光顾。

喧嚣、热闹、光鲜已成过去，家乡已非昔日模样，再找不到从前的温馨和欢乐。

这次回老家，我站在门前的小路上出神。想起曾在这条路上学骑自行车，摔倒时隔壁庄的大男孩大笑，我忍着疼爬起来，倔强地大喊："我又不痛，你们笑什么……"

以及后来学骑摩托车，从这条路上出发闯荡。这条路见证了我的成长，从童年到成年，成为人妻人母。

小路和村庄的变化，也见证了时代的发展。在时代潮流面前，个人只能顺应和接受。

恍惚中，我又看见那个小小的我，站在路旁，摇着石子，折着糖纸，昂着头，想象着神秘的远方，幻想着未来。

门前的这条路，承载了我太多记忆：快乐、悲伤、欢笑、流泪、向往。唯有在梦里，才能找寻它过往的模样，怀念那段单纯宁静的时光。

这一生，无论要走多少路，家乡门前的小路，永远是我心中最深最美的眷念。它一直在我心上蜿蜒，伸向远方……

## 我们都是年味变淡的"稀释者"

又是一年的年底，小年已过，大年将至。放眼望去，无论是城市还是乡村，都感受不到过年的气氛，年味似乎一年不如一年。

由于环保部门的监管，鞭炮烟花已很少见到，到处显得冷冷清清，与平日并无二致。有人说过年只是农村人的节日，城市人早已不再重视，但现在连乡村的年味也变得淡薄。随着社会的不断发展，过年已不再像过去那样热闹。

记忆中，从腊八节开始，孩子们就每天倒数着过年的日子，每天早上都会问母亲，还有多少天过年，哪怕心里清楚，也要再确认一次。

过去，一进腊月，大人们就开始忙碌起来，打扫卫生，置办年货，准备各种食物。杀猪、做豆腐、炸红薯干、炒花生、炸爆米花、炸圆子、炒南瓜子、做米糖和芝麻糖，每一样都能让孩子们欢呼雀跃。

杀猪在农村是件大事，猪肉通常一半留着腌制，一半卖掉。唯独我家只留下猪下水和几斤肉，其余都卖掉以支付学费。

做豆腐时，要提前泡好黄豆，然后挑到村里的豆腐作坊。因为过年每家都要做豆腐，豆腐作坊的生意异常火爆，必须提前预约。轮到我家时，我和妹妹们总是兴奋得手舞足蹈，因为可以喝到新鲜的豆浆。

现在回想起来，觉得那时的自己很可笑，同时也感叹社会的快速发展。如今，豆浆再也喝不出小时候的味道，不是豆浆变了，而是我们长大了。

腊月里，母亲炒花生时，我们总是急不可耐地抓起来就吃，炒好的花生装在小铁箱里,可以吃到正月底。妈妈还会把存好的锅巴用油炸,又香又脆,美味无比,用袋子装好可以存放一段时间。

过年时,即使是家境贫寒,也会给孩子买新衣服、红头绳,以增添节日的喜庆。

年夜饭上的红烧鱼一直到正月十五都保持完整,这象征着"年年有余",人们非常注重这种仪式感,那盘鱼就是不下筷,这也是一种对美好生活的期待。

那些年的春晚,是每个家庭必看的节目,也是全球华人关注的焦点。倪萍、曹颖、陈佩斯、赵本山等人成为我们几代人心中的深刻记忆。

70后和80后对那个物质匮乏年代的年味有着深刻的体会。我们盼望的不是过年,而是过年时才能享受到的美食,才能见到的人,以及那份闲适。归根结底,味蕾才是情感的闸门。

现在,我们都在感叹"年味越来越淡",觉得越来越没意思。其实,我们每个人都是年味变淡的"稀释者"。

拜年走亲戚变得像送快递一样匆忙。每个人都在忙,都在不停地抢时间,却无法停下来好好享受生活。我们到底在忙些什么?生命的意义又是什么?

即便是亲朋好友难得相聚,大家寒暄过后,往往各自玩手机。"世界上最遥远的距离不是生与死,而是我在你面前,你却在玩手机。"

社会节奏发展太快,电子产品和自媒体平台的兴起,以及小视频和多元化娱乐节目的流行,分散了人们的注意力,使得一家人围坐谈笑、看春晚的场景变得罕见。

现在,人们的心态变得浮躁,什么都追求效率。拜年恨不得一天之内全部完成,而瓜子、花生、米糖等年货,只需在手机上一点,就能送到家。

生活水平提高,让人们不再需要等到过年才能享受美食。这减少了过年的仪式感,人们也不再那么期待。

一些大城市的居民甚至不再过年,选择全家出游或在手机上预订年夜饭。一部手机就能搞定一切,吃喝玩乐应有尽有。

我们从当年收压岁钱的孩子,成长为发压岁钱的成年人。最不喜欢过年的可能是中年人,因为过年意味着对过去一年的盘点,以及面对比较和攀比,让人感受到无奈和心酸。

从童年、少年到青年、中年,我们对过年的热闹记忆到如今的年味变淡,甚至消失,这或许是社会发展的必然趋势。

曾经浓浓的年味、乡情,以及热闹的办年货场景,都已成为记忆中的画面。唯愿中华传统节日能够永久传承。

# 因为没有学历，我用了 18 年才活成一个体面的普通人

## 01

读小学时，我的作文曾被老师当作范文。初中时，我的语文成绩在全年级七个班中排名前三。

记得有一次作文满分是 50 分，我得了 45 分。考试的作文题目是根据一份资料写文章，资料讲述了因将合同上的"乌鲁木齐"误写为"乌鲁木齐"，导致 500 万损失的故事，意在形容粗心大意的人。

因家庭原因，我在初三那年离开校园，为了节省考试费用，我没有完成初三课程。14 岁半的我，开始了谋生之路。起初，我在村里打零工，比如在堂哥的厂里制作啤酒瓶颈上的锡纸套。

那年下半年，我开始学习缝纫。由于村里借不到钱，母亲从小姨家借了 450 元，其中 420 元用来购买了一台蝴蝶牌缝纫机，20 元买了一把 12 号的张小泉大剪刀。

我不确定自己是否喜欢这个行业，但我记得曾在缝纫机上刻下"有志者事竟成"的字样。

第二年，我前往镇上继续学习缝纫，因为村里的门面没有太多活干，学不到东西。我每天骑自行车四五十分钟到镇上。镇上的师傅家里有《读者》杂志，还有毕淑敏和梁晓声的书，这可能是我首次接触文学作品。

当时我们有七位师姐妹，几乎没有多余的时间看书。师傅在场时我们也不敢看。每天还得帮师傅家拖地、带孩子、洗衣服、干杂活。作为最后一个加入的徒弟，拆线头、缝脚口、熨衣、锁扣眼、钉扣子等杂活都是我的任务。

除了这两本书，我的童年和青少年时期几乎没有读过其他课外书。不怕大家笑话，我连新华字典都没有，家里也没有作文书。与许多有家族文化底蕴的人相比，我在阅读方面落后了很多年。

## 02

在镇上学习了一年缝纫技术后，我前往沿海地区打工，目的地是福建泉州晋江东石镇潘径村的南星服装厂。

在厂里，我和闺蜜是两个特别的存在。其他人说我们说话喜欢文绉绉的，在他们看来，这是贬义词。我们都是花季雨季的孩子。那时，工作时间非常长，从早上8点到凌晨2点，但经常拖到凌晨三四点才下班。

每天晚上10点是夜宵时间，几乎全年无休。除非一批货做完了休息半天，或者中秋、端午节晚上不上班。

有时饭还在嘴里，我们就赶回车间，只为了比别人多踩几下平车。在福建的第一年，我仍然是学徒，一年到头辛苦工作，回家时只有900元。我赶上了师徒传承的末期，总共学了两年半。

即便在忙碌的情况下，我还是喜欢摘抄歌词，如张信哲、刘德华、任贤齐的，后来还有阿杜、刀郎的。只要有同事买了磁带，我就立刻借来，抄下歌词。

厂里有时会有多余的口袋布或有瑕疵的布料，我就把它们整理好，看着内心非常满足，并在口袋布上写字。有空时，我就在上面写东西，有时抄歌词，有时写日记或感慨。

在那种封闭的环境中，我对未来一无所知。大家比较的是谁更节省、谁做衣服更快、谁的工资更高，但没人知道梦想是什么，人生该何去何从。人如机器，如工具。

忙里偷闲时，我睡前会看10来分钟杂志，如《南风》《花溪》《读者》《意林》《知音》和《特别关注》等。

隔壁的老乡嘲笑我们，说我们宿舍那么晚还不睡觉，不是在看书就是在练字。他们认为我们几年后仍然是村妇，不相信我们的命运会有所不同。

在他们眼中，我和闺蜜成了厂里的异类。但我想，即使是村妇，我也要做一个有思想、有情怀的村妇。

我在福建的厂里待了4年。2007年，我还在温州茶山大学城的一个女装品牌厂工作了一年。此外，我还在老家的羽绒服店工作了两次，每次半年。

2007年，在女装厂的墙上有很多口号，我把它们全部摘抄在笔记本上，比如"既要争分夺秒，又要针针计较"。

现在回想起来，或许热爱文字的种子早已种下，只是没有遇到合适的环境生根发芽。多年来，我一直在为生存而被迫谋生，生活麻木枯燥。社会上有太多人仅仅为了活着就耗费了所有精力。

我人生中最美好的青春年华是在闭塞的工厂里度过的，那些远去的花季、雨季、梦季啊！

## 03

在接下来的几年里，我曾在电子厂工作，也尝试过自己做生意，卖小吃。我的足迹遍布河南的漯河、河北的宽城、浙江的温州和陕西的西安。

2013年到2015年,我开始学会使用手机QQ,并在QQ空间无意中结识了许多文友。从一个文友的空间跳转到另一个,我仿佛进入了一个全新的世界。他们的日志配以图片和音乐,显得格外唯美。

我感到非常高兴,因为无需花费金钱购买书籍,我就能阅读到这么多优秀的文章。

我喜欢认真地为他们的日志留言和点赞,非常珍惜这些作品。尽管他们可能对我这个读者没有什么印象,但我偶尔会在QQ空间发一些动态。他们文章中提到的书籍,我也会购买来阅读,幸运的是,我工作的地方旁边有一个旧书摊,我在那里阅读了许多文学名著。

2016年年初,我通过QQ群了解到了简书,并顺藤摸瓜下载了简书App。起初的几个月,我只是在阅读,自己并没有动笔写作。

直到那年年中,我才正式开始写作,并注册了微信公众号"齐帆齐"。至今,公众号已经更新了1700多篇文章。

在写作初期,由于我白天还需要工作,我只能在晚上熬夜写作。从最初的10天写一篇文章,到后来每周一篇,再到稳定的每周三四篇。

那一年,我大部分时间的睡眠时间只有五个多小时。我尽可能地抽出时间来阅读、写作、排版和研究自媒体。我认为这可能是改变命运的最后机会。

我写了许多关于底层草根人物的故事,因为他们就是我自己或者我身边的人,他们的故事真实可感。

对于平台来说,这些故事非常新鲜,阅读量也非常好。我写过快递员、做早餐的老乡、卖面条的、开馄饨店的、卖油漆的朋友等,这些都是接地气且深入人心的人物故事。

2017年5月,我申请出版了电子书,并在豆瓣上架,这本书被推到了首页,霸屏了很长时间。

同年7月,我成为了简书签约作者。8月底,我的文章在人民网发表,阅读量在两小时内就超过了10万。同时，我还签约了百度平台。也就是说，在正式写作一年多的时间里，我签约了两家大型平台。

当时，平台支持签约作者开设课程。每个签约作者都有自己的经纪人。通过微信公众号、课程收入和百度平台的收入，我的收入已经远远超过了我的主业。

2017年11月，我成为了一名全职自由写作者。2018年，我签约了出书合同。2019年1月，我的《追梦路上，让灵魂发光》出版。2021年，我的学员合集书《遇见梦想，遇见花开》上市。

掌阅上现在有我的4本书籍。同时，我还推荐学员们出书近200部，推荐他们加入各类作协、中国散文学会等，以及签约各类平台。

让我觉得最幸福的事，不仅是我自身因文字获得了成长，还有许多人因为我而坚持了写作之路，实现了文学梦想，看到了未来更多的可能性。

希望朋友们都能找到内心的热爱，热爱可以帮我们寻找幸福之光。做热爱之事，内心充满欢悦，也是最容易出成果的。我们要有坚持下去的决心，让读书写作成为精神的呼吸。

人生没有白走的路，人生没有白写的字。

因为家庭环境原因，没有学历，没有背景，我经历了18年的兜兜转转、颠沛流离，在命运的洪流里沉沉浮浮。所有的经历都成了我写作的最好素材。

我很感恩遇见了大好的自媒体时代，让普通人持续输出内容就得以"被看见"；感恩遇见简书平台，给了我写作的动力之源。

写作没有年龄、学历、地位、性别之分，没有时间和空间的限制。希望大家能坚持到底。

# 本来无一物,每进一寸都是欢喜

## 01

同一件事情,不同的人感受到的快乐是不同的。那天,我读到一位同行朋友的文章,里面有一句话:"本来无一物,每进一步都特别欢喜。"让我深有感触。

那位作者说他是从山区走出来的,小时候觉得拥有一座新房子就是最大的梦想。后来,他读了文学硕士,在读研期间,他的文章多次上稿大号平台,出版了三本书籍。去年刚毕业,他就靠书籍版税在某省会城市付了房子首付。

这是一个普通男孩通过读书写作改变命运的故事,看得出他对自己的人生非常满意。

我是一个连中考都没参加的人,现在每天抱着手机就能工作,可以随时读书写作,行走见人,参加文友会,去自己想去的地方,趁时光正好,趁年华未老。

这一切是我过去所不敢想象的。即使我和同行们相比有很大的差距,但我仍然有很强烈的快乐感。这是由每个人的心态以及他弹跳的高度所决定的吧!俗话说,知足者常乐!

我在 2019 年就注册了文化传媒公司,只是为走账需要。我并不喜欢说自己是公司创始人、CEO之类，倒是更喜欢说自己是自由写作者、网络写手，这样让我心里更舒服。

直到今年，我才慢慢接受了这个身份，有时会说自己是文化传媒公司创始人。一开始不习惯这样宣称，可能还是内心自卑的原因，以及对新事物接受程度慢，心境需要一个适应的过程。

在我写作之前，做得最长的工作就是在厂里做衣服，还做了几年的个体户小生意，摆过地摊，做过几个月营业员，在电子厂也做过一段时间。

今年是我读书写作的第9个年头，我感觉只是一眨眼的时间，一切如梦如幻，蓦然回首，人生已到中年。

## 02

大前年，我二妹在安徽省城合肥买了套小房子，她说激动得三夜没睡好。

我们在小群里面聊天，说大合肥有多少人买的是四室的房子，有的还是洋楼、别墅、高档学区房，面积是她的房子数倍以上，但他们可能还没有她这样强烈的快乐感，肯定不会激动成这般模样。

其实我二妹在县城中心有一套学区房，120多平方，装修比较不错，但她依然为省城有个小房子开心不已。这就是一个人的快乐感吧！

如同小妹所说，每当看到好天气，看到花开就欢乐得想唱歌，这也是一种心态良好的体现。

有的人生活非常优渥，不需要像我们这样辛苦，但是他的内心却没有这么大的一种愉悦感。

从这点来说，我们姐妹非常幸运，能吃能睡不长肉，幸福快乐感极强，一点点小确幸都有莫大的喜悦感。

每天我们在小群里都有说不完的话题。有个文友曾评价，你们姐妹这么好，必定是精神思想相当，要不然没有那么多话可讲。

我们这代出生在农村的人，如果又没读什么书，圈层眼界有限，完全靠自己从农村到县城再到省会，必须得耗费大半生甚至一生的全部心血精力。

从农村到城市的第一代，注定是要被牺牲掉的一代，下一代相对会好点。

今天在微博看到一句话："奋斗吧！你一个人的努力可以改变三代人的命运。"

## 03

前不久，我发了条朋友圈感慨，我是老天"赏饭吃"的孩子吗？零基础写作一年，上稿《人民网》，签约两家知名大平台，写作一年半后，签约出书合同，加入安庆市作协会员，再后来成为安徽省作协会员，拿到自考大专学历等等。

我觉得很大程度上是来源于机遇的加持以及大环境的综合因素所得。也许对很多同行大咖们来说，这不算什么成绩，但对于我这样在写作之前都没有真正写过长文的人来讲，这是一种很大的鼓舞。感恩因缘机遇。

我做视频两个月的时候，出现两个爆款，分别为26万+和19万+。我做第三场直播的时候，观看人数突破1000多，新增关注30多人，这些都有截图发在朋友圈，这些都是我的小确幸。

我时常感叹人生机遇各不同，在写作之前我做过好几种不同的工作，浑浑噩噩，一事无成，心想，这一生就这样吧！

自从写作后，一切顺风顺水，似乎是找到了合适的土壤，适合自己的发展赛道，实现了曾经所不敢想象的一切。

现在的我，每一天都过得非常有意义。我通过文字影响很多心情状态不太好的人，用我的文字去温暖他们，给他们力量和信心。

同时，写作让我有一种使命感和意义，很多人说因我而坚持读书写作，心情明媚，精神状态越来越好。原来文字既能自我救赎，也能救人。

我的写作社群可以说是市场上出书和加入作协较多的群体。有个文友对我说，你会链接资源，精神引导力很强，所以学员出成绩的多。我总觉得这些都是我的运气，他们中很多人本身就比较优秀。

## 04

今天，我与一个文化公司签约了网课上架的合同，我的第4本书正在进行第三次审稿，有望年底或明年初上市。我没有像同行大咖们那样年入数百万。也没有像有的人那么胆大自信，刚做一两年却发展得特别神速，我就像个小蜗牛似的爬行。

至少有五个人说我坐在金矿上要饭，认为我太佛系，不会营销打造，自我价值感太低。

他们举例说，你看某某某才进入互联网两年，人家现在的收入已是你的N倍。

每个人都有他的发展时区，人生是一场马拉松；每个人有每个人的活法，还是要一步一个脚印，踏踏实实去前行。

名和利是永远赚不完的，在自己可驾驭的范围内稳中提升就好。

本来无一物，所以每进一寸都是欢喜，我的价值快乐感，并不比他们大咖少。

# 写作最终是思想洞见和心智模式的比拼

很多人认为写作是遥不可及的事，觉得只有专业人士或高学历者才能从事。然而，无数事实表明，只要你愿意写，就能成为写作者。正如王小波所说："只要会说话就会写作。"写作和说话一样，都是表达方式，只是形式不同。

写作不仅是文学水平的较量，也是心智模式的博弈。除了少数人拥有真正的文学天赋，大多数写作者都依靠后天的大量练习，不断锤炼语言，提升笔力和语感，从量变到质变，最终实现梦想。

有些人自我怀疑、自我设限、自我内耗，时间在自我否定中流逝。当他们老去，留下的只有悲伤和懊恼。

常听到有人说："等我孩子大一点再写，等我退休了再写，等我换个大房子有安静的地方再写，等我换份轻松的工作再写……"这样的人通常不会再写作，因为他们总觉得没有时间，总能为自己找到借口。

想做的人会找方法，不想做的人会找借口。每个年龄段都有相应的烦恼，总有琐事缠身。但时间就像海绵里的水，只要愿意挤，总会有的。

热爱玩游戏的人总能抽出时间，爱打牌的人也总有时间。如果真心热爱文字，有决心成为写作者，就能找到时间规划写作，享受写作乐趣。创造性工作能带来最高级的快乐感。

海明威、梁漱溟、村上春树等作家都选择在早晨专心写作。早晨是记忆力和精神状态最好的时候，大脑经过一夜休息，效率更高。把重要的事情如写作安排在早晨，能让一整天心情轻松愉快。

有些人很早就确定人生方向，坚定地走下去，这样的人生更顺利，没有走弯路，没有纠结内耗。而大多数人由于早年缺乏环境和氛围，梦想早已搁浅。

现在，我们赶上了移动互联网的黄金时代。自媒体平台需要大量内容创作者，各平台也有多种激励政策，如保底签约制、稿费、分成、奖金征文活动等。只要你有持续的内容输出能力，就不必担心没有机会。

现在是信息透明化的时代，不存在怀才不遇。不必担心年龄、学历或写作水平，关键在于你能坚持多久，一年、两年？是否能写到50万字或百万字？

村上春树说："喜欢的事情可以坚持下去，不喜欢的事怎么也坚持不了。"如何坚持是个常见问题。首先要热爱文字，其次要自律。最好有几个志同道合的文友互相鼓励，或加入写作圈子，不断激发潜能。

写作最终不是比拼文采或文学水平，而是比拼思维和见解，即心智模式。从我个人经历看，写作是人人都能学会的事。只要你有想法，就可以用文字表达。写作时，想象对面坐着一个人，与他聊天谈心，说出你的所思所想。

生活中，许多人被传统思想束缚，认为写作高不可攀，是神圣的存在，被太多条条框框限制。他们没有理解新媒体时代的写作。自4G网络和智能手机普及以来，已是全民写作的时代。

无论你是普通农民工或保洁员，尝试用手机写下一句话、一段话，日积月累，就能完成整篇文章。只要你愿意，注册一个账号，就能成为写作者。随着写作量的增加，驾驭文字的能力提高，你就能成为别人眼中的作家。

# 从来不用想起，永远也不会忘记

## 01

在阅读同行写作者的第一本书时，我注意到他们经常会写到自己的发小和闺蜜，这让我也有了写作的冲动，希望将来能将这些故事纳入我的书中。

我的发小齐小艳比我大一岁，我们一起从学前班到初二都是同班同学。即使在初三分班后，我们每天上下学依然形影不离。

初中毕业后，我们一起在村里的加工厂工作，烘制啤酒套。但那年下半年，村里的小厂关闭了。小艳去了桐城市学习缝纫，而我在家附近的一家店铺学习缝纫。和我们同一批不再读书的同学一样，我们都选择了学习一门手艺。长辈们常说："大荒年饿不死手艺人"，学一门手艺才是长久之计。

小艳是一个简单快乐的人，她乐观的性格与我的悲观和多愁善感形成鲜明对比。

在我记忆中，读一年级之前，她总是听从我的意见。我们一起玩耍，挖掘泥巴，甚至有时会玩得打起来。但后来，我更多地听从她的意见。

小学时，我们用本子的钉子做成鱼钩，用蚯蚓做鱼饵，用竹签做鱼竿，在池塘边钓鱼。有一次，我不慎掉进水里，幸运的是，小艳及时把我拉上了岸。

我们还一起上山砍柴，去田里挖泥鳅，捡拾桃核、挖猪菜，用野葡萄制作葡萄酒，跳绳、跳房子、踢毽子等，一起经历了许多乡野趣事。

初三最后一个学期，面对400元的学费，我决定不再上学，而是去啤酒套厂工作，一天能赚10元左右。小艳一直劝我继续上学，说最后几个月了，我们应该坚持到底，拿到毕业证，这对将来走上社会很有用。

她本能地劝说我，也许是希望我们能一起上学，有个伴。我又回到了学校几个月，但最终在预选考试时，因为180元的考试费，我放弃了学业，告别了学校应试教育。

我们家所在的村庄是全校最远的，骑自行车单程需要40多分钟。每天天还没亮，小艳就会从屋后到我家门前喊我，我们一起上下学，形影不离。

小艳每天自己做早饭，而我则是母亲做好后叫我起来吃。尽管我家条件不好，但母亲是最宠爱孩子的人。

## 02

我们在老家学了一年半缝纫后，都找到了不同的师傅带我们去福建工作。

在福建的第二年，我和同事在村子的集市上逛街买衣服时，小艳突然从远处喊我，就像小时候一样向我招手，那一刻我几乎分不清是现实还是梦境。

我们来到离家几千里的地方打工，却在同一个集市上相遇，原来她的厂就在我们隔壁镇。我在东石镇，她在石井镇。我们厂生产沙滩裤，她厂生产夹克衫。

偶尔，她和同事也会来我们这边的集市。她说只要遇到其他厂的老乡，她都会打听我的消息。那时大家都没有手机，联系起来比较困难。现在终于见到我了。

世界太小了，福建太小了。

从那以后，我们知道了彼此的厂址，每隔几个月，我们会骑摩托车去对方的厂里玩。我还带了厂里的几位同事去她那里玩。

每次，小艳都会做好吃的给我们，她很早就会做各种菜肴，还会买很多零食。现在看来这很平常，但那时我们觉得非常幸福，可以休息放松，还能聚在一起享受美食。

## 03

今年年初，我在福建的老同事发微信告诉我，他在桐城某地见到了我的发小。她可能不太记得他，但他记得她。他们在街头擦肩而过，但没有说话。

我问，你还记得她吗？老同事说，我曾带他去过小艳的厂里，看过我们的合影，还有一年腊月去我家玩时，小艳也来了，所以他印象深刻。

小艳当年在厂里表现不错，做事麻利。那年泉州市举办活动，厂里庆典，挑选 12 名女同事排练节目参加，她和她的表妹都被选中。

想想我们安徽桐城的水土真是养人！在那么大的厂里，她俩都被选中了。

前几天，我和女儿聊天时提到了我的发小艳子。女儿问她现在生活得怎么样？我说挺好的，她性格好，人又努力。她在福建打工几年后，通过叔叔的介绍认识了一个木匠，婚后就留在家中，家离桐城很近，在附近的厂里上班。8 年前，她们家拆迁分到了 3 套房，过着普通的小市民生活，简单安逸。她有一个儿子，和你一样大，考入了桐城市第一重点高中，可能成绩比你还好一点。

我年轻时总想离开桐城，远离家乡，觉得自己在家乡没有得到足够的爱与尊重。多年后才明白，每个人向往的远方，何尝不是别人想逃离的家乡？

如果我像艳子一样没有离开桐城，大概率会少经历很多颠沛流离。毕竟从我们家到桐城市中心，骑摩托车只需十来分钟。后来交通更加便利了。

小艳是个会操持家务的能手，她选择的生活很适合她。我年轻时，总想去越远的地方越好，以为远方会有精彩的世界，直到中年后才知道自己当时的想法有多简单。

## 04

我很羡慕小艳的性格，她这样的人无论在哪里都能过得幸福。

我时常回忆起小时候，我们经常拍着巴掌，边唱边跳："小燕子，穿花衣，每年春天来这里……"

大约在二年级时，有一天放学路上，我捡到一个鸭蛋，是浅绿色的。我一路拿着它编着顺口溜，小艳就在一旁听着。我与生俱来的发散思维、敏感和悲观性格，她似乎都没有，她一直活得比我快乐。

五年级时，我们曾幻想小学毕业后一起去镇上做刷子或鬃毛，梦想着将来买什么样的漂亮自行车，想象着美好的上班生活。每天上下学的路上，我们都聊着这些话题。

谁知当年一纸政策普及了初中教育，我们必须去离家6里外的初中读书，没有人敢不去。

## 05

  如果我没能赶上九年义务教育的第一届，我肯定就不会去读初中。那样的话，我还会写作吗？

  其实我的初中语文成绩反而比小学时好很多，可能我是属于开窍很晚的人。初中时，我的语文、英语、历史都能轻松拿高分，语文成绩多次在全年级名列前茅。

  小艳在初中时学习有些跟不上，离我家近的几个女同学中，我的初中成绩是最好的。

  如果我们那一届还是通过小考选拔上初中的话，我们俩都没通过小考，80%多的人也没通过。

  初中时，我们好几次早上把时间看错了，分钟和小时看反了，骑自行车到了学校，天还没亮，我们无奈地哈哈大笑。

  我们去学校的路上，大清早都要经过一个山头，四周黑乎乎的，都是坟墓，一个人走的话真会毛骨悚然！

  小艳是陪我走过幼年、童年以及青春时光的人。我人生中最美好的年华都是她陪伴度过的，我所有的成长、不幸、波折、疲累、快乐和进步，她都一一知晓，参与并见证了。

  时光飞逝，现在我们的孩子都已是高中生，人生真是如梦一场。

  现在我们偶尔在朋友圈点个赞，有时腊月见面聊几句，平常没有太多沟通，但这并不影响我们在各自生命中的重要位置。

  从来不用刻意想起，永远也不会忘记。

# 我用 7 年时间从底层生活爬了起来，成为内容创业者

我用了 7 年时间，从底层生活爬了起来。内容创业是最适合普通人的方式。

我是一名左手抓着月亮、右手拿着六便士的网络自由工作者。近年来，我的月收入至少达到 5 万 +，但这离不开我前几年的积累和铺垫，以及互联网这个放大器的巨大作用。

互联网内容创业非常适合我们这些"三无"人员——无背景、无资源、无学历。

我是一名 80 后，初中未毕业。据我所知，我的父母和上三代都是文盲，一个字都不认识，可以说是底层中的底层。

我学过两年半的缝纫，做过 6 年的服装厂流水线工人，当过电子厂工人，做过营业员，做过电话销售，开过早餐店数年……

我是如何从底层生活中走出来的？

1. 找到自己内心的热爱。每个人都有一种能力超过 1 万人，那就是你的天赋所在。

从小，周围的人都说我记忆力好，多愁善感，喜欢文字。我在理科上是超级学渣，但在文科上表现不错。

2.30 岁后，我接触了自媒体，智能手机的普及给了我用手机写作的勇气。

我开始以"齐帆齐"为笔名在全网写作。从最初的一周写 800 字都

很困难，到现在可以轻松日更 3000 字 +。我不畏嘲笑，不畏打击，坚持写作，看好互联网自媒体的趋势。

3. 以文字为中心，多元化发展。我写文案、接商稿、写书、带货、分销产品、做社群、直播等。

4. 把一个人活成一支队伍。我是写作者、编辑、运营客服、销售、知心姐姐、带货博主。我还是安徽省作协会员，签约出版了几本书籍，是一个典型的复合型工作者。

5. 我已是 7 年的自由工作者。只有自律，才能实现真正的自由。

我用整整 7 年的时间，把自己从底层的泥潭里拽了出来。我的生活状态发生了质的飞跃，成为了自己喜欢的模样，也影响了数万网友。

6. 学习力比学历更重要，成长比成功更重要。自媒体内容创业主要比拼的是毅力、思维迭代能力、行动力、与时俱进的能力。

7. 要把热爱当成事业，要有长期主义者的思维，和时间做朋友，享受时间带来的福利。

8. 适当加入一些圈子学习，无论是付费的还是免费的，它们的学习效果和能量吸收能力截然不同，重视程度也不同。

## 中年后常恨过去的自己

我们安徽桐城市是一个县级市，属于地级市安庆市管辖。人们常说桐城市是安庆市下辖的八县一市中经济发展最好的，甚至超过了古城安庆。（近年有所改动，划走了一个县）

我的老家闺蜜曾在安庆上过两个月班，她听到最多的话就是："桐城人干嘛来这里上班？桐城多好呀！桐城人聪明什么的……"（这也可能是桐城人自己宣扬出去的）

我们老家镇上随处可见刷子厂，羊毛刷、钢丝刷、漆刷、滚筒刷厂……大家开玩笑说，瞎子走在路上都能碰到刷子厂。我们镇中心的十字路口挂着巨型的大标识"中国制刷之乡"。很多山区的人会到我们镇上来打工，也有小部分外省人。

我们的隔壁镇——桐城新安渡镇是塑料袋的出产地。据说中国的70%的塑料袋产自这个镇上，包装厂、印刷厂也很多。

我当年为什么要花两三年学习缝纫技术？又为什么要千里迢迢跑到3000里之外的福建去打工做打工妹呢？开始的两三年打工，每天夜里要做到凌晨三四点，通宵也是常有的事。早上八点就要上班，直到后来把我累到吐血。

如果我在本地上班，不就是别人眼里羡慕的本地人了吗？更不用熬夜那么晚，把身体累出毛病。在家乡的镇上或者桐城市里上班，都是早出晚归，骑自行车上班，后来骑摩托车也挺方便。

我只能说当年年少，脑子就是进了水。吃饱了撑的要找罪受，人到中年真是越想越恨自己。顺路不走，要走倒车路。

更内疚的是我母亲是一个儿女心特别重的人，她后来生病主要是劳累，还有部分原因就是太思念我们了，思念成疾。正月出门到腊月过年才能看到我们，我每次出门走，她都会哭很久很久。

我更没有料到母亲的生命是如此短暂。如果我们没去外地打工，我可以多陪伴一些时日，甚至可能她可以多活一些年。

年少无知啊！当时听说外地工资高，比我们家高好几倍。我的发小和一班小姐妹都是去外省打工的多，极少人选择在家门口上班。这应了古人说的"远香近臭"吧！

真正到了外地厂里后，论时长性价并不比我们老家工资高多少。但我又为了所谓的面子，怕别人说怕吃苦在外面待不下去，并没有及时回到家乡来谋生，继续远在他乡受苦受累。

从我朦胧懂事起，我就渴望远离家乡，觉得在家乡没得到尊重和爱，长大后我要离老家越远越好。可我唯独没有为我母亲设身处地去想。

我不但自己去外地，还把二妹也带出去。本来她在老家桐城市印刷厂干了两个多月。前几天二妹还说起当年妈妈送她去桐城上班，家门口这点路，妈妈都是边走边哭，心疼她这么小就要每天在厂里干活了。何况后来我还把她带到福建服装厂里……

周围人都说学个手艺是长久之计，大荒年饿不死手艺人，有个一技之长傍身稳当。让你妹妹跟着你学手艺才是更好的选择，姐妹在一起攒钱快。

数年过后，我们早已都不从事缝纫这个行业了。我曾经哭着闹着跳着吵着让我母亲借钱给我买的缝纫机，最后也是当废品卖掉了。

一切的本质就是那时候没有见识，没有网络，家里没有收音机、电视机、课外书，人又晚熟，没有自己的主见。周围多数人怎么做，我也就随大流怎么做。

内心懦弱，不敢大胆做自我。

我这人呐，就是没有一颗自己的心啊！

人到中年后，越来越恨曾经的自己。

## 文学是世道人心最后的温暖

曾有很多网友对我走向全职写作之路充满好奇。回想起2014年、2015年，那时，我正在西安高新区某个城中村做早餐小生意。其实就是一个临时的大棚子，铁架子上搭着帆布，一长排，由村子里收租。

那条街在上下班高峰期人来人往，周边都是各种小吃店，锅碗瓢盆叮当作响，充满了人间烟火和市井气息。

那时，我无意中用手机进入QQ空间，沉迷其中。每天下午切菜洗菜，准备第二天的食材后，我就守着店铺，一边掏出手机看QQ空间文友们的日志。从一位文友的空间进入另一位文友的空间，仿佛哥伦布发现新大陆，让我看到了一个远离繁碌世俗的另一个世界。

记得我还写了一段关于西安到处拆迁的动态，感叹被拆迁的后代如何找到他们的精神家园，灵魂栖息地在哪里。我常常看着城中村的人们发呆思考，感慨人与人之间的差距。经常看到戴着钢玻璃帽、工装上有泥巴的工地农民工来买馒头。他们都舍不得吃肉包，以馒头为主，因为馒头更耐饿。我有时看着那些漂亮的高楼，心想，如此努力的农民工们何时能住上电梯洋房呢？

我与生俱来就喜欢多愁善感。其实我也住不起那洋楼。记得一位安庆QQ空间文友给我留言："看不出你还思想深刻啊！还为被拆迁的人感慨万千的，人家补偿款利息也吃不完……"

城中村的傍晚，卖水果的吆喝声、三轮车的响铃声、上班族的匆匆脚步声交织在一起。我最喜欢的是旁边的那家旧书摊，书籍超级便宜，成为我的心头好，阅读量大幅提升，也是我对那村子最大的眷念。在文学大省陕西西安的四年，对我后来从事写作有很好的铺垫。

2015年4月，我转让摊位回到老家，在老家镇上的服装厂做了几个月，每天套裙子里布、做袖口。那厂里都是附近中年女性为主，按计件多劳多得，适合照顾家庭带孩子，总比做营业员自由点。

我依然忙里偷闲，见缝插针也会在手机上看看QQ空间文字，阅读手头为数不多的书籍。

家里镇上的房子也装修好了。本来一直这样在厂里做下去，但厂里工资比我想象的更低。早上7:30去厂里，晚上10:30回来，一个月只有1600-2000元。内心总有一丝丝不甘心。

2015年8月，小妹打电话让我去上海看看。我想再去试一试吧！如果没啥出头的，年底还是要回来在老家上班。开始准备去给家早餐店当营业员，包吃住一月4000元。

我在老乡店铺帮忙了几天，小妹想想还是说："算了吧！你做这还不如在老家呢！"她说找机会问问他们公司经理，看能不能把我介绍进去。

妹妹所在的公司是一家互联网公司，员工80%都是销售为主，只有几个程序员和设计。

小妹的部门经理也是我们安徽老乡，85后女子。她问小妹："你姐姐电脑办公软件都会操作吧？"小妹说："没问题，基本的我已教过了。"

经理认为小妹工作优秀，她姐姐应该也不差。我就绕过了投简历这步，直接内聘加入了小妹同一个部门。我成了全公司学历最低的一个人，年龄偏大，虽有年龄相仿的但人家是多年老员工了。

好在做销售也没有太深奥的东西。开始有老师培训了一周，关于公司发展历程、产品介绍、打电话话术等等。

每天要打两三百个电话，我可以做到不用看电话机都能拨电话。客户有意向的就把信息摘抄在本子上。每天下班前要把意向客户邮箱数发送给经理，抄送总监。表格都有现成的模板，不太复杂。

我座位两边都是刚出校门的大学生，电脑知识不会的都是他们教我。

只是我的客户本上每页速空都会写一些好词好句，涂涂画画。如："生如夏花之绚烂，死如秋叶之静美"，"当你老了，睡意昏沉……"。有时候自己会写几句感慨的话，都是断不成章。

这份工作是我人生中第一次有周末的工作。虽然周六经常还是要去公司培训开会，实质上只是单休，但对于我来说还是非常知足开心。

那时下班周末我会看很多公众号文章，内心蠢蠢欲动，感觉有很多情绪想要迸发出来，对这个世界有很多话想说。

我就是处在这样的环境和心态下，有同事的帮助下，2016年注册了微信公众号《齐帆齐微刊》，正式开启了写作之路，也因此改变了我的命运。

2017年下半年，我的副业已经远远超过了主业，我回到老家，开启了全职写作之路。2018年签约第一本书《追梦路上，让灵魂发光》，加入安庆市作协会员、安徽省作协会员、中国散文学会会员。注册文化传媒公司，做MCN内容矩阵。2021年出版《人人都能学会的写作变现指南》以及4本合集书。

我跌跌撞撞地成了一名自由写作者，内容创业者，通过文字为支点，实现了精神物质大跃迁。可以自由支配时间，财务自由，实现了生命价值和意义。

我的过往人生——学缝纫机生涯、8年沿海服装厂流水工作、做过营业员、电子厂工人以及数年的早餐店经历——这所有的人生过往经历叠加在一起，让我在写作路上不缺素材。更重要的是让我更深刻地体验了底层普通人的生活，感受世态炎凉、人情冷暖，让我的文字拥有更强的共情力，因为我就是其中的一员。

很多读者网友说我的文字感染力代入感特别强，很真实接地气，有时代感。也许这是对我的鼓励，但我深知我的文章也有很多不成熟的地方，也希望本书的读者能多多包涵指正。

出书只是对过去这段写作路的总结，对自己的鼓励。自己满意的作品，应该永远在下一部。

这本书中很多都是我个人的成长以及对生活一路的心路历程。虽然我是80后，但我的文字也能让60后很多人产生共鸣。我走上社会很早，记忆力不错，同时又身处网络自媒体洪流中，因而实现了个体崛起。相信95后的人在我的文字里也能找到些许价值。

关于乡村生活，那些久远的记忆、童年、少年，文字把我们逐渐消逝的往事重新打捞备份，让其成为永恒。

写文字的人是幸福的，我们可以把一辈子活成别人的两辈子：一个是现实世界；一个是精神世界。

感恩时代赐予普通人机会，有这么多写作平台可以安放我们的文字梦。

在《追梦路上，让灵魂发光》《只做唯一的我，不做第二个谁》《左手月亮，右手六便士》之后，我将继续探索、思省、记录。

# 时常感到彷徨

微信和微信社群极大地方便了广大人民群众，让社交触达变得更加便捷。如今，即便是农村 70 多岁的老人也能熟练地使用微信。早些年人们常说年轻人沉迷手机，但现在这群老人似乎更加沉迷，他们喜欢刷抖音、看爱奇艺视频。

在老家，有许多生活服务社群，如推荐工作的社群、拼单群、拼车群等。比如从我们老家到安庆、合肥、杭州等地，都有人专门提供相关服务。只要有人发布出行信息、手机号码和乘车人数，很快就会有人联系。还有人专门做推荐介绍，负责接送，价格非常实惠，比自己开车或乘大巴都要方便、划算。

有一次我坐拼出租车经过安庆长江大桥时，司机特意绕了一圈再上桥。我们问他为什么这样做，他说这样可以节省过桥费。十来分钟就能省下 21 元钱，司机觉得非常划算。旁边的几位大姐也表示下次让家人亲戚也这样做，能省点钱。我笑着说这是在"薅国家的羊毛"。

司机聊起他们行业的辛苦，每个跑车的司机都是一身职业病，为了三四块钱的生意有时要开一两个小时。还有人因此腰部做手术，再也无法从事开车工作。

每个行业到了后期都不再有红利，只能赚些辛苦钱。作为一个开车师傅，这既是技术活，又有车辆的消耗和保养，需要高度的注意力，耗费时间和精力。在如今的物价下，如果没有月入 1 万 +，真的觉得非常不值。付出和收获已不成正比。

出租车司机在2014年之前是一个非常红火的行业，那时营运牌照非常值钱，被炒作得很火。如果某家有属于自己的营运牌照和车辆，当时的日子是过得非常滋润。还有人转让车辆牌照给别人开车，自己躺着赚差价。

然而，网约车的出现对出租车、跑车拼车行业是一场重大革命。

印象最深刻的是有一次在合肥乘出租车时，司机聊到让他悔恨终生的事情。他的老表在同一时间用钱在合肥买了房，他自己还借了钱给他老表。在差不多的时期，他咬牙凑钱买了出租车营业执照。

很快，营运执照大幅跌价，而他老表的房子几年后迅速升值，房子升值的钱是他跑出租车6年赚的钱还多。那位师傅说他自己借过好几次钱给亲戚们买房，就是不知道自己也去买。等到他自己儿子长大时，买房只能选择楼顶的隔热层，没有电梯的老楼。他遗憾自己错过了最佳的买房黄金时期。

不得不说，很多时候选择大于努力，但每个人的选择都是结合自己的思想认知，权衡利弊后的结果。

有时，我思考互联网上做社群的、做IP的、直播带货的、做职场咨询的，有的人赚钱似乎很轻松。传统线下和线上已经是两个世界。

那天在依米群里有一个网友说线下与线上已经是100倍的震撼度。我说传统线下和线上形成了很鲜明的割裂，已经无法同日而语了。

我近距离地观察着线上线下两群人，常常感慨万千，同时也很焦虑彷徨，内心分裂。互联网又能持续多久？人工智能如此发达，可能不久的将来就会颠覆淘汰我们。BAT或许都将沦为传统公司，没有任何商业是长存的，没有任何模式是不会被改革的。

时代的列车最终会走向何方？

昨天，我在一本书里看到，一个90后的女孩被称为"富二代"。她的父母在 1992 年辞去体制内的工作下海经商，曾做到 9 位数的资产，在张家界当地已经算是头部之一了。

她说父亲 60 岁就已经退休了，每天钓鱼，每年固定被骗些钱。自从女孩做互联网之后，父亲被骗的概率少了很多，因为他父亲什么事会问她。

她的母亲回忆当年时说，在面对巨大的财富时，人的内心冲击力很大。改革开放下海创业那一代很多成功者是无法守住那么多财富。能驾驭财富是一种更深奥的学问。

这个女孩认为她母亲在生意眼光方面更具有天赋。在 2002 年时，她的母亲就大量地买土地使用权，而她爸爸觉得当"地主"这个事很没意思。他是医生出身，从小开始学中医，他先学儒学再学医，他总觉得应该去做研发，为这个城市创造更大的价值，结果基本上全部亏光了。如果不是因为当年买公司的时候，还有一些城市中心土地的话，现在绝对是资不抵债。她母亲的预判成真。

由于她母亲和父亲对于社会经济发展眼光的不同，2002 年后他们离婚分开，这才使当年下海创业的成果保住了大半。

这个女孩认为家庭也是个组织，也是个原始的最小单位的生产组织。当组织不具备增加生产力的时候，自然会考虑换一个能够共同造势的最佳伙伴。

女孩说她父亲后来再也遇不到像她母亲这么优秀的人了。

她父母享受到了时代的红利，她认为自己这辈子无论如何也超越不了父母。但她想证明自己不比父辈能力差，靠自己完全可以实现财务自由。

她做本地美团业务，公司成熟后她每年拿一半收入，另一半给团队做奖励。她抽身去杭州做互联网相关的一些事情，也足够实现财务自由。

在滚滚的时代洪流面前,父辈的选择会影响整个家族,甚至后几代人。但任何人在面对选择的时候,谁也不知道对还是错。

Living like this.

## 我的村庄，我的梦

2002年，我家已经盖了新楼房，但无数次在梦境中出现的都是我家老房子，我父亲盖的三间土坯房，下雨天，外面下大雨，里面下小雨。但回忆起来依然是很多欢乐的时光，以至于新房，从未出现过在我的梦境里。

记忆中，母亲扯着嗓子喊：帆儿，吃饭了，回来吃饭啦！还不回来，天天跟野人似的，在外面疯。

我懂事很晚，不开窍，只顾自己贪玩，貌似其他事都不大懂。

我就喜欢跟着小伙伴们在外面玩，打架，捉虾，游玩，疯跑，不归家，反正就是不爱在家里安安静静地待着。我妈常骂我就像个"野人"。家族长辈戏说我是投错了胎，适合做男孩子。

我家房子右边是一个山坡，那里是我家的地，种过花生和绿豆，还记得有一次下雨天我和母亲在那边地栽红薯的一幕。还有常在道场上打小麦，打油菜籽的片段。

我们村庄一个人八分田，一家有几块地，一块地一般就三四条埂。属于小丘陵地带，田地并不肥沃。不种荒掉又舍不得，累死累活，田地其实并不能带来多少实质创收。

小时候听奶奶说，她那时不只是贫农，是贫下农，是村里有名的特困户。当年实行分田到户制度的时候，村里看我们家实在太苦了，多给三分田给奶奶，作为福利，照顾贫困对象。

那不得了，小队里有几户人家跳手跳脚地闹，整整闹了一个月。有人的地方就江湖，自古都是，任何环境都是如此。

在我读书的时候，奶奶一个人自言自语又有点小嘚瑟地对我感叹道：当年村子里多分一点田照顾我这可怜人，屋后那谁谁闹得这么凶，骂得这么狠，现在田大家都不爱种了，三十年河东，三十年河西啊！

现在我种田的儿子也有，我吃商品粮的儿子也有。田也没人太稀罕了。

我大伯能吃上商品粮，完全是他自个儿的主意。我奶奶哪有这个远见和想法，家庭更没有那个能力。

我大伯从小读书挺聪明，读到二年级爷爷奶奶让他别读了，没钱读，回来帮家里做事。我大伯从小懂事勤快孝顺。

当他在重要事件上挺有自己的主意，大伯身高一米八出头，他自己偷偷地去村里报名当兵，待一切成为定局，村里到家来通知的时候，我奶奶才知道这事，一脸懵逼，随后大哭。

据说我奶奶那天坐在地上哭一天，她哭是家里没人做事了，爷爷身体一直不好，脾气又暴躁还好打人，这大儿子走了，少了得力的干将，这日子还怎么过……

周边好心人劝说，大家会搭伙做事帮忙。当兵是去锻炼还能学习，这是为国家做贡献，大家各种安慰。我大伯这一主动也直接改变他自己的命运。

当了两三年兵过后，回到老家，再又被通知转正到安庆化肥厂上班，带城市户口。当年各地工厂紧缺工人，是人才匮乏的年代，我的堂哥堂姐后来都成了安庆城里人。

我们齐屋队一共只有两个吃商品粮的人，我大伯是其中之一；另一位是中学校长。

爷爷奶奶目不识丁，家里又那么贫寒。只读了两年书的大伯却成为正式工，吃上国家饭拿工资，也只有在那个年代才有机会实现吧！这也是命运的神奇之处。

前几天大娘还跟我说，当年大伯那个最早的集体宿舍，还分了房款，足够她养老的了。2000年的时候，他们全款买了商品房，那时候多数人还没有按揭贷款的意识，完全可以用那本金搞两套。后来堂哥又在合肥定居安家。

如今，大伯快到80岁的年龄了，我认为，他已经是在他所处的时代，那样家庭起点境况下已达到了天花板。已经算是很幸运的人了。

前些年，大伯为照顾奶奶回到老家，他们也早计划回农村盖小院养老。

大伯现在每天早晚散步锻炼，精神状态特别好，热爱花花草草，他还会种田地，养鸡鸭，好让堂哥吃上老家的农作物产品。

我的村庄，我的梦。这是我们生命的根，更是写作者的创作源头。回一趟出生的村庄，至少能写上十篇文章……

## 自我疗愈之路

从前，每次回到我出生的老家齐屋队，都会有很多悲观情绪蔓延。人到中年，我逐渐学会了自我疗愈，与命运、与周围的一切和解妥协。

我们姐妹站在老家门口的稻谷场上聊天，或在池塘边洗东西，总会有一些看着我们长大的老人窃窃私语。他们的话题主要是说这几个孩子长得都算很齐整，很上进能干，不输人家男孩子，可惜她们的父母就没有福气，要是还在，睡着都能笑醒。

还会有老人说，没想到她父母这样的老好人，养的几个孩子，却比我们这些人的孩子都能干，只可惜好人苦命。

回到老家，看着我的发小一家，看着那些小时候的玩伴，心里就会感叹，为什么别人的父母都健健康康，为什么那么多人比我的父母多活了两倍的岁数以上，怎么会差距这么大？为什么别人都那么幸福？

为什么那么多人都能轻易自然地拥有了世俗里的圆满？

前天小年那天，我问小婶，我小时候的那些玩伴发小，他们现在忙什么呢？在老家还是在外地？小时候玩得好的我们有4个人，他们分别比我大一岁、两岁、三岁。

小婶说，一个在桐城市工地上做制模，房子楼顶的那种模子；一个在外地做展览馆，搭展览架；还有和我玩得好的小伙伴艳子在街上厂里做衣服。她的儿子读书非常聪明，在我们桐城市第一重点高中的重点班，他们家靠近市边，因为扩建，拆迁也有几套房子。

小婶说你不用问他们，比你事业好的少。我只是习惯性地问一下。我从没有觉得自己有多好，他们这样也都挺好的啊！

脑海里，回忆起过去和发小几个一起丢手绢、玩警察抓小偷、一起去山上打柴、去河里抓鱼、一起搭锅、一起抓石子、一起玩生娃娃、去田埂打猪草、学骑自行车等等。那是生命里最快乐，最无忧的时光！

我和小艳从读学前班到初二，都是在一个班，还坐过同桌。三年级学毛笔字的时候，我们俩一不开心，拿着毛笔在对方脸上衣服上涂鸦，一起被老师叫到办公室。

那时，每天都是她等我一起去上学。初中毕业后，我们又一起学习缝纫技术，又跟随不同的师傅都到了福建晋江厂里上班。

我大娘笑说，你是齐屋村庄女性发展比较好的。其实人生只有到老的时候才知道一生到底如何。

听到长辈的一些话，我更多的是一种压力，更多的是一种感叹。每个人都沿着自己的命运轨迹在行走，都在努力认真地生活着。

如果命运可以选择，可以调换，我肯定不要所谓苦难这样的财富。我肯定希望有一个平顺圆满的人生。

曾经在我写父亲那篇文章里，我写道，我情愿生得矮几公分，黑一点，胖一点，能换到他的健在长寿。

看到很多人五六十岁的父母健在，真是人和人从来没有可比性啊！我只有心生羡慕的份儿。

现在每当我有悲观情绪的时候，学会了自我疗愈，想起安妮宝贝所说的要站在宇宙的高度看待这个人世间。

人生在世各自要完成他的使命，然后奔赴下一个轮回。生老病死，都是每个人要面对的课题。前世因果循环，而每个人面对的时间早晚不同。

下一世的我们，在不同的时空里又会经历怎样的人生？

去年有一个文友跟我说,2017年某个平台专题编辑采访我后哭了三天。我大为惊讶,觉得自己真是罪过,让别人哭了几天,而之前我压根不知道,我甚至都已想不起来那专题编辑叫什么名字。

我只是平静地叙述,那些背负在身上的经历,一种抒发,如同在讲述别人的故事。除了偶尔心情不好的时候,我也没有觉得自己多难。世界上有很多比我更早经历不幸,历经更多苦难,活得很累的人们,我已经比较幸运了。

人总是一个矛盾的存在。没有人绝对地幸福或不幸,快乐也只是短暂的刹那感觉。更多的时候,每个人在这人世间都要面对生活里的一地鸡毛,生命里的刀光剑影,直到临终,才算是完成了这一生要走完的生命体验。

当我们思绪进入死胡同的时候,必须学会自我调节,自我疗愈走出来。

看,又是明媚的一天。

# 每个人都在自己的命运里沉浮

从前,我总觉得自己这辈子就这样了。别人优秀是他们的事,他们有好的起点、美满的家庭、优秀的学历。而我,初三就早早辍学,母亲是农村里俗称的"老好人",是周围人共同轻蔑的对象。父亲早逝,这样的家庭背景,是命运的安排,我无从选择。

当年老家人常说,"大荒年饿不死手艺人"。我和辍学的小伙伴们都去学缝纫,男孩子们则去学做木匠、瓦匠等。我也顺其自然地加入了学缝纫的行列。

离开学校时,内心满是欢喜。

学了一年半缝纫后,2000年,我跟随老乡师傅们前往几千里之外的福建泉州晋江东石镇的某村工厂,做流水线工作。在那里,我又继续学习了一年电机。在那个厂,一待就是四五年。

后来,我在温州和杭州都做过服装,还在家门口的门店给别人做过羽绒服。现在回想起来,都不知道那些年是怎么走过来的。

在福建那个厂的时候,每天工作到凌晨两点到四点多,常年无休。每晚十点是吃夜宵时间,吃完再继续工作。夜宵不过是一块钱的馄饨,或者锅巴泡饭,或者一碗面条。这就是传说中的"血汗工厂",也是中国工业化的上半场,而我只是其中数千万人中的一个小小的螺丝钉。

工厂的大院子像牢笼一样。我曾经幻想一边打工一边学习,提升学历,改变命运。但现实是不可能的,每天累得倒头就睡,上班都会打瞌睡，连上厕所都能睡着。村庄偏僻，周围全是工厂，哪里有夜校或职校？根本没有时间、环境和金钱去学习。

外面的世界并没有想象中的好，虽然繁华精彩，却也很无奈。人是斗不过命运的，总得学会与自我和解。

常常看到厂里的大型发货车，那一箱箱包装好的衣服都是我们同事的劳动成果。据说衣服会发往香港，再转到非洲国家。我们厂的老板只是一个三年级文化的人，他们兄弟几个都办工厂，但曾经都是卖牛卖菜出身。他们后来遇见了改革开放和所在区域的红利。他有一个姐姐在香港专门接外贸单子，兄弟几个迅速发家，成为那个村庄比较厉害的人物。

我们这些外地来的打工仔、打工妹都是他们赚钱的工具。当年我那厂里员工主要来自四川、江西、贵州、湖北和安徽。

时光匆匆，数年过去，新时代来临了。移动互联网普及，用一部手机就可以写作发布，我就是这波浪潮的受益者之一。从开始只能写出六百字到一千字，再到两三千，一个字一个字地写，一本书一本书地读，加倍努力来弥补先天的不足。

感恩上苍厚爱，我用手机写作一年半后，实现了全职自由写作，签约平台，出书，加入省作协，自考大学。全职五年后，我实现了全方位的跨越成长。

在移动互联网正火爆的时期，我也迈入了30+。通过网络，我打开了眼界，提升了视野，实现了自我觉醒。女人一旦觉醒，她将坚不可摧。往后余生，努力绽放，实现生命的意义和价值。

当年我所在的福建工厂，自2010年后一直在走下坡路。外贸本身附加值很低，给到员工的待遇有限。很多人后来宁愿选择在老家上班，也不愿再去那么远的地方。

福建那个村庄，许多老板把厂搬到了云南、缅甸。我曾在温州做过的那家女装厂，做内销品牌，这几年国内环境和同行竞争激烈，大概率也越来越难了。

我还给老家两家定制羽绒服店做过衣服，她们后来都没有开了。一个转型开饭店去了，一个转型做电商。她们说现在半成品羽绒服太多了，成品衣服卖得那么便宜，又很时尚，手工定制羽绒服根本没有市场竞争力。

有个老板娘小冰姐，我曾写过她的成长故事。前年正月我去她家玩，她惊讶于我走上了写作之路。她现在在天猫开店，弟媳妇给她做客服，家里有几个人做衣服。小冰姐不用像过去依赖街上的人流量，在自己家的客厅里做衣服就可以了。

小冰姐比我大4岁，她的人生是另一个版本的励志故事。她从小读书每年年级第一。四年级末的某天，她带着奖状开心地回家，她母亲却离家出走了，再也没有回来。她无数次站在路口眺望，希望母亲的影子出现。

她母亲曾说，小冰学习这么好，以后砸锅卖铁也要供她读书，终究还是走了。她的父亲是比较少有的父亲，死活不肯给她再读书。都是小冰姐求亲戚说情，想尽了办法，才勉强读到了初二。

小冰姐12岁时，她的父亲为她量身配置了锄头、扁担、箩筐，他们一同外出干活。她只要走慢了点，她父亲在后面大声呵斥她，用脚踢她、打她。她父亲认为女孩子读书无用，在家干农活，做到30岁嫁给本村庄里的人。后来小冰姐学缝纫技术是找她堂哥借的缝纫机，都是靠自己和父亲多次抗争谈判来的。

她曾说小时候很恨母亲，为什么离家出走不管她了。长大了她明白，这样的父亲真的很难相处，难怪母亲过不下去了。

我给小冰姐店里帮忙做衣服时，她还跟我讲过她小时候母亲带着她一起离家出走，边走边要饭。人家给了一块肉给她母亲，她拿起来就往嘴里一塞，从此别人给她起了个外号叫"好吃佬"。她母亲有过几次带她短暂出走的经历。或许是曾想要尝试带小冰一起走的，终究是无能为力，把她丢在了家里。

小冰姐在上海打工，在服装厂做杂事剪线头，做小烫、到做流水、做整件，再到做样衣、打板设计。她也很喜欢看文学书籍，懂得的知识挺多。

小冰姐最让我感动佩服的一件事，她当年问一个老乡借了一本服装样板书，那本书整个上海很难买到。她就用下班时间把那本厚厚的样书全部抄下来了，这是什么样的一种精神呀！她在做样衣的几年里，一直在业余自学打板。

她在我们镇上开店，设计衣服，打板能力全是靠自学自悟的。这个世界上很多人是那么认真用力地生活着，这些才是沉默的大多数。

我常想，如果小冰姐的母亲没有走，如果她出生于稍微好的家庭，如果遇见过更好的平台，凭她的聪明好学和身上这股劲儿，她的人生应该比现在更好上百倍千倍吧！

作为底层中的底层出生，遇见那样的家庭，那样的父亲。现在小冰姐在同等出身中，也算是生活圆满，事业小成，完成了自我超越。

她在30岁后结束了打工岁月，回老家开店。几年后又转向网店运营，我们都是在30岁后觉醒，实现自我成长。

回想我曾在小冰姐家冬天做几个月羽绒服的时光，每天还是蛮开心的。她性格开朗，说话幽默搞笑，是个热爱生活、能量满满的人。再苦的往事，她都能笑着说出来。

有一次，有个顾客来问哪个是"老板娘"。我正在埋头做衣服，小冰姐正在扫地，她说："看看，扫地打杂的肯定是老板娘呀！就是我。"还有一次，我问她要拉链辅料配件，她用长尺子指着地面上的地板砖，

Living like this.

身子一转，大笑着说："一二三，帆齐，请看大屏幕……"简直把我笑得肚子疼。

小冰姐还说起她老公当年在她厂附近的地方搞装修瓦匠。下雨天有空的时候，他会和她一起出去玩。为了她坐在车前面，他把自行车后座给下了。这又是一个笑点故事。

她刚开始学缝纫机三个月培训班需要150块钱学费，她父亲不支持，自己又一分钱没有。她堂哥答应借缝纫机，她想了个点子，去找培训班老板，用缝纫机抵押学费。多次去磨去谈，最后老板发好心总算成了。

往事如烟，转眼之间距离我在小冰姐店里做羽绒服已经十多年过去了。她说过的好多事情，很有趣有意思，有的让人思考，有的让人觉得沉重。泪中有笑，笑中有泪。这就是人生吧！这就是众生相！

像小冰姐这样的人不管在什么境遇里都能生活得很好，欢悦知足，擅于创造快乐和幸福。这样的心态和精神值得佩服学习。

社会的滚滚浪潮，时间的车轮飞逝，各行业的不断迭代，企业、工厂、个体门店和个人都在自己所在命运轨迹里探索沉浮。我们都是这苍茫人世间的过客，有着各自的宿命。

## 无常才是人生，好心态最重要

我今天听说，我们老家隔壁某县城的公务员从今年四月份开始降薪，下月开始改为两个月发一次工资。这是多少年才会发生一次的事啊！

据说2千万元不够发县城所有公务员的工资。县城还有一家公立幼儿园，以前不管放不放假，老师都是按月拿工资的。现在老师轮流值班，一人上一个月班，没上班的老师那个月就没钱拿。

突然感叹，我们这代人在见证历史啊！我们见证了房地产快速发展的20年，犹如脱缰的野马快速奔跑。及时抓住房地产红利的人赚得盆满钵满。房价成了磨灭年轻人梦想的最好"武器"。

过去没有跟上房产这趟列车的人，财富在无形中也被收割了，货币在大量贬值。

我本人还亲身经历过沿海血汗工厂的压榨，全厂工人每日每夜地工作，真的是人如机器。每天工作到凌晨才下班，夏天下班洗个澡天就亮了。常年无休，只有在中秋、端午、国庆的晚上没有加班，那就是老板眼里的"放假"。

更荒唐的是服装厂，包括那附近所有的工厂，都是到年底才一起结账给员工。每年正月元宵节后到厂，腊月回家，仿佛一年到头卖给别人了。

平常只有每个月的10号、20号、30号借生活费。有同事借50元，有的借100元，有的借70元，大部分借100元。

我们就这点生活费钱，都会省吃俭用扣下点，夹在信封里寄回去。我至今还在困惑，明明是我们工人自己赚的辛苦血汗钱，还要用"借"这个字。

我还记得每个月10日的晚上，老板的女儿背个包来到车间，同事们就一阵骚动，很兴奋，可以借钱啦！有的同事吹着口哨，有的打着响指，难得的片刻欢愉。

我们每个工人拿着自己领衣服的小黄账本去排队，老板女儿在账本上写某人某号借100元，然后我们员工签名，拿到她发的100元，谦卑地说着："谢谢，谢谢。"好像是老板赠送给我们似的，感恩戴德。

我们当时做衣服用的缝纫线都是自己的，大家当然都喜欢抢那个S号的衣服做，能节省线，还能节省时间。S号和XXL号相差很大，偶尔因抢小号衣服有争执闹不愉快的时候。

现在看来，那厂的哪一条工厂规定都不符合劳动法，为什么大家都觉得理所当然？周边村子的工厂都这个样子。

为什么我还在这个厂待了四五年呢？后来还在温州、杭州、老家也做过服装。为什么自己没敢跳出去那个圈层，哪怕是做营业员、销售员，也比在厂里封闭着好，思维眼界也会早一点打开。

为什么我就没有去广东那边呢？后来听说那边都有单休，有的厂里面还有图书馆。

我咋就不懂得去找人，办个中专证去应聘销售前台之类的呢？上次在某视频里看到一个女子同样早早辍学，但是她花钱办了中专证，应聘4S店销售，后来又做奢侈品销售员，思维开阔，自信满满。

前几天我看到社群里面另一个女子的分享，她也是辍学很早，但是她就比我有勇气，胆也大。厂里干了半年过后，她就果断去学电脑，后来应聘跟单员。

看着她们的故事，就觉得她们头脑好灵活聪明，自己怎么当年那么傻，在最好的年华里活成了工具人。

我那个时候人好像是麻木的，师傅、老乡们怎么说就怎么做。脑子每天只想着怎么省钱，怎么努力再提升自己的干活速度，怎么早点把家里债还完，何时能给家里盖栋楼房。万一换工作，换环境一折腾就没钱了，所以想都没敢想换行业，哪怕是换厂都不敢想。

营业员之类的工作不管吃住，反而攒不住钱，到底还是人穷志短啊！

总之那时候的我是没得选择。如果岁月可以穿越回当年，肯定还得继续在服装厂待那么多年。

2013年过后，智能手机的出现和普及，标志着一个时代的结束，另一个时代的开始。各大自媒体平台横空出世，你方唱罢我登场，犹如古时各方诸侯，每一个平台有不同的调性特色，熙熙攘攘，热闹非凡。

微博、微信公众号、今日头条、简书、百家号、网易等平台，让普通草根都有了发声的机会，也因此成就了无数人。

移动互联网的普及，让每一个人都能快速获取到信息。即便在遥远的国度、遥远的省份发生的大事情，一两分钟后，整个网络就铺天盖地，任何人打开手机就能看到。互联网让世界变得平坦。

抖音视频平台更是在两年多的时间里就达到了数亿用户量，简直是奇迹般的存在。不论是4岁的小孩还是80岁的老人都喜欢玩抖音。TikTok（抖音海外版）在国外也是大受欢迎，据说有超过推特的趋势。

哪里有市场，哪里就有需求。美团外卖上，手机上一点，想吃的食物就送到你手上。出门有需要，在手机上提前预约网约车，有专业人士为你当司机。不用操心开车，不用操心找停车场，还可以在车子上打盹休息。

微信转账汇款，在手机上用银行APP转账都是秒到……

我们这代人还经历过去邮政局填写汇款单寄钱，那个熟悉的邮政绿色标识。我小时候还看到过发电报，曾写过无数封手写信，用过磁卡电话，高额的电话费时期。现在只要有无线网，即便相隔千山万水，也能彼此看见。

直播带货、人工智能、无人驾驶……

曾经有人说："淘宝不死，中国不富。"现在各平台的直播带货风生水起，这是时代的趋势。

一个行业的崛起，无形中会有另一个行业在没落。每一次巨变都是社会财富资源的重新再分配。

这些年来，社会在翻天覆地地变化，我们都是亲身经历者，也是参与者。我们都是在见证历史啊！

未来我们这艘社会"大船"，最终会走向何方？在时代的狂涛巨浪下，我们个体又将有怎样的生命轨迹？

## 你有这样的房东阿姨吗?

不管你是在北京、上海、广州、深圳,还是在其他任何一个城市,在我们的记忆里,在我们漂泊的岁月里,一定都会有一个令人难忘的房东阿姨。

我看过许多名家写过自己的房东,犹记得迟子建笔下的房东老人,是一位近八十岁的流亡哈尔滨的犹太后裔——吉莲娜,她爱干净、整洁、考究,热爱音乐和美术……

我也想用清浅的文字记录下我的房东。我在上海待了两年,租住的房子位于浦东近世纪大道的一个相对高档的小区,其绿化、安全性和地理位置都让我相当满意,且毗邻地铁六号线和七号线。

房东阿姨是一位50岁左右的上海本地人,笑容似乎随时挂在她脸上,说话细声慢语。近看她的皮肤非常光洁,根本没有她这个年纪该有的皱纹。她说她心态很好,不爱操心。就连我租住的这房子,都是十几年前,她的好友再三拉她一起在这个小区买的(十几年前劝人买房的都是贵人啊)。目前她在浦东和浦西各有两套房子,她的独生女正在美国留学。

她说她租房首先是看人的,是看人谈房租的。因为之前我妹妹也在她这租了四年的房子。去年初她回老家合肥发展,有了空位我就搬过来了。房东本人只在一年一次的签合同时才来,有时顺道过来看看,平常我们也只是每季度在微信上给她转账。

她并不像别人所说的上海人那样难说话、算计小气,相反,她非常豪爽、干脆，很有人情味。在我们这么好的小区，她一套近120平米的房子租给我们，才只要3000元。

有住在我们同一小区的同事，他们一间房也要2500元，而且是合租的，卫生间常常都得排队。加上二手房东的缘故，他们的每月电费、网费都比一手租户贵了两倍多。他们对我所租的价格都表示羡慕嫉妒恨，有的甚至不敢相信，说我们房东是不是钱太多了⋯⋯

钱这东西，有谁会嫌多？想一想，自己真是莫大的福气。我也问过房东阿姨为何对我们这么好。她说：她的房子也是要人住的，遇上投缘的人，象征性地收些租金。你们姐妹都非常讨人喜欢，租给你们哪怕价格低些我也是乐意的。你们住里面，一定要注意水电安全，帮我把房子看好，总共人数别超过四人就好。

她还反倒每次对我们说："谢谢，谢谢！"收房租时，还会带些国外比较新鲜的食品让我们品尝。

房东阿姨还同我分享她刚在美国芝加哥所拍的冬日乡村摄影照片。之前她业余一直很喜欢拍照片，正式学摄影有一年多了，经常到各地去拍摄，是很有情怀、有追求的一位阿姨。

她常去美国看望她的女儿，她也一直有关注我的公众号。后来知道我爱写文章，说以后文章中需要时可以用上她的照片。

看到她所发来的图片，我脑海中只蹦出了"如诗如画，如梦如幻，美得想哭"这些文字。

我把她发的图片全都备份保存了起来。心里一直有句话：遇上这样的房东阿姨真是我前世修来的福气，是生命里的一种福报和加持！唯有珍惜，感恩！

我想每个外出谋生过的人，一定对"房东"这个词不陌生。其实它不仅仅是利益上的关系，也是一种感情的所在。它不像酒店、宾馆招待所，没有太多的联系。

许多年后，我们回忆起打拼漂泊的时光，回忆曾停留过的城市，必定会回忆起关于那个房东的种种。

## 关于门前的那条火车路

儿时的记忆里，家门口不远处一直在修建铁路。放学后，我们常会沿着铁路边走，这样的路线更直，算得上是一条捷径。

有一次，听大人们说不要再从铁路边走，因为前面有一条大河，即将架设一座铁路桥，以便火车能顺利通行。我们这些小屁孩调皮地反问："不就是修桥吗？我们从边上小心地走就是了。"

大人们却说，修桥是一项大工程，大型桥梁能顺利建成，往往伴随着"收魂"的说法。时至今日，我仍不清楚这究竟是迷信还是人们的想象。有传说称，某地的桥梁数次无法顺利完工时，就会采取招魂术，用牛或人的魂魄去支撑桥梁。

这些传说被描述得栩栩如生，说是有道士用一个系着红布的瓦罐，当有人经过并回应时，魂魄就会被招走并用红布系好。而被招魂的人就会消失。

那段时间，大人们告诫我们千万不要再从铁路附近走，如果陌生人叫喊，也绝不能答应。我们虽然对这些说法半信半疑，但又因畏惧大人们的权威而不敢违背。耳边常常听到某地的铁路桥已牺牲了多少老牛，才能将桥梁架设得严丝合缝。

还有传言说，某地的老奶奶牵着孙子经过桥边，听到修桥道士叫喊，小男孩干脆地应声，结果回去没几天就去世了。关于小男孩的死因，有各种说法，有的说是因为他答应了道士的招魂，被带去了极乐世界帮忙背桥梁，有的则说是因为吃馒头撑死的，众说纷纭。

人们都抱着宁可信其有，不可信其无的心态。我的父母和其他小伙伴的家长商量后决定，以后每天轮流送我们上学，直到桥梁完工。

我们只能每天远远地望着铁路，乖乖地跟着父母绕道走，直到铁路桥竣工，合九铁路顺利通车。我并没有亲眼看到或听说本村有人因修桥而被招魂丧命。

那些传说中活灵活现的主角，往往都是指某地的某人，只是经过口耳相传，添油加醋后的结果。

此刻，我躺在床上，敲打着手机，听到由远而近的火车哐当声，想起小时候的那些传说，总会不自觉地笑出声来……

## 奶奶陪伴的童年时光

我童年的大部分时光都是在奶奶身边度过的,夏季总是让我产生更多的怀念。

奶奶屋后有一棵两人都环抱不过来的大柳树。酷暑难耐的夏天,这里就成了最天然的避暑纳凉好场所,尤其是在物质贫瘠的90年代初。

晚饭后,左邻右舍纷纷搬出凉床,带着蒲扇,谈论今晚的南风或风势大小,也有声音说,今晚凉快了,能睡个好觉。此时的我,在边上跟着萤火虫欢快地奔跑。

奶奶忙着用井水擦洗家里的凉床,喊我过来安静坐下,别跑得满身是汗。我嘴贫地说,我过去坐着,你就给我讲故事。奶奶连声说好。

我躺在凉床上,仰望着天上的星星月亮,听奶奶讲《嫦娥奔月》的故事。奶奶还不忘在我身上来回摇着蒲扇。那把蒲扇的边沿用布条包裹了一圈,手柄因用得久而光滑无比,带着岁月的痕迹。奶奶给我扇的风幅度不大,动作轻缓,凉风徐徐飘来,没有一个蚊子敢来叮我。

有时奶奶会讲《七仙女》《牛郎织女》等故事。听着听着,我就进入了梦乡。有时深夜热得醒来,奶奶似乎有心灵感应,马上从睡梦中惊醒,继续帮我摇蒲扇,直到我再次进入梦乡。

第二天晚饭后,奶奶会继续昨天的故事,摇动蒲扇,有时还会变戏法似的掏出杏子、桃子给我。后来,我渐渐长大,才知道她自己舍不得吃水果零食,手头微薄的零花钱也省着,给我们姐妹上学买本子用。

奶奶在我心中就像个无所不能的人，有着说不完的故事。因此，我成了村子里小伙伴们羡慕的对象，被称为"故事王"。

奶奶有时会用故事引申出做人的道理，如"小时偷针，大了偷金"等朴素而富有哲理的话语，教导我们要不卑不亢，靠自己努力争取所想要的。她希望当别人提到我们时，是竖拇指称赞，而不是摇头不想提。

奶奶还会带我去附近的山上砍柴。我会拽着她的衣角，她去哪儿我就跟到哪儿，一路上蹦蹦跳跳，非常快乐。后来，她失明了，这样的时光再也没有了。她成了需要我们牵着的人。

虽然奶奶已离开我们多年，但她的音容笑貌，夏夜给我摇蒲扇讲故事的情景，像电影镜头一样定格在我的脑海里，成为我心中最温馨难忘的画面。那些没有手机、电脑、空调的日子，因她的陪伴而变得充实。

或许，是这位我深爱的老人的影响，让我成为了一个写故事的人。

# 记忆里的粉蒸肉

每个地区都有自己的特色菜。在我老家安徽安庆,粉蒸肉是待客必不可少的一道菜,我们当地也叫它炸肉粉。你们家乡有吗?

我记得第一次吃粉蒸肉是在同学小美家。某个周末,我去她家玩,她们家正在吃午饭,桌上有一碗青菜和一碗粉蒸肉。她妈妈热情地给我盛了米饭,夹了好几块粉蒸肉。那香喷喷的味道让我特别感动。

那肉裹着一层粉,吃起来不油不腻,鲜美异常。我羡慕小美家的生活条件。我们家已经好几个月没吃过肉了。估计小美的妈妈早就看出来了,想让我尝尝她的手艺,补补身子。她笑着说,碗里还有,你和小美把这些肉吃干净。那是我第一次吃粉蒸肉,吃了两大碗饭,把碗里的蒸肉粉吃得点滴不剩。

后来,村子里办了个厂,妈妈领着我们加班加点干活,贴补家用。生活环境逐渐好起来,妈妈一直记得我想再吃粉蒸肉。

于是她开始准备,用大米、糯米、八角、茴香、桂皮等,将米浸泡洗净,让我点火热锅,她把米放进去小火翻炒。米的颜色变化,摸上去滚烫后,加花椒和掰碎的八角一起炒。炒到米粒膨胀,闻起来很香就可以停了。然后妈妈用手捣碎炒好的米和调料。

接着,她把切好的五花肉薄片和蒸肉粉一起调拌,撒入盐和味精,大火蒸。蒸一小时后,粉蒸肉的香味扑鼻而来。

当妈妈要掀锅盖时,我总是不顾烫手,赶快夹起一块肉,那肉入口即化，肥而不腻，口感润滑。妈妈看着我吃得满足，乐呵呵地笑，自己却吃得很少，说等家里宽裕了要天天做给我吃。

粉蒸肉的美味，主要看蒸肉粉做得如何。蒸肉粉味道调得好，粉蒸肉自然味道鲜美。

这些年在外地，很少吃到家乡的粉蒸肉。超市里的蒸肉粉，虽然包装精美，但怎么也做不出老家的味道。记忆里的粉蒸肉，是家乡的味道，妈妈的味道，那里有家庭的温馨，母亲的慈爱，我们的童年。

## 阅读与智者对谈，与灵魂共舞

"腹有诗书气自华"、"读书百遍，其义自见"、"书中自有黄金屋，书中自有颜如玉"、"我害怕阅读的人"、"爱读书的孩子，不会变坏"、"书籍是人类进步的阶梯"……这些经典句子，无一不是在阐述阅读对人的重要性。阅读能重塑我们的精神品格，它让我们拥有强大的内心力量，从容地应对这个瞬息万变的社会。

在物质生活贫瘠的年代，获取书籍的资源渠道极其有限。只要我逮到机会，看到自己喜欢的字句，就迫不及待地摘抄，恨不得把每一个字每一句话都融进骨髓里。

时间稍微宽裕后，每天下午和傍晚，我会抽空在旧书摊淘书回去看。周而复始，光阴流转，那些看过的书，一本一本都在潜移默化中影响了我，储存在我的血液中。每读一本书都是在与智者交谈，与大师对话，与自己的灵魂共舞，那是属于自己愉快的心流时光。

我在西安做早餐生意时，每天早上三四点起床，会在面板的一角放上收音机，一边做事，一边听路遥的《平凡的世界》《白鹿原》等名家经典书籍。争分夺秒地汲取精神营养，让我在忙碌繁琐的现实世俗生活之外，看到了另一个精神世界。

这些养分让我在面对生活的打击、身体出现毛病时依然能坚强面对，因为我的心中拥有更加辽阔的时空。如同毛姆所说："阅读是一座随身携带的避难所"。一个热爱阅读的人是不会被轻易打垮的。

早期热爱文字的习惯，让我在移动互联网的大潮下，想要表达，想要倾诉，想要"被看见"。我像是必然又是偶然地成了一名自由写作者，签约出版了5本书籍，实现了时间自由，经济独立。

如果没有从前的阅读与积累，我是不可能抓住现在的自媒体写作机会的。

曾经看过一句话：任何一个行业都有低学历的成功人士，但这个人一定是热爱阅读、热爱学习思考的人。我不敢说自己算是成功者，但爱阅读的习惯的确改变了我的命运。

前年，我受邀在某学校报告厅做了一场《阅读与写作》的分享会。我告诉这些学生：大家一定要保持阅读的习惯。当你看的书多了，你就有更深的思考，心中有了更加广阔的世界。你能更早地知道，自己想要什么样的生活和人生，或许也有机会成为一名作家。古今中外，哪个名人不爱阅读呢？

如果你觉得生活一切如意，你也要阅读，在书中体会他人的悲苦与不幸，增加生命的厚度；如果你生活中遇见风雨坎坷，你也要阅读，因为你在阅读中，才知道这世界有人比你更痛苦，看他们又是如何面对那些磨难，又是如何走出人生至暗时刻的。

阅读是门槛最低的投资，阅读是最好的精神救赎，也是最好的修行道场。

Living like this.

# 岁月如歌，每个人的人生都是一部书

## 01

辍学之初，我在村中一家熟人店里学习缝纫。我在缝纫机的左边刻下"有志者事竟成"，右边则刻着："精诚所至，金石为开"。那时的我，其实并不清楚梦想究竟为何物。

那时，我拥有一本厚重的笔记本，专门用来抒发心情和记录日记。我给它起名为《人世间》，模仿着书本将内容分为1、2、3等章节，记录下在师傅家听到的周边村庄的人事，每一页都密密麻麻地记载着少女时期的所见所闻。

多年后，当我看到梁晓声老师编写的电视剧《人世间》，不禁感慨自己当年竟也大胆地取了这样一个宏大的题目。

那时，14岁多一点的我，对这个世界的理解还只是一知半解。

由于村中缝纫活计稀少，次年，我便转至镇上继续学习缝纫技术。骑自行车前往镇上需要40多分钟。我常想，我现在的大长腿，是否就是那时骑自行车锻炼出来的？

在镇上的师傅家中，我读到了梁晓声和毕淑敏的作品。那时的毕淑敏还是文坛的新星。

这两本书似乎是师傅参加活动时被赠送的。师傅家中还订阅了半年期的《读者》杂志，每当她去安庆批发布料时，我也会偷偷翻阅。

在镇上学习时，我最爱听人谈论服装厂的赚钱故事。一听到这些，我就聚精会神地听。那时的我，对于梦想、人生规划、读书改变命运等概念一无所知，心中唯一的念头就是赚钱改善生活。

我的大师姐下半年去了天津做服装，腊月时她回店铺玩，告诉我们她一个月能赚600多元，让我们这些学徒羡慕不已。

我们当时共有7个师姐妹，我和另一个女孩是最后加入的，自然承担了拆洗、打扫、带小孩等杂活。

师傅偶尔让我烫衣服、卷裤脚、缝扣眼，但当我在缝裤腰头时出了错，被师傅严厉批评，之后我又回到了杂活中。我必须承认，自己学东西慢，脑子没有其他人灵光。

镇上的这位服装师傅是位30岁出头的女子，身高1.7米，气质非凡，被誉为镇上四大美女之一。她是镇上第一个想到结合布匹和窗帘销售的人，也是喜欢设计新款衣服的人。用现代的话来说，她具有超前的思维、前瞻性的眼光和商业头脑。

至今，我仍记得她美丽的容颜和她记尺寸本子上漂亮的字迹。

有一次，师傅去安庆参加台胞台属联谊会（她有个舅爷爷在台湾）。开会回来后，给我们师姐妹每人带了一点小礼物，虽然只是宾馆里的一次性小香皂、小洗发液和一些零食，但对我们来说却是新奇的玩意儿。

分给我的是一个小盒香皂，我把它当作宝贝一样珍惜，每次只使用一点点。师傅说，别人不想要的东西她全部带回家送给我们。我记得那咖啡色的小盒香皂，我用了很久很久，直到用完，还把小盒子像文物一样珍藏着。

在村子里学徒时，因为活计太少；在镇上学缝纫时，因为人太多，自己接受能力差，感觉没有学到什么技术，无法独立裁剪并制作出一件完整的衣服。现在回想起来，总是有些遗憾。

Living like this.

## 02

在镇上学习了一年缝纫后,家里通过熟人的介绍,帮我找到了一位师傅带我去福建的工厂。由于信息和认知的局限,我在福建又做了一年的徒弟。我的缝纫技艺并不精湛,却前后拜了三位师傅。

读初中时,附近的人都说在外地的服装厂一年能赚一万多块钱,这让我和发小都无比心动。我曾计划在外面的工厂干三年,给家里盖一栋漂亮的楼房,也好扬眉吐气。然而,当我真正进入这一行,才发现收入并没有别人说的那么多,或许是行业的红利期已逐渐退去,外贸服装的工价一降再降。

我所在的福建泉州晋江东石镇潘径村,几乎家家户户都是服装厂。即便在老家学过两三年缝纫机,到了外地依然要学习一年电动缝纫机(平车)。实际上,电动缝纫机踩上三四天就能熟悉,之后便可以慢慢摸索着赚钱。

但那时,大家普遍认为第一年应该白干,师傅们则从中赚取差价。师傅的主要作用是带路。他们垫付了来回车费,这对我家来说,省去了一大笔费用,非常有吸引力。临出门前,母亲担心我在外没钱用,卖掉了自己的头发,给了我20块钱。邻居老太太和我奶奶也分别给了我5元钱,这些钱都是她们省吃俭用攒下的。

厂里的师傅通常每10天给徒弟15块钱,用来购买零花和日用品。饭是和师傅一起吃的,年底则给1000块钱带回家。我每月的零花钱是45块钱,我连5毛钱的包子都舍不得吃,经常饿着。一袋五毛钱的飘柔洗发液,我要分三次使用,用完后还用塑料袋包起来,留待下次再用。我省下的钱,会在写信时夹在信封里寄回家,通常是5块,有时10块,最多的一次夹了50元。

当时和我一样当学徒的老乡女孩大约有 15 个，其中一对师傅夫妇带了 12 位徒弟。据说那对夫妇一年到头净收入 3 万多，那是在 2000 年。

初到福建的半年，我的脚因不适应沿海的碱水，右脚背烂了一个洞，化脓且奇痒难忍。我只能左脚踩电动缝纫机，每天穿着校服（对我来说，校服是最好的衣裳）。记得初中那套红色校服要 60 块钱一套，学校规定每个同学都必须购买。

校服真是好东西，它保护了我的尊严和体面。我以为左脚踩电动缝纫机，右脚就会好起来，没想到情况越来越严重，走路都要一瘸一拐的，伴随着疼痛。厂里的江西同事给我取了个绰号"左脚大侠"，在全厂独一无二。

年少时，我对一切浑然不觉，师傅不提带我去诊所，我也不敢开口。每天只知道吃饭干活，吃饭干活，像个工具人。我甚至担心看脚的钱要从那 1000 块里扣除，做梦都希望脚能自愈。

直到有老乡提醒师傅，我的脚再不看可能要残废。师傅当时的回复是："残废就残废呗……"不过，她还是带我去诊所挂了盐水。经过半个多月的治疗，伤口逐渐愈合。现在，我的右脚背上还有一个模糊的疤痕，阴雨天还会隐隐作痛。

治疗期间，除了去挂水，我并没有耽误太多工作。我提醒自己要提升速度，甚至比以前更努力，以补偿去诊所的时间。我的师傅相比其他师傅要温和许多。

我见过其他师傅罚徒弟站在车间柱子旁，大声斥责，甚至用脚踢她的电动缝纫机和装衣服的框子，全车间的人都看得见。只因为那女孩做衣服时打瞌睡。

我第一年所在的厂里，每天晚上工作到凌晨三四点，早上九点又要上班。徒弟早上要比师傅到得早，怎能不打瞌睡？上厕所都能睡着。现在看来或许不可思议，但那时是常态。

其实，我师傅从老家出门时，还带了另一个女孩徒弟。我们一起坐绿皮火车，一起住在一个宿舍（宿舍有6个上下铺）。她在家里没学过一天缝纫机。到福建后，她每天踩机子就头晕，说身体不好，想回家，总是难过，想家。

她大概待了一个月，师傅送她去车站，她家人接走了。然后师傅和老乡们常说那女孩怕吃苦。从他们的角度来看，估计都会这样说吧！"师傅们"也是食物链的底端。

我不想被别人说怕吃苦。其实我也很想家，很想回去。但我连车费都没有，不敢再有这念头。离家三千里，每天工作17个小时以上，年底才1000块钱。而我五年级周末打零工，一天都快10块钱了。这个时薪还不如我在老家的待遇，我却为了不想被别人说怕吃苦，为了不被老家人笑话，在外面苦撑。

当时的舆论环境认为，外面待一段时间就跑回来的人非常丢脸。我恨自己没有主见，现在想来，真是咬牙切齿。那年的自己真是傻。为什么不想法和那女孩一起回家？回来骑自行车到镇上上班，做刷子，去包装厂，塑料袋厂，还可以去桐城市里上班，还可以照顾家人，在农忙时帮家里干活。

我在镇上学缝纫机时，同学陈金睇在对面做钢丝刷，一年有三四千元。我们经常早晚骑自行车遇见，家门口的厂里还不用熬夜。

人到中年，我意识到，做学徒的那两年半，选择去外省打工，简直是让人生开倒车，走了倒退的路。难道就为了给我今天的写作提供素材？这代价未免太大。人无法用后来的认知去衡量从前的自己，一切都是命。

深层次的原因是，我一直不喜欢家乡。从小受尽冷眼，没感受到太多的爱与尊重，总渴望快快长大，远离家乡，越远越好。真到了外面，发现没有想象中那么好，也不甘心回家。

其实，我们所渴望的远方，何尝不是别人待腻了的家乡？

## 03

  那时,常有山区人来我们镇上工作,我们镇被誉为"中国制刷之乡"。桐城市更是塑料袋的主要产地,据说占据了全国60%以上的市场份额。

  如果我早知道母亲的寿命如此短暂,我无论如何也不会选择去那么远的地方打工。每年都是正月出发,腊月才回家,感觉自己像是卖给了别人一样。哪怕在家门口少赚一些,至少我的身体不会在美好的青春年华里累到病倒。

  那时候,在福建的工厂里,我们一年只回家一次。安徽人非常重视回家过年。而四川、贵州的同事们,有些人三四年才回家一次。我隔壁车间的一位四川同事,回家时她的女儿甚至都认不出她了。

  现在回想起来,这是多么悲凉。当年经历这一切或见证这一切的人,反而没有那么多感慨。思想和内心没有那么多感慨的人,自然也就少了很多悲伤。

  2002年时,我们厂里的下班时间已经改到了凌晨2点。

  那年,我曾做过几个月的服装检验员。加工厂的衣服送到我们总厂的库房里,有时需要人手检验,就会找老员工去做检验员。检查衣服哪里掉线了、跳针了、不对称,不合格的就用黄色胶带贴一下,让别人拿回去返工。检验员一天的工资是30元(到了2004年时是40元一天),都是住在厂里,吃自己的。

  如果自己做衣服,是多劳多得。一条沙滩裤平均一块钱一件,我平均一天能做三四十件。因为干活麻利,我在厂里算是工资较高的几位之一。

  厂里生产的是非洲难民穿的沙滩裤,设计复杂,大口袋上贴着小口袋，大口袋侧面还有拉链，表面还有立体袋，斜插袋，膝盖处有口袋，屁股后面还有贴袋，袋口有魔术贴。算下来，一条短裤上有十几个口袋。

在厂里工作得又累又倦时，还时常面对大量返修，有时真恨不得把衣服扔到海里去。我常常想，到底是谁发明了做衣服？

当年，我们边做衣服，边听收音机。记得听过《激情燃烧的岁月》等一些广播剧，以及一些问答情感互动栏目。

《真情花园》是我们最喜欢的节目。节目的开场白是："在不远处的海面上，有一只白色的帆船，静静驶向心灵的彼岸。"

那档节目的主持人叫白帆。以至于我在2016年写作时，取笔名时也带了这个"帆"字。那档节目主要是读一些打工人写去的信件，还可以给别人点歌送歌。

主持人的声音亲切动听，读信中穿插一些歌曲，如伍佰、张信哲、任贤齐、刘德华、阿杜等人的歌。

每当有同事买回磁带，我总是抢先去借那张有歌词的纸，让她把歌词抽出来，我要拿去摘抄，把歌词抄在口袋布上。

……

往事如烟，岁月如歌！

滚滚红尘，时代变迁！

每个人的人生都是一本厚厚的书，一本具有独特韵味的书。

## 04

看新闻说现在的00后，工作上一不高兴就抬腿走人，炒了老板鱿鱼再说。我们那群85后的人却吃了那么多苦头。听说比我早两年进厂的一位江西同事，曾被老板打，用烟头烫他的手背……

比我晚几年进厂的同事，有的人一天缝纫机都没学过，不需要师傅，自己进厂由组长带着做流水线就可以赚钱。

再后来，不管学木匠、瓦匠、油漆等任何手艺，都不用学几年，边学边做就有收入了，更不用仰仗师傅和任何人的鼻息。

由于工业化的普及，民间师徒那种传帮带的习俗已成为历史。近几年去沿海打工的工作时间也在逐年缩短。

你看，早几年或晚几年，一切都截然不同。

人不过是时代的产物，身处那样的大环境（小环境），自身又弱小，真是无力改变。

想起前辈作家陆天明老师曾写道："任何一个人，当然包括你和我，其实都是历史舞台上被动的扮演者。总编剧、总导演只能是时代和社会。"

## 那些远去的手艺人

从前，有人脖子上挂着相机，到各处村庄转悠，吆喝着："照相，照相，谁要照相？"那时候，能拥有一部相机，从事这个职业的，肯定是头脑灵活、有点门道的人。

记忆中，我只有一张5岁时的黑白照片，照片中的我站在隔壁的儿童车旁，留着小光头，穿着围兜。至今家人亲戚都说我从小像男孩，性格更是如此。

在我读初中后，这种挂相机上门照相的人已经不见了，随着时代的发展，他们被淘汰了。

后来，流行去照相馆拍照。那里有很多衣服可以选，拍照时可以搭配几套衣服，再选几个镜头，一个镜头多少钱，洗几张，种类繁多。

近些年，照相馆也受到了新发展趋势的影响。我在西安做小生意时，隔壁就是照相馆，店主是和我同龄的河南女子。她说证件照没什么人照，来拍生活照的人更少，因为很多人已有数码相机，而且手机拍照功能越来越强大。

她回忆起曾经的风光时光，2003年有两个月，仅拍证件照就月赚近万元。那时是非典时期，很多地方需要查验证件，智能手机还未普及。

她感慨地说，当年钱好赚时没有好好珍惜，现在越来越难。只有转型做大型影楼拍婚纱照才能存活，而且要做成品牌，但那需要大量投资，不是每个普通照相馆都能顺利成功转型。

社会的每一个发展时期，既能成就很多职业，也会淘汰一些。

回忆起那些消失的职业，小时候，还常看到补鞋匠，他是个瘦小的中年人。只要他一到，村庄里家家户户都把破了洞的鞋拿出来，有妈妈做的手工布鞋，有军用式的黄球鞋。孩子们也会跟着凑热闹，围着补鞋摊子叽叽喳喳，犹如过年般开心。

补鞋匠进村时常挑着一个担子，一边是补鞋机，一边箩筐里装着补鞋用的辅料。鞋子撕口的，脚尖踢破的，都可以被补鞋匠那双巧手缝补起来，被人欢天喜地地当新鞋穿。那时的人们并不觉得生活苦，反而很容易满足。

记忆中，离我家不远的地方还有家铁匠铺，两兄弟整天在火炉边忙碌，生意兴隆。两人肩膀上常搭着条毛巾，赤着胳膊，整个人黑乎乎的。现在想来，在没有空调的夏天，他们是如何每日在高温下作业的？

村子里人用的砍柴刀、割稻镰刀、铲土铁锹都是他们打造的。童年的我觉得这铁匠简直有鬼斧神工，满心钦佩。

随着我逐渐长大，路过他们门口，发现他们的生意越来越冷清。直到有一天，村子里都在讨论那铁匠兄弟到外地打工，店铺关门了。外面赚钱可比这多，他们家三代打铁的手艺就这样荒废了。大家一阵感叹！

我的亲小叔曾经是个篾匠，擅长编织睡觉的席子、洗菜的篾箩、挑秧苗的筐子。去小叔家时，他总是围着块破布，把竹子剖开，再一片片削成薄片，经过他神奇的手编织成一个个人们所需的物件。

大家拿到手工编织的物品，反复触摸、翻看，自有一种喜悦与幸福。

三叔过去是补锅匠，像补鞋匠一样挑着担子到各村庄。那个年代，锅碗瓢盆破了也不会轻易扔掉，等到补锅的来时，补好再继续用。

我曾跟着三叔后面走街串巷，他悠长的声音喊着"补锅，补锅咯"。每到一处村庄，都会引起一阵沸腾热闹。只见三叔拿起锅，对着光照照，确定好碎掉的位置，用锡烫，窟窿大的得换锅底。一个个手艺人敲敲打打，便产生了破镜重圆的效果，补过的锅除了很小部分有明显痕迹外，更多的是要完好如新。

　　90年代后期，补锅的行当也突然消失，和三叔一样的补锅人都出去打工了。

　　从前还有上门的剃头匠，而不是现在叫理发师、美发师。那时的剃头匠拎个木制的小箱子，到每个村庄给男士剃头，到年底一起结账，经济实惠。

　　我的篾匠小叔后来去了武汉做塑料袋生意，如剃头匠、铁匠、补鞋匠一样，重新改行谋生。

　　那些手艺人是特定时代的特殊人群，是时代的产物。在市场经济还没有正式发达时，他们是人们眼里走南闯北、眼界开阔的人，他们骄傲有底气，因为有一门手艺。"大荒年，饿不死手艺人嘛。"

　　但随着社会的发展，产品的分工越来越细，机器化、科技化的迅猛发展，让那些老一辈匠人消失在人们的视野，退出了历史的舞台，成了某个特定时期的符号。

　　我从有手艺人的岁月中走过来，目睹过那些老手艺的制作过程，见证了他们的繁华与凋零。能看懂每件物品背后的故事：是享受，是成全，有温度，有喜悦，更是对生活和人生难以割舍的挚爱。

　　我们现在火热的职业或技术，未来20年后又会怎么样呢？唯有时间会给予答案吧！

## 老屋和土灶台

算起来,家里新房子已经盖了有些年头,但很奇怪的是,午夜梦回时,所梦见的总是小时候住过的老屋,而不是后来建的楼房。

老屋承载了我儿时绝大多数的回忆,无论是无忧的快乐还是自卑的贫穷。

家里土坯砌成的三间老屋,是爸爸在我出生那年修建好的。听奶奶说,为了盖这三间瓦房,爸爸每天起早贪黑,所有盖房用的土坯都是他一人亲自在田地用木模子做出来的,再晒上好些天才可以使用。屋顶上的木梁也是他独自一人去外婆那边的舒城大山区一步步一根根步行驮回来的。

在那物资极度匮乏的年代,尤其是贫苦人家,即便是再普通不过的三间土坯房,也是耗尽一家人的全部心血。奶奶提起这些辛酸就会不停地抹着眼泪。

老屋的左侧是厨房,进门便是大大的灶台。听老人说,砌灶台是个技术活,高高的烟囱通风要好,否则很费柴禾。有的砌得不好的会满屋烟气,锅与灶台要严丝合缝。

大部分人家的锅台上会安有两口锅,一个主锅用来炒菜,另一个大锅用来煮饭。中间会有两口水井罐,用来煨热水。饭好了,热水用来洗脸和刷碗。后来有了铝井罐,热水开了也会装在水瓶里,这样能节省柴禾和时间。

灶台的上方挂着铁铲、铜勺、筷笼子等物件,贴着春节时写的四个字："水火平安"。锅台的一端下方会放一个大大的水缸，里面放着一个用半边干葫芦做成的水瓢，用来舀水盛水。

那时都是用的木头锅盖，煮饭时锅沿常常会用洗碗布围一圈以免漏气。我常常会坐在灶门口的蒲垫上帮忙塞柴禾，有稻草、油菜秸、松毛和树枝等等。有时用棍柴树枝时总会容易把燃着的火弄灭了，即使我鼓起腮帮子使劲地吹，眼睛时常会呛得流泪，火总是还着不起来。

妈妈就会告诉我，"人要实心，火要空心"。要把树枝架起来，中间留个空隙，这样火才会旺起来。也有人家会安个风箱，遇上柴禾不好着时，就会拉一拉风箱，有利于柴禾的通风。

灶台、木锅盖、柴禾、大锅煮出来的米饭格外香。起米汤后，再添几把小火，饭就会慢慢溢出香气。远远地都能闻到香气，直叫人馋涎欲滴。每每饭后，我会把底下香而脆的锅巴泡上米汤吃，别提有多美了。

下午放学回家后的第一件事，就是跑进厨房找中午剩的锅巴泡开水，就着咸菜吃得津津有味。

秋天是红薯收获的季节，我们姐妹常常在灶洞里放进红薯，让火星火种一起覆盖起来。一个多小时后闻到香味再取出，管不了外面那黑乎乎的一层皮，也管不了多烫手，我们左手换右手，右手换左手，掰开就吃。那金黄的瓤咬一口，哇，好吃！别提有多爽了。时至今日，那香喷喷、热乎乎的烤红薯依然是我心里最美的美食之一。

随着液化气、电饭煲、电磁炉等电器化厨具的普及，如今再也很少见到记忆里那样的土灶台了，那样的木锅盖、那样的大锅、那样的烧红薯味……这一切都将淹没在时光深处了。

以后的我们只有花高价去农家乐体验了吧？

灶台、火光、妈妈，那都是我们心中永恒温暖的存在！

## 所有的一切都有它的局限性

10多年前，中央电视台曾经主办过一次"品牌中国"的大型宣传活动，评选出消费者最喜爱的本土品牌榜单。当时上榜的有40个本土品牌：大宝、小护士、波导、步步高、万利达、同方、奥克斯、波士顿、恒源祥、雅戈尔、七匹狼、李宁、森马、杉杉等。

这些品牌中，我对森马、美特斯邦威、李宁、小护士比较熟悉。森马是温州的本土品牌，当时温州还有个美特斯邦威也挺火。2008年，我做生意的那条街上就有森马和美特斯邦威的专卖店。森马在温州话中意为"什么"，其广告语"穿什么就是什么"。这两个品牌价格适中，适合大众消费，当时很受人欢迎。

我二妹曾在上海做过森马店的导购员。记得二妹曾说，她在的那家门店一天销售额能达到1万多，节假日更多。但导购员是按自己的营业额拿提成的，二妹说她的性格不太适合，每天饭都是抢着时间，随便吃几口，同事间抢客户，明争暗斗，她大概只做了三个多月。

时代汹涌澎湃，这些品牌好像都逐渐销声匿迹了。2007年，我在浙江温州茶山区大学城附近的一家品牌女装厂上班，商标叫"雪凡妮"。老板的姐姐的厂做得更成功，在全世界100多个国家都有专卖店，她的品牌名叫"雪歌"。当时温州有名的几条大道上都有这个"雪歌"品牌的广告牌。

据说这老板的姐姐是非常传奇的人物，17岁就带家人做服装，从小门店到自己学设计一步步做大，也率先意识到品牌的重要性。她出嫁前还为这个厂和娘家打了官司，最后她只带走了"雪歌"的商标。厂房设备所有的一切留给她弟弟了，就是我待的那个厂"雪凡妮"。

我在那里上班的那年，老板和他姐姐年龄可能比那时的我大不了多少，有同事看到"雪歌"创始人回娘家办事，都夸她看起来年轻漂亮有气质。虽然她出嫁时只带走了商标两个字，但只用几年，她依然远超他弟弟的发展状况。

由于浙江地区和大环境的机遇，以及自身的努力拼搏，他们成立了自己的品牌，我们外地人为他们打工，在他们那里讨生活。据说更早一点，在五六十年代，浙江人几乎都来我们安徽谋生。他们的盐碱地长不出庄稼，不出来营生混口饭，真会饿着。那年代他们羡慕"中原"人呢！真是三十年河东，三十年河西。

在2015年之前，传统品牌的成长模式都是先注册一个商标，再用一切资源宣传，如同"雪歌"在高速路口都有巨型广告灯牌展示，温州广播电台都有他们的宣传推广。再用品牌名气吸引各地的加盟商，开专卖店。品牌、加工、生产、销售一条龙，属于自产自销的内贸。

我刚走出社会上班的福建那个大厂，他们做的是外贸，用大货车集装箱从香港发走，转运到非洲各地。那些年外贸非常红火，后来美元贬值，内地人工成本增加，外贸厂越来越没有利润，我们很多老乡宁可选择在老家厂上班，也不再去沿海了。2012年后沿海的很多服装厂都已经搬到云南、越南和缅甸那边去了。

去年腊月，偶然遇见当年在温州女装厂的老乡同事，我还问起她，我们当年的"雪凡妮"以及他姐姐的"雪歌"现在怎么样了？她说也不知道。这位老乡姐姐以前是在那厂带组长。她年前请我吃火锅时，说得最多的话就是感慨我怎么成了"作家"。

我说，按照这个网络时代的发展趋势，我们当年待过的女装厂，如果没有及时转型重视网络营销，大概率是已经没落了。我三叔是补锅的，我小叔是做篾匠的，编农村里面挑秧苗的箩筐、洗菜的箩筐、挑稻谷的箩子等。

我还记得小叔坐在地上打凉席的样子。我也曾跟随三叔去看补锅，用那个锡把锅底小洞给补上，实在是没有含金量的工作，没几年就被时代淘汰掉了。一个锅一共才值多少钱？再过几年，小叔的行当也被时代淘汰了。机器化的批量产出，这种手工劳作品没有可比性。现要买凉席，买现成的成品快捷又便宜。那时候我小叔打一床凉席都要几天几夜，时间成本太高了。

小叔曾在背后感叹说，认为我奶奶没远见，同龄人家里学木匠、瓦匠，我奶奶给他们学补锅和篾匠。我小叔读书时候成绩非常好，年年拿奖状的。家里贫苦以及缺少读书的意识，让他早点回来为家里做事，再找师傅学篾匠。只能说，每个人和家庭都有自身的局限性。

在我辍学的时候，我们家族没有一个亲戚能带我一条出路，更没有一个直系亲戚能帮忙。七拐八弯，找了一个远房亲戚介绍的师傅带我去福建。那是个比我大一岁（12岁）的女子。我也算幸运了，在当年厂里的所有师傅中，她是最温和的，不大声说话骂人，更不会打人。

等我在福建厂里稳定了，便把小叔介绍到我的厂里烫衣服，小婶介绍到流水车间做衣服。两年后，小叔在我和老乡们的鼓励下，承包了厂里后道车间的整个烫台。他们干了几年后，家庭收入得到了很大的改善，现在他们家的那栋漂亮房子还是当年在福建赚的钱所建的。

后来我离开了福建那厂，听老乡说，老板每年请客请大餐，叫几个代表，小叔必定是其中之一。他是老员工又是烫台的承包人，那几年也是小叔存在感最强的几年。后来福建外贸厂走下坡路，老乡都离开得差不多了。小叔最近这些年一直在工地上做事，出苦力那种，经常是跟随各工地辗转。

想当年，他在工厂里，有自己的独立宿舍，干净明亮，还有专门烧

Living like this.

饭的地方，安徽派在厂里又受人尊敬，比起现在在工地上的环境和处境不知道要好多少。现在，我们每次回老家，都会带点牛奶或者红包给小婶，她死活都不肯收钱，顶多留下一箱牛奶。

每次我问小叔怎么样，小婶总是说没人带，这辈子还能怎么样？小叔那些年常年不怎么回家，对孩子也不怎么管，唯一的儿子，也就是我堂弟，初二都没读完。作为独生子的堂弟，居然辍学比我们还早。现在也是在工地上，三天打鱼两天晒网。

每次听到这类话，总是有种深深的无力感。我小妹当年十几岁在街上自己找工作，一家一家地问，自己打印资料投放找工作。从初到上海100块钱床铺一个月的拼租间到超市导购员，到日本料理店包吃包住的工作，再到成为公司行政工作者，在上海张江高科的小区和表妹以及老乡合租了单间，一步步地置换稍微好的居住环境。

她后来又分期按揭交学费，自考本科，自考日语二级，自考司法考试等。每个人、每个职业、每个家庭、每家公司，都有它所处的时代环境以及个人性格的各种局限。

想起在两千零几年，各地方有很多开摩的工作者，我也坐过很多次。后来被共享单车给淘汰了。以前还用过那种万能充，一闪一闪的，现在压根不需要了。以前我有一个邻居是开照相馆的，一个河南姑娘，她当时已经意识到危机了。她说如果不转型做婚纱影楼就要淘汰了。记得她还跟我说 2003 年非典，需要查照片，仅靠洗印单人照这一项，一个月能赚 8000 多。

好在，他们一大家人意识蛮超前，在西安房价三四千的时候就已经买了两套房了。这河南姑娘现在还是我的 QQ 好友。时代的列车轰轰而过，没有及时跟上，没有完成基本的财富保值，慢慢的就容易滑落到最底层，形成恶性循环，越来越难。

要么后代有人读书智商超高，通过高考改变阶层命运，只是现在的高考"性价比"也没有 30 年前高了；或者看准趋势红利，抓住机会实现突破，这得要眼光、运气、行动力等综合能力了。今天我在读《时代之巅：互联网构建新经济》时感慨太多了，那些被消失的行业，那些转型失败的公司，那些没有与时俱进，然后越活越累的人们。

诺基亚当年被收购的时候，高层领导黯然地对记者说，"我觉得我们没有做错什么，但是不知道为什么，可我们就是失败了"。历史的车轮滚滚向前，它不会因任何人的消极缓慢而停止。

我有那么多可写的活生生的素材，可我总是没能写出自己想要的文字，写了这么多年也是不温不火，这也是我的局限性。人世间的一切都有它的局限性。

# 抓住一次风口能少奋斗10年？

## 01

风口总是在成为过去后，我们才意识到它的存在，总是在事后才被追认为重要的机遇。当身处风口之中，我们往往无法辨识，更不知如何把握。

实际上，能够抓住风口的人，通常在风口来临前就已经开始相关领域的积累。如果等到风口来了才从零开始，那将无法抓住机遇，因为一切都来不及了。

因此，你必须置身于信息源的边缘，否则你无法看到自己所处的信息层级，这将决定我们成为什么样的人。我们需要设法靠近重要的信息源，这非常关键。

自2017年以来，每年都有人说微信公众号不好做了，自媒体没有机会了。但每年依然有人成功运营公众号，靠公众号过上滋润的生活，享受自由。

我的老学员邓姑娘，她在2019年开始做公众号，仅用一年半时间就吸引了十来万粉丝，实现了自由职业。

即使到了2023年，依然有人成功运营公众号，基本生活无忧，能够通过公众号养活自己。

如果你总是因为信息渠道不足，信息来源落后，就会不断错过这个时代最好的机会。有时一步错，就会一路错过。

例如，过去二十年来的几次互联网机遇，1970年以前出生的人大多几乎抓不住，他们对网络不敏感，接受能力较差。例如，2000年代初的淘宝造就了无数人，2013年的微商，2015至2016年的自媒体火爆期，但大多数人完美错过了。

做淘宝起家的人大多是80后，做微商成功的大多是90后，而小红书、B站和抖音平台的主要是90后、95后，这是由他们的敏感度、适应度以及平台的调性决定的。

60后中有的人对这些平台的某些新潮词汇一时难以接受。

如果你看好某个领域，就要设法朝这个方向努力，多读相关书籍，靠近这个领域的圈子，从物理到心理，即使你现在起步晚了，只要你持续正确且坚定地努力，你总会抓住下一个风口，迅速完成能力迁移。

很多人问我，现在写作、做自媒体还来得及么？

我总是说，任何时候觉醒、想行动都不晚。当你觉得为时已晚的时候，恰恰是最好的时候。

今年，许多人通过公众号获得了不错的副业收入，还有通过视频号获得关注的人。有位网络同行，通过视频号上的一个视频给公众号涨粉3万+。在小红书、快手和抖音上，每年每月依然会有人崭露头角。

## 02

我有一个前同事小亮，1987年出生。我们曾在福建的一个服装厂工作过。不过，他来厂没多久，我就因身体原因回老家了。但我对这位老乡同事还有些印象。

后来，他换到浙江的服装厂工作。他在听收音机时了解到电商的发展趋势，仿佛看到了希望，业余时间开始研究这个领域，从淘宝的基础操作学起。但由于进货压货，资金周转困难，他不得不回到服装厂工作几个月，然后再继续做淘宝，这样断断续续折腾了三年多。

直到2012年，他开始全职做淘宝。2014年、2015年，他的事业有了小爆发，最高一个月赚了50万+。到2018年，他又抓住了拼多多的红利，一款裤子在拼多多上月销售额突破900万。虽然对于那些成功的大牛来说并不算多，但他的起点只是一个没学历、没背景、没人脉的三无人员。

有了不错的收入后，他在浙江买了3套房，在老家桐城市投资了店铺，都是在房价暴涨前下手的。这些年，他还带领了许多桐城老乡通过网络增加了不少收入，改变了命运。

今年，他开始尝试抖音电商。在当前的大环境下，虽然没有过去那么好做，他也与其他主播达人合作分成，以及参与一些其他项目。幸运的是，这位老同事已经完成了原始积累，即便什么都不再做，也可以超过80%的人。

他也遗憾地说，刚到浙江的那几年黄金时期，因为没有人带，手上没有本金，走了不少弯路。全靠自己一步步摸索，资金周转困难时，再回厂里打工，一步步坚持至今。

每个人的一生中都会遇到风口机遇，只要你能抓住一次，你就可以实现蜕变。我的这位前同事，虽然淘宝这块并没有赶上最好的红利期，但让他接触到了电商，看到了电商的无限可能性。有了一点积蓄后，他全职投入电商，独自带着一个包跑到义乌。

这些都是他后来起飞的重要基础。如果没有淘宝运营经验，没有深入电商圈子，那后来就不会抓住拼多多的风口。

如果他一直只是在服装厂里，每天接触的都是做衣服的同事，没有去和电商圈的人交流接触，那他的思维自然会有很大的局限。

幸运的是，他果断地一个人从福建跑到浙江嵊州找厂，探索其他可能性。浙江嵊州的厂里工作时间比福建的短几小时，工资稍高，偶尔淡季时，晚上可以不用上班，这让他有了时间思考和学习。

而当年我们绝大部分福建厂里的老乡和同事是万万不敢轻易换厂的，更不用说跨省换厂了。

当时大家觉得天下乌鸦一般黑，只有在一个厂里不动，才能存住钱。大家都害怕试错成本。主要还是人穷志短吧！我们现实社会里有多少人本可能有更大的作为和前途，但因自身各种局限和不得已。

## 03

我这位老乡同事在尝到淘宝的甜头后，再次一个人前往浙江义乌，辗转打听找到做电商的圈子，出门遇见的每个人都是电商人。

他在他们居住的地方租下其中一处地下室落脚。当他看到义乌遍地都是物美价廉的产品时，两眼发光，心想，这回真是来对了。

这些决策都是基于他自己的主见，也有命运的眷顾。前年夏天，他又及时出手卖掉义乌的一套房子，扣除各种成本和税后，还净赚了100万。这是一次明智的决策。如果现在才卖那套房子，结果就差太多了。

之前看他在朋友圈发动态说，遇见风口，猪都能飞起来，说自己运气好，踩上了电商红利。我想说，风口并不是只吹向一个人或一群人，而是整个社会所有人。

虽然，我这前同事小亮不是从事自媒体领域，但他也是因互联网而成就的人，是这个移动互联网时代大潮下的受益者。他的一些成长决定，放在自媒体领域底层逻辑也是一样的。

我也听说过许多人在2010年以前就开过淘宝店，也就是在最好的红利期入局的，但并没有坚持下来，最后还是回去上班了。这样的群体也不少，并没有像我这个义乌老同事这样能把电商做出一份事业，还能养活几个员工。

因此，你不用担心做自媒体晚了，写作晚了。只要提升认知，找对方法，坚持深耕，你总会吃到属于自己的红利。我们只要比昨天的自己有所进步就好。

## 人强得过命吗？在命运面前，休论公道……

我是个记事很晚的人，10岁以前的事情，能记得的极为有限，只有为数不多的几个片段。

大约在读一、二年级时，有天放学路上，我和发小们一起回家，途经小山坡时，突然看到奶奶远远地拄着竹棍迎面走过来，喊我说："帆儿，你陪我去小吴医生（村庄赤脚医生）那看看，我的眼睛突然像是蒙住了，看不太清楚了。"

我年幼无知且贪玩，我说自己要和小伙伴回家了，不陪你，你自己去吧。

奶奶一个人去村庄看赤脚医生了。可能就是从那天起，奶奶的眼睛就慢慢走向失明。

记得有次，在安庆的大娘回老家，和叔叔一起带奶奶上我们县城医院去看，医生说是可开刀可不开。有个女医生还说："老了还开什么刀……"

后来，我曾听奶奶无数次唠叨，就怪那女医生那句话，更后悔自己当时不坚定，没有坚持要开刀做手术。主要是她自己也没想到后来多活了几十年的寿命。同村有老人眼睛开刀治疗后就能看见了，奶奶可羡慕了。

奶奶是个自尊心极强的人，哪怕后来眼睛彻底看不见了，她也要坚持自己单独居住，用她的话说："想吃早一点就早一点，想晚一点就晚一点，落得自在啊！"

她每天在三间土坯屋子里一个人摸索着过日子,生活在黑暗之中。

村庄里人都说奶奶的眼睛是生生哭瞎的,她是泪腺极低的人,无论开心或不开心的事,她都会流泪。

我爸爸的去世对奶奶的打击特别大。奶奶在门口塘边井里提水时,把水放在边上,坐在土墩上休息时,想想就会哭起来,想她苦命的儿子,哭诉命运的不公,为什么让她白发送黑发人,也担心我们姐妹几个的成长,那时小妹才一岁。

有时在菜园地里干活时,奶奶坐在地沟里也会哭很久,好像唯有哭是她向这个世界最想表达的内容。

年少的我常常听到她的哭声,有时晚上,她房子边上的邻居又在喊我们:"你奶奶又在家哭了,怕她会想不开,都去劝慰她。"

有几次大半夜哭得比较严重时,门口大娘说:"要不要拍电报让你家东祥(我大伯)回来。"奶奶总是会说:"我一会儿就好了,可不能麻烦他,他在安庆上班工作过日子也不容易。"

她真是没日没夜地哭泣了两个月,奶奶以双目失明为沉重代价。

原来这世界上真有人能把一双眼睛生生哭瞎,这是多沉痛的双重悲剧。

我懂事晚,脑子好像少了一根筋的人,对于那时奶奶的悲痛无法共情。看她在我面前痛哭时,我从没有跟着哭过,哪怕流一滴泪,如同在冷眼旁观地看着一个不相干的老人。

而今,中年的我,成为职业写作者,在写这类回忆的文字时,会泪如雨下。在一些无眠的夜里,想起奶奶时,也会泪水滂沱,曾经没有流过的眼泪,终究是加倍流了出来。

奶奶真是个极其苦命的人,她的一生就是走完饱含苦难悲情的一生。

她曾多次祈祷上天,让她早点离开人世。她说别人多活一天是福气,那是寿。对于她来说，每多活一天是孽没有做满，老天不肯轻易收她，那是在惩罚她。

在那动荡饥饿贫寒至极的年代，我奶奶童年就丧失了父母和爷爷奶奶，跟随她唯一的亲人（她老太太）来乞讨生活。老太太年迈为继，在我奶奶8岁时，把她许给我爷爷，由这头老人带着再继续要饭。

关于那些要饭的岁月，她在我面前说得最多的一幕，她最怕的就是地主家的大狼狗，有的狗比人还高，哇哇地叫，她吓得躲在拐角瑟瑟发抖，宁可挨饿也不敢出来。

奶奶再稍微大一点时，她就到地主家打长工了。虽说一年忙活到头没有一分钱，但可以管着嘴，也就是最基本的生存，总比要饭稳定也有了尊严。

还是孩子的她，在地主家冬天敲冰洗衣、洗被子、收拾卫生、做各种家务活，每天天没亮开始干活直到晚上。

她说的这家地主的女老人，在我十来岁时，还见到了。那地主一家早就搬到城里了，后代都发展得非常好。那老人那次回老家走亲，还特意到我们庄来了，一双小脚，穿着看起来就很有贵气。

她想打听我奶奶生活得如何，听说我爸爸那么年轻去世了，她坐着哀叹了会。临走时，那位曾经的地主老人还给了我奶奶20元钱，非常热心。

听到我奶奶在门口和庄里另外老人说："真是某人某命啊！她（那地主）年轻时，家里田地那么多，许多穷人给她家干活，现在子孙个个又都如此成功，家族兴旺。人是狠不过命啊！"

地主，也算是特定年代的精英阶层，祖上优秀基因在那里，通常家族都不会差。而我奶奶依然还是整个大村庄最穷的人家，还是很不幸的人家，自身眼睛还瞎了。

此刻，我在想，奶奶何尝不想做个能给予帮助别人的人，毕竟施比

Living like this.

受幸福，奈何命运就是不如她愿，她孩童时给人家打长工，老年时，还是得受人家的恩惠。

奶奶常在我们姐妹面前说："可怜你爸爸走得早，不然你们吃穿哪样不比你们同龄孩子差，你爸爸多勤快，连日带夜地做，日子越来越好了，别人家有的，我们家也有了，可惜是人强命不强啊！"

每次听奶奶絮叨过无数次的陈年往事，我只要一会没有回应，她就把手摸一摸："你还在听我说话吗？帆儿，你在吗？"

奶奶也是人强命不强啊！

奶奶生前对我们说无数次的话："我这瞎子奶奶什么也没有，伸手不见五指，不能帮你们一点点，还要你们常照顾我。我唯有死后，一定要保佑你们……"

大多时候，奶奶独自摸索着在塘边用小铁桶提水，洗衣做饭，到门口菜地里种菜。不敢想象，我那耳背眼瞎的奶奶，是如何才能做到这些的啊！

有时周末，奶奶让我帮抬粪去菜地浇菜，每次给我2角钱。

她的钱是大伯给她买油的零花钱，她是从牙缝里抠出来变相倒贴给我们家了，大多是鼓励我们干活的。

我们姐妹在山上打的柴按市场价10元100斤，过秤给她，牵她去菜地，提水抬粪，她都会给我们一点零花钱，我们如获至宝。

奶奶说去别人那买柴也是给钱，这钱不如给自己孙女赚，买本子和笔也是好的，也提高她们做事积极性。

回想起来，我人生中第一个打工的对象，那就是为我自己奶奶打工。

还记得奶奶和我抬着柴称秤的慈祥微笑模样。我们星期日一天能搞好几十斤松毛柴回来，作为孩子的我能把自己的劳动换到钱，特别开心有成就感。

我奶奶年轻时应该是个五官棱角分明、双眼皮大眼睛的人，也是个非常心地善良的人。

我多次看到她给要饭的人，都是半盛米的往人家袋子里倒，别人只是用手抓一点点米打发要饭人。

奶奶说我自己是苦命人，我心疼苦人。

奶奶个高、美丽、能干、好强，奈何她所处的时代和家庭没能给她一点点机会，更没有顺遂的命运。她斗大字不识一个，我爸爸也不认得字。

奶奶中年时，我爷爷就去世了，真是劳苦一生，悲苦一生。

在纹丝不动的命运之下，到底是什么力量在掌控人的命运走向，强悍的终究是命运啊！

冬天，对奶奶说是一种折磨。瘦弱的奶奶最怕冷，她说她身上没有什么血气，老了更怕冷了。

她走的头年腊月，我回老家看她，晚上给她装好了暖瓶，放在她被窝里，奶奶非常激动又满足。

2012年，奶奶在冬至的第二天离开了人世，据说早上叔叔送饭时喊她已经去世了。

没有空调、电热毯、没有暖气的南方农村，她终没有走过那年冬天，而我在外漂泊谋生，不知我当年是怎么想的，奶奶的葬礼我并没有回去。那年我是在西安做早点生意，是舍不得歇业，还是舍不得车费？反正就是没回去，成了生命里的遗憾。如果是现在，无论如何也会立马飞回去。

在另一个平行世界里，希望我亲爱的奶奶不再有苦难不幸，贫穷悲痛。拥有健康幸福，耳聪目明，能识字读书，能拥有美好的一切。

因为奶奶，我看到的每一个老人都像她；因为奶奶，我成为一个良善的人。

Living like this.

# 命运之神的力量

曾有读者朋友说，网络上许多博主多半出身于普通人家，但你是真正从底层草根家庭出来的，韧性极强，太不容易了。

社会上有无数人也可能有类似的出身或不幸经历，大多可能就会深陷泥潭，爬不出来，压根再没有勇气去追求梦想了……

其实，谁不想有平顺的人生，顺遂的命运？都是前世因果，轮回中，总会有不幸降临于某个人或某个家庭身上。

一个人的出生区域和家庭环境，早期的一切，个人哪有什么选择权？都是命运的安排啊！

人们都说苦难是财富，如果我能选择，我才不要这样的财富呢！我是无从选择的！

## 01

安徽舒城和桐城这方热土共同孕育了我们。

我的母亲是1963年生人，她是兄妹7人中唯一没上过一天学的人。大姨还读了一、二年级。

她是安徽六安舒城人，外婆家是那种开门四处环山的大山沟里。

我的父亲是兄弟4人中也是唯一没上过学的人。大伯还读了二年级。我父亲出生于安徽安庆桐城郊区的农村。

15岁的母亲和32岁的父亲经人介绍相识。一个家庭是希望能嫁到山外去，为贫困家庭寻找突破口，至少能换些粮食贴补家里，哪怕一年多两担米也是好的。

一个家贫又文盲，年龄又大了，当地不好找。盼望在大山区探访个贫困家庭里的憨厚听话女孩，完成传宗接代的使命。

可以说，我的母亲和父亲都是各自大家庭的牺牲品。在那个能吃饱吃好都是奢侈的岁月里，又有多少人能拥有自我命运的选择权？

我的父亲和母亲就在这样的境遇下，几年后结婚，完成了他们的人生大事。

如此这般的他们结合在一起，有了我们姐妹三个。

小时候，从桐城到舒城的中间路程是坐三轮车，咚咚咚，灰尘漫天，两头还得步行很久很久。到舒城那头的路真是叫山路十八弯，弯弯绕绕，总是看不到头，所以母亲回趟娘家都是一两年为单位。

有时候母亲为了节省路费钱，她全程全部步行，天没亮就开始出发。

早些年交通不发达，大家生活都很困顿的岁月，亲戚见面很少。我15岁之前都没有见过大姨家的表姐长什么样子。

路远加上交通不便，我大姨以前身体不太好，晕车严重，直到我母亲2002年去世时，大姨才第一次来到我家里。

后来，去舒城的道路有所改善，在去舒城和桐城两地交界处，有块石碑备注：这边柏油路是桐城，那边土路是舒城，很明显地区分。那是桐城人引以为傲的谈资。那些年，桐城在经济发展方面是优越于舒城很多的。

毕竟我们桐城私企特别多，我们镇上走错路都能遇见刷子厂、塑料袋厂，被称为"中国制刷之乡"。60%的刷子来源于我们这地方。

数年过后，舒城和桐城两边道路已经一样是水泥路，也有多种可直达的车。

现在的舒城被称为"合肥的后花园"。和桐城已经是并驾齐驱,都是风景优美、人文底蕴深厚的城市,都是安徽重要的人才产出地。

二妹在小姨的介绍下,在舒城成家生活,舒城现在是我比小时候去得更勤的地方。

时光一晃而过,而我们也人到中年。我成了自媒体人,全职写作者;二妹是公司白领,副业是摄影师、美食博主。我们都是靠后天自学而成。

## 02

2004年,我因大咯血回家养病。

下半年,我买了部手机,诺基亚蓝屏手机1200元,是我前一年在福建打工时的积蓄。那时在家养病,同事在外赚钱,我却在花钱,内心是无限悲凉,也曾有段时间悲愤上天的不公,埋怨命运的吝啬。

在服装厂里时,我总想拿到高工资,总想拿第一名或前几名。因身体原因,不得已停下。到老家,我用了好长时间做心理建设,必须接受事实,我的身体匹配不上厂里超负荷的劳动强度。

我在一本杂志上看到,有时,上天让你生一场小病,是看你太累了,想让你休息休息……

我就退一步来想这件事,用积极正面的角度来对待面前的不幸之事。

在福建确诊为结核时,医生就说现在各地有这相关的医院,可免费治疗。各地有专属机构,是由日本资助的,全球这类病都可免费治疗。我回到老家前,我三叔已帮打听到我们桐城市专属治疗机构的具体地点了。

我想到过去年代很多名人家世那么好，得同样的病，用很多年都治不好，过去被称为"痨病"，早几十年农村很多得这病就直接没命了。

我只是幸运比他们晚出生了几十年，而我所处的时代，这类病只是个重感冒，半年到一年就完完全全好了。

农村人也称为"富贵病"，吃好喝好不做事才好得快。

那半年，确实是我成人以来最清闲的时光，吃了玩，玩了睡。手边为数不多的杂志都被我写写画画，涂得满满，日记本也是写些句子，段不成章。那时，实在是太无聊了。

后来，我干脆不去想我的那么多老乡同事都在外努力拼搏，而我在家坐吃山空，我也不再和谁比省钱、赚钱、存钱的事了。我在老家认得的新同事都有手机，我也就一咬牙也买了部。

老家认识的新同事和在福建厂里的同事们消费观是截然不同的两类。

03

当我把手机递给奶奶时，她摸在手里，反复抚摩，照来照去，还用手摇摇，笑容可掬。

奶奶说："这东西没电线，这怎么能打电话呢？说话能听到？声音怎么来的？电话有线还情有可原，这是什么宝物？"

我奶奶又开始感慨："你们这一朝人真是好，都是享了时代的福，都是享了党的光。"

据说穷人家的后代，对教员是有着深入骨髓的爱，这话肯定是有道理的。

2007年，我在温州茶山大学城边上一家女装厂做流水线。坐在我前面的同事和另一个同事不知怎么聊起关于教员的事，说什么想不通人民币上为什么是他头像，还说什么不是教员，他早开上宝马了……

我坐在后面一边做衣，一边听着他们对话，真是气不打一处来，就跟他们抬杠起来。

虽然读书有限，历史知识有限，但对于教员这种爱，已然是一种来自灵魂的信仰，来源于奶奶在我很小时就种下的种子。那是神一样的存在！

奶奶说，我们那时布是织着用，每天早上三四点就起来织布。她指指木楼上的纺织车："米是捶着吃，天天用手工锻（我们当地方言，就是用手工磨出米），上哪地方去都是一双脚量一二一，柴是上山砍着烧，那时候需要柴的人多，只有往更深的大山里才能搞到柴……"

奶奶找人拍过电报，找人代写过信，为联系大伯时。对于新型通讯工具——手机，老人是一时接受不了。

1996年，我所在的安徽桐城县改为县级市。那些年安庆管辖下有8县1市，那个市就是我们桐城市。民间大家聊天时说，桐城的经济增速是要超过安庆古城了。

县改为市的晚上，到处都在放烟花，放电影，一片热闹繁华的感觉。个人和家庭似乎也跟着都要好起来。

我和村庄小伙伴还隔壁庄同学一起去村支部门口看电影，貌似都在为家乡从"县"改为"市"而骄傲，其实也就是跟着凑热闹。

那天，我们看着露天电影时，大家不知道怎么聊到关于"公平"这一话题。我最后总结了一句："只有死亡是对每个人公平的。"

1998年时，我们门口不远处就有公交车直达桐城市广场，当时车费是一元钱，车程近20分钟。也就是说从我们村庄步行五六分钟到公交车站就有直达公交车到市里了。

1998年，正是洪涝灾害很严重的那一年，农作物大幅度减产。村里发了很多救济衣服，我们是如获至宝，比我们自己家平常的衣服好太多了，时髦洋气，款式新颖。那是离不开城里好心人的帮助。

我们家常常得去街上卖菜来度生活，家里从不买菜，更别说吃荤菜。菜地里的菜得省着吃，还得卖点补贴生活。（除非杀猪时有猪下水，鸡瘟时或者有犁田的来干活时，伙食好点）

初中三年，我每天中午都是吃早上从家里带的咸菜，日日如此。学校老师家属有卖做好的菜，摆在食堂边上卖，至今仍记得蔬菜叶子加豆腐汤是三毛钱一份，也就一铁瓢。如果是菜里有点肉末，那就是五毛钱一份，整整三年，我只有羡慕别人能有钱买新鲜菜的份儿。

特别是镇上的同学们，居然还有一个人会带两份菜，还花钱再买新鲜蔬菜吃，我看他们简直都是天外幸运之人，真是和我来自不同的世界。

1998年，稻谷跌到35元一担，庄里人都是唉声叹气。听说当年稻谷大跌是因亚洲金融危机影响，是让农民承担了大部分，这都是农人闲聊的话。

自古以来，任何时期若是发生了时代悲剧，底层人一定是最苦的，生活肯定是雪上加霜。历来如此，这是不争的事实。

奶奶说她过去挑柴去桐城街上卖，全是靠步行。她说："你们现在真是好，上街买个东西，还有公交车搭，又是自行车或摩托车，你们这一代人真是好命。"

你爷爷生前最大的梦想是什么时候能把米饭吃个够就好了。他说："米饭多香啊！那是他终生未如愿的梦。你爷爷只要多活10年就能实现，多活10年就可以了啊！"

奶奶还常提到自己当年挑柴比男的走得还快，她做哪一样农活都不输整个大村庄的任何人。

此刻，我在想，如果奶奶生活在我们现在这个年代，她肯定能生活得好很多，也许还能成就一番小事业。一个人就算再有本事，也得有大环境来支撑。一个人在时代面前是很渺小无力的。个体命运和所处的时代是息息相关的。

即便现在，我们社会或者身边的一些大咖牛人，他们如果生在中东一些国家，就未必能拥有现在的一切。

现在回想，我在家休养那年，没和奶奶说过我生病，也不知可有庄里人提过，奶奶也没问过我怎么突然回来了。

2004年，是我自辍学以后，和奶奶相伴时间最多的一年。再后来，每年只有过年那几天在家，看望她，听她聊天了。

我要是知道自己未来能成为职业作家，当年应该拿个小本本，把我奶奶所说的每一句话都记录下来。

感恩命运的一切恩典，不管是好的还是坏的。

## 那一年在镇上学裁缝的时光

1999年,因家门口的缝纫活不多,我家通过熟人介绍,让我去镇上的师傅那里学缝纫技术。我每天骑着加重自行车去镇上,单程大约需要40多分钟。

师傅是一位32岁的高个子美女,被誉为镇上四大美女之一。当时,她店里已经有6个师姐,我是最后一个加入的师妹。师傅是镇上第一个经营布匹的裁缝,也是第一个开展窗帘业务的裁缝店。

在裁缝店对面的大马路那边,有一家钢丝刷加工厂,我的小学兼初中同学陈金娣就在那里上班。听说她一年能赚近4000元,那是我们镇上刷子行业比较兴旺的几年,吸引了很多外地人来镇上工作。

后来不知哪一年,我听说陈金娣因精神失常,在一个冬天冻死在桥洞下,让我唏嘘不已,沉默了很久。回想起1999年,我们少女时代在路上相遇,一边骑自行车一边谈笑,对未来充满幻想。世事无常,人生变迁。

我学徒时交了100元押金,并自带缝纫机。因为前面已有好几个师姐,我这个新来的小徒弟,每天的工作主要是打杂:拆洗、缝补、锁扣眼、挑脚边、烫衣服。我做得最多的是帮师傅做家务,如扫地、拖地、擦地板、带孩子、洗衣服。当时师傅家有两个女儿,大的8岁,小的两岁多。

师傅的小女儿长得非常可爱,皮肤白嫩。我常牵着她的小手在街上走,有时抱着她在后街转转。记得有一次,师傅让我带小宝宝出去玩,买几个旺旺雪饼。我把雪饼一点点尝了，觉得非常脆香。我当时感叹世上竟有如此美味的零食，那美味让我久久回味。我当时暗暗想，将来有钱了，一定要吃个够。

当年这个想法是真心的，但现在，即便雪饼摆在我面前，我也没有想吃的欲望。

还有一次，师傅让我带小宝宝出去玩，顺便买几斤水果。我特意抱着师傅的小宝宝去车站附近的我家门口大娘那里买水果。大娘看到后吓坏了，担心我带这么可爱的孩子过马路太危险。她嘱咐我下次别再带小宝宝特意来她这里买水果。

我这位大娘是个心怀悲悯的人，对每个人都很好。她不会因为我家是庄里弱势家庭就另眼看待，也不会因为我奶奶是盲人就对她不好，反而在各方面非常照顾我奶奶。现在我终于明白，她当年为何那样关心。

师傅家有个大师姐叫海霞，她跟随师傅多年，已能独立做衣服。当年师傅每月给她250元，让她帮忙协助干活，相当于我们的"小师傅"。师傅常去安庆进货，不在家时，很多事情都由海霞师姐负责。

那一年，我并没有学到多少做衣服的本领。有一次，我上了一条裤腰头，结果衣服拿出来裤腰是扭的，很不平整。师傅让我拆了，她重新上那条裤腰，让我看着。从那以后，师傅再也没有给我做过有技术含量的工序，我继续以打杂和带孩子为主。

除了没钱用，我每天过得也很简单，挺轻松。看到师姐们买方便面做零食，我只能羡慕。我要是回去要钱，妈妈就会不住地说，我现在不读书了，怎么还要钱？我也觉得开不了口，何况家里确实没钱。

还有个小师姐秋香，她家离镇上不太远。我曾去过她家，她姐姐非常优秀，是我们那年初中学校成绩拔尖的学生，全校有名。当时，她姐姐已在安师大读硕士，每年拿奖学金。这位小师姐家里有她姐姐买的很多书，包括《钢铁是怎样炼成的》和几本线装书，如《毛泽东选集》。那是我第一次真正读名著，粗略读了《钢铁是怎样炼成的》。

几年后，在福建的服装厂里，坐在我工位边的小邱也是那个小师姐一个村庄的。我问她小师姐的事，她说，她姐姐后来读了博士，发展得很好，还把她妹妹带起来了。说我那小师姐后来也发展得不错。

在师傅家，我也是第一次看到《读者》杂志，有单行本，也有年度合集本。师傅不在家时，我有时会翻看。师傅裁剪衣服的桌子抽屉里还有毕淑敏和梁晓声的随笔集，我都看过一些。

几年前的某个腊月，当我再次经过镇上，那个曾经学习裁缝技艺的店铺位置时，我本能地探头望去，却发现一切早已变了模样。我没有看到我的师傅，即使偶然相遇，她可能也认不出我了。或许我还能依稀认出她的身影。

在过去这20多年的时光里，我再也没有遇见过那6位师姐。人生漫长而又匆忙，像过客一般，我们各自匆匆前行。岁月的流转中，那些年轻时遇见的美好人和事逐渐变得模糊，但我希望用文字将它们记录下来。让这些记忆在我的文字中得以永存。

## 往事如烟——继父篇

很多事不愿过多回忆，记忆也自动屏蔽了许多细节。

我已记不清继父是何时来到我家的。他在我家的岁月里，每年在家的日子并不多，常年在外打工，主要在工地上做苦力，因此记忆并不深刻。

只记得继父正式从隔壁村庄搬到我家那天，举行了一个简单的仪式。那时我还小，跟随村里的姐姐们玩耍，我说我也想闹新娘，手里攥着土坯。一旁的村里姐姐大笑道："你知道今晚大家来看热闹的是哪个吗？"

我感到疑惑。她们说："那是你妈妈呀！"

这件事我只记得那个片段。其实那时我应该也不算太小，不知为何，我小时候的许多事情都记得不太清楚。

父亲去世后，很多人建议把小妹送人，这样家里能轻松一些，甚至已经联系好了人家，但我妈妈舍不得。

后来，不时有人给妈妈介绍对象，我记得其中有个四五十岁的杀猪佬，看上去不太舒服，头发梳得很油腻，让人害怕。幸好妈妈没有同意。

奶奶和小叔都劝妈妈不要改嫁，留在老齐屋村庄，那里都是熟人，一个村庄的人都姓齐，大家能相互照应。尽管也有不好的地方，但总比妈妈一个人去外村要好得多。

我们家那时已有三间土坯房，有院子，有田地，有风车，电风扇，我们姐妹都在身边。如果妈妈改嫁，别人不可能一下接受这么多孩子，何况妈妈是个特别重视家庭的人。

她听从了奶奶的建议，留在齐老屋本庄是明智的。

在过去的岁月里，女人走投无路时往往选择结婚，男人走投无路时则可能被动离婚。

在这样的背景下，我的继父来到了我家。他是隔壁村庄的人，听说是继父的堂哥介绍的。他认为，尽管我们家有三个孩子，但总比一个人强，至少有了一个家，有了希望。

我的继父姓谢，他是一个从未结过婚的人，长得高大帅气，比我母亲大6岁，看起来比我妈年轻，也是个文盲，但人很好，特别爱干净，勤快。

印象中，他每天都会把自己收拾得很整洁，家里的毛巾即使很旧，也总是晾得平平整整。

现在回想起来，母亲和继父之间可能真的有感情。毕竟当年我父亲被介绍给母亲时，她才15岁，什么都不懂，完全是听从外婆和家人的安排。

父亲在世时，在陶瓷厂工作，早晚还会干农活，每月发工资都会交给母亲。父亲比母亲大17岁，听说他很疼爱母亲。

母亲也和我说过，她当年在村支部做绝育手术时，父亲守在窗外，心疼得哭了起来。

继父和母亲年龄差距小，他们看起来很恩爱。继父太老实，在工地上做最重的活，却拿着最低的工资，常年不在家，只有在农忙时才会回来。更让人无奈的是，他经常拿不到工资，这在当时很常见。

当我五年级周末和暑假打工时，每天的收入已经接近继父的收入了，而且我的钱不会少一分，那是邻居家哥哥开的小加工厂，工资很靠谱。

有时候，二妹和小妹下午放学后去帮忙数啤酒套子，干两三个小时，那些大人会提前垫付现金给我们。

她们还笑着说，几个孩子傍晚干几个小时，就够一周买本子的钱了。

母亲和继父看我们能识字，做事灵活，那么小就能赚钱，也不比大人少，乡邻们经常在他们面前夸我们姐妹。

他们似乎认为我们将来会比他们更有出息，对我们很宽容。我是最爱顶嘴淘气的一个，他们只好由着我，甚至有点怕我。

我周末打工的那家是村里第一家有电话的，记得花了2500元安装，周围乡邻的电话都从他家转。他们家是热心肠，为人非常好。

继父难得和同事一起上街打电话，堂哥喊我和妈妈去接，继父第一句话是："家里猪还好吗？"

这成了他同事们之间传了很久的笑话。

他的同事们都是农民工，每年正月扛着大包小包去各个工地。能干幸运的人还能带些工钱回来，像继父这样的老好人常常白干。

奶奶也夸继父好，继父对奶奶也不错。在工地上如果能拿到工钱，他都会给每个人带一份小礼物，有好吃的也会送给奶奶，看到有活都会抢着做。

不知道为什么，我对他的印象不太深刻，相处的时间不多，他大约在我家待了七八年。

后来在工地上从大车上摔下来，听说脑浆都摔出来了，一命呜呼，母亲伤心了很久。

那时我在福建打工学徒，收到二妹的信后，才知道继父已经去世几个月了。

至今记得二妹在信里说："叔叔已离开这个美好的世界，姐姐要更加努力地赚钱……"

继父去世后,村干部和小叔带妈妈去出事的工地。妈妈不识字,表达能力又不太好,他们就让她见到包工头就哭,最后工地给了三万多元安葬费。

几年后,母亲生病,有算命的说是太思念继父,有的说是父亲和继父都缠着她。

不知道在另一个世界里,他们是否又相遇了?

## 我就是矛盾的人

在我身上似乎有着很多矛盾的点。很多人夸我记忆力好,我的妹妹、发小们、以前的多位同事都这么说,但我自己从未觉得自己记忆力好。

青春期时,在服装厂里,有段时间我和一些老乡同事在做检验员。我们厂有很多分厂,分加工厂的衣服拿到我们总厂要由老员工检验。检验员的工作,就是坐在库房车间的检验台上,看到做好的衣服有哪里不好的地方,贴上黄胶纸作为标记,让人返工,如有不平整、跳线漏针、不对称等。

我还记得那时候做检验员是30元一天,后来涨到40元一天,它是固定的,不按计件,自然比做衣服要轻松不少。一边干活一边和同事聊天,也不影响收入。那段时间,有位叫小邱的老乡坐在我旁边,她是我们老家一个镇上的人,皮肤特别白皙细嫩,看起来很妩媚可爱。

她有次收到一份信件,看完后随手往我这边衣服堆上一放。我问:"我可以看吗?"她说:"可以。"我就大致看了一下。过了些天,我们聊天时再次提到这封信,我就从头到尾把主要内容复述了一遍。她大为惊讶:"你怎么会记忆力这么好?小齐啊,简直有过目不忘的本领!"我一点都不记得了。

其实我也只是选择性记忆。对抽象的东西,方向感很差,超级路痴,还有数字盲,怎么用心记,总是记不住。出门有三个岔口我就会迷路。不是谦虚,是真心从没认为自己记忆力好。

15岁以前的事记得不太多。也有人说能走上写作之路的人都有一个敏感细腻的心，但我对很多时候又是极其钝感的。我的父母亲去世都不曾流过泪，母亲去世时的哭，那还是二妹在边上哭，还有大姨在边上哭她苦命的妹妹，长一声短一声，撕心裂肺，我是被她们带哭的。

因我母亲是跨地区跨县城的远嫁，娘家人都隔得远，大姨晕车厉害，身体不好，直到我母亲去世，大姨才第一次来我家。不知道她内心可曾遗憾过，曾经没有克服困难来看看自己远嫁的老实苦命的妹妹。

我是对痛苦不幸钝感到极致的人，这无形中也有好处。对于别人看来是苦难，跨不过去的坎，而对于我来说完全是麻木，好像那与我的生命个体是无关的事。

多年后到现在，我成为一名专职写作者，我依然有很多纠结矛盾的地方。有时候很想安心地成为一名写作者，不直播、不搞视频、不搞社群等，但是残酷的社会环境下，那我就无法拥有收入来支撑。你想埋头写得好了，就有出路，其实比我们写得好的大有人在。即便你很优秀，社会上同样很优秀的人，也是大把大把的。这是内卷的本质。

只能把文艺行为和商业思维相互结合，赚钱养活梦想，如同我的书名《左手月亮，右手六便士：以自己喜欢的方式过一生》。希望在不远的未来，我能靠书籍的版税收入就能足够养活自己。每天只需要安静读书写作就好，那会是我无上的荣光，也是最最美好的梦想。

# 她先天残疾，出身农村，在网络创业第 3 年时就实现年入百万

她先天残疾，出身农村，在网络创业第 3 年时就实现年入百万。这是一个极为神奇的故事，正如我曾说过的那句话：传奇不在天边，传奇就在身边。

了解安然老师的成长故事，你会觉得电影都不敢这样拍。真是艺术来源于生活，但有时还真没有现实生活更精彩。

她身高一米四，脊椎天生弯曲，身体畸形。自小，她就是在别人的嘲笑打击中度过的，没有玩伴，没有同龄人的围绕，在孤独中度过童年和少年时光。

她曾说，梦想是当老师。同学们都笑话她："你人还没讲台高，还想当老师？"有的男孩放学拦住她，嘲笑说："你怎么长成这个样子，你就是个侏儒……"

当村里面的人议论纷纷，对她指手画脚的时候，有的村民也会提议："养这样的孩子，还不如扔掉省心……"

但安然的奶奶为她种下了爱和相信的种子。每次有人用异样的眼神看她时，奶奶就会对她说："孩子，你一定是佛祖派来人间的，不用在乎别人怎么看你，好好学习，你会成为很厉害的人……"每次安然都含着泪水，使劲点点头。

小时候，安然在外面一个人玩时，只要看到妈妈的身影，她赶紧往回跑，因为她妈妈会骂她。她妈妈总是说："生这样的怪物女儿丢人。"如果不是奶奶的护爱，她妈妈是很想把她扔掉的。

安然上大学时，可羡慕别人谈恋爱了。看别人都是成双成对的，自己却形单影只，但她也知道自己的实际情况。

她的同学也有给她介绍过对象，别人一见，没说几句话，就会说："我有事要先走了。"

她也有注册过一些相亲网站，都是类似结果。她已经做好了独身一生的准备。

在她不再抱有什么希望，开始安心读书，周末兼职做家教时，有一天在外面发传单遇见一个男子，就是现在的老公。当时他是在校外开培训机构的，安然是研二学生。男孩对她照顾有加，第二天，就为她搞了一个办公室带课。这个男人从认识安然的那天起，就把她当作未来一生要照顾陪伴的人了。

她的同学们反过来又来羡慕安然了。有的同学男朋友都换几个了，有的还是单身，说安然一次性就到了顶配，就是奔着结婚了，而且是这么帅的人，还是创业小老板，还对安然这么好。

安然准备结婚时，她20岁的弟弟因交通事故身亡，全家陷入了巨大的悲痛之中。安然又和老公商量，他们婚后住到安然的娘家。

他们那边重男轻女的氛围很是严重。其实，她老公是独生子，我们很佩服她老公和她父母的大格局，包容，支持儿子的一切想法和决定。

安然父母开过公交车，后来也做煤炭生意。她老公觉得碎末浪费太可惜，想用这些来做蜂窝煤卖，打算做活动先送后卖。传单都已经发出去了，村庄的人来领时，安然母亲却把别人拦在外面，说这可不送，只能花钱买。搞得安然老公很是无奈，觉得自己处处为他们考虑，却得不到一点肯定。

因安然老公的一些生意销售理念和安然父母不同，有过一些小小的争执。每次安然都是站在她父母那一边。那时，他们夫妻也陷入过对峙、茫然。

直到后来安然自学心理学之后,才慢慢体会到她老公的不易,看见他的诸多付出。

在他们还在谈恋爱时,安然母亲让她去找现在的老公借钱。当时,她的老公还是一个住在地下室的小青年。听到安然的请求后,刷了10张信用卡,凑了三万给安然家换了一辆新公交车。

安然回忆起老公一路走来对她的支持,她提出不在娘家住了,和老公到城里住,避免年龄代沟、思维习惯造成的不愉快。

我们一群人现场听着安然老师的故事,总觉得真实的电影都不敢这样拍,不知道是小说照进了现实,还是现实写进了小说?

安然后来也一直在学习心理学、能量学,她现在所做的心理学能量极强,让很多小伙伴通过副业变现了。在安然的强大能量加持下,很多人因此改变了命运,他们都称安然老师为自己的贵人。

能把网络副业做好的人也是不简单的,考验的是人的共情力、转化力、内容力、营销力等,最终销售的是个人能量。

安然老师在网络做副业的第三年就实现年入百万,她是如何做到的?

安然老师在月薪5000元的情况下,用两个月的工资去报名线上课学习。她每参加一个社群,都是10倍赚回学费。这勇气和魄力也不是每个人都具备的。

她是带着ROI思维去使用自己的每一分钱,实现自我增值,不断破圈,敢想敢做,还能现学现卖,还卖得极好。

本身,安然老师就是10年教育工作者,又是二级心理咨询师。她学过线上各类知识,如文案、朋友圈成交、营销系统等,她把这些知识点融合在一起,形成自己独有的安然教育体系,帮很多人收入增长了10倍到40倍。

她懂心理学,能量强,口头表达能力也非常好,还擅于提供情绪价值，同理心极强。其实很多时候，线上教育卖的就是自身释放的能量和未来预期。

上个月，有个浙江客户，也是一名在校老师，她一次性全款付给安然老师15万元，要跟着安然老师学习。这也是安然老师的人格魅力，毕竟哪个人的钱也不是大风刮来的。金钱也是价值和能量的交换。

安然老师在网络上做副业才三年，就实现了年入百万。她办的线下课，有很多人特意坐飞机飞到山东，只是为了能亲眼见到安然老师。

她说未来会考虑成立安然教育基金会，帮助失学儿童重返校园，会走遍七大洲，在世界各地演讲，像尼克胡哲一样，让更多人重新站起来，点燃更多的梦想。

安然老师总是强调人要心存感恩，感恩的人容易遇到贵人。贵人不仅带来机会，还带来更重要的资源，带来了新的视野。

她是这么说的，也是这么做的。与她相处，如沐春风，温暖热情，她对人还非常舍得，真正践行有舍才有得的理念。

她说，持续地给予别人价值，持续地付出，自然获得好人缘，自然获得粉丝，获得贵人，获得机会。从营销角度说，利他是顶级的销售战略。

当她的同行也就是大多数老师在原地踏步的时候，安然老师这么多年一直在不断地学习，不断地精进。她把这些新知识融入课堂之中，她就能给学生更多的启发，也成了更特别的老师。她让很多厌学少年重返校园，不少后来读到了名校博士。

安然老师说，别让你未来的生活对不起你曾经承受过的苦难！要用爱赋能，用生命能量驱动生命能量！影响更多人向上向善，实现个人价值放大100倍。

我非常相信安然老师能实现在全球大学演讲的那一天，无数听众会被她的精彩演讲所震撼，很多人会借着她的光走出人生的至暗时刻，找到自己的使命，进而活得热烈绽放。

（ps：安然老师并没有很好的先天资质，读书时课代表帮她讲数学题，说了三次，她仍然听得一头雾水，还是解答不来题目。那课代表无奈地摇头说："你好像少了一根筋。"安然老师无数次因学习不好而无法接受，她认为身体的残疾是先天的，是无力改变的，但上学成绩不好，是自己的原因。她奋力参加两次高考才勉强上了大学，但安然老师可能是属于开窍晚的人，后来考研是一次性通过。2012年，以第一名的成绩考上当地重点中学编制老师。人生有梦不觉晚，上天会厚待有强大韧劲的人。）

Living like this.

# Only relative, no absolute

### 01

The village in the city, as the name suggests, is both urban and rural, is an awkward existence. For city managers, they can't wait to quickly flatten it and replace it with a unified high-rise building, so that the city appearance and political achievements will appear better. But for us migrant workers, we want more villages in the city because there are cheaper houses to rent.

I lived in the village for seven years. In 2008 and 2009, I was in a village in the city near Liming Industrial Zone in Lucheng District, Wenzhou. We sold breakfast under the 1 row of mobile iron houses. At that time, the monthly rent of the house I lived in was 250 yuan.

In 2007, I worked in a women's clothing factory near the university town in Chashan District, Wenzhou. Every weekend there is a day off, I will take a bus back to the store in the village in the city to improve the food. The 1 Hubei elder sister in our group always said enviously that I have green vegetables to eat at home on weekends and the shop is still open at home.

The wife of our team leader is specially responsible for sleeve-up, which is the highest-paid process. Everyone secretly envies her because her monthly salary is as high as 3000 or 4000 yuan. In 2007, my highest salary was more than 2000 yuan, usually around 1,45 yuan, which was much better than my previous treatment of foreign trade clothing in Fujian. I had a single break every week, and my evening work ended at 10: 30.

The Wenzhou clothing factory where I work produces brand clothing. The clothes are sold in specialty stores at home and abroad. The process requirements are particularly high, and the work pressure is also great. A little carelessness may require rework.

Why can eat vegetables will let a person envy? Because the bell of the women's clothing factory 1 rang every day, we rushed to the canteen, like 1 people who had just been released from hunger. Only in this way can we get better dishes in the canteen. Fresh vegetables are very limited, and there are no people who come late.

There are 1 buckets of soup in the cafeteria, which are finely crushed eggs and tomatoes, sometimes seaweed. We often have to scramble for slightly larger eggs and tomatoes. There are often eight or nine people around the iron barrel where the soup is placed, just to catch slightly larger tomatoes and eggs.

The cost of food in the factory is 150 yuan per month, which is deducted from the salary. The boss wanted to make a profit from the meal, so the food was very rudimentary. The so-called two meat 1 vegetarian 1 soup, two one-inch-long small fish is even a meat dish; Two 3 small peppers dipped in a little egg foam are even scrambled eggs with chili. Green vegetables are usually eaten only by those who come early. The so-called soup is the kind of clear soup I described earlier.

Some people may ask, why don't you go to a restaurant? Because it takes a lot of walking to eat out, it takes time, and the food outside is more expensive. 150 yuan a month is enough to eat in the canteen. If you eat outside, this money is far from enough.

We also live under this blue sky, in this vast land, we are born as human beings, but our lives are different. Everyone's life is like a thick book.

Some of my readers and literary friends, who have lived in cities for generations, may find it incredible to see these experiences I wrote about, but this is indeed what happened.

I was also shocked and heartbroken when I read Ding Yan's "Factory Girls" series. Many of the books describe the life of the post-95s. They work in underground breweries and mold factories. Their hands are broken for many years and they have to put band-aids on them every day. There are also underground black factories, where workers will be physically injured after working for half a year, and then a new group of workers will be replaced. There are injection molding factory workers broken toe accident...

I am a post-80s generation and may still understand such a life. But is there still a factory like this? Are there still so many people in society living like this?

In 2008 and 2009, I lived in the village in the city of the industrial zone. My neighbor was a woman from Henan. She was the same age as me. She was very beautiful, with a melon-faced face and white and red skin. Every morning, I have to get up and do things before dawn, and I always envy those friends who are still sleeping. My cousin has holidays and a decent job. She doesn't go to work until 9 o'clock in the morning.

However, the life I hate is the envy of others. My neighbor always envies me. She has two sons, one is 3 years old, the other is over 1 years old, and there is another in her belly. Her husband works as a porter at Wenzhou Station, earning 1300 yuan a month and especially loving playing cards. She has little spare money and sometimes has to pick up garbage bottles to sell.

She often goes to the supermarket in the evening to buy discounted tomatoes and other processed dishes. Some of her fellow villagers envy her because she has a good relationship with us and often gets free rolls and steamed buns. Our family also sells fresh milk. If there is any left, it will be sold and given to her family.

In retrospect, even in factories and urban villages, everyone's life was different. What you are accustomed to may be envied by others.

Every time I think of the village in the city where I lived in Wenzhou, I think of the beautiful neighbor, the housing building, and the large rows of iron houses 1 shops. Later, the industrial area was to be demolished and we moved away. She may have returned home to have a third child. At that time, a Wenzhou native wanted to adopt her third child, but she did not agree.

At that time, communication was underdeveloped, and the neighbor and I did not leave any contact information, so we disappeared in our respective lives.

Life is long, passing in a hurry.

## 02

We have a post-60s teacher in Hefei, who has also published books. She used to work in a well-known state-owned enterprise in Hefei, and also served as a teacher in an undergraduate college.

After reading my work "On the Road to Dreams, Let the Soul Shines", Teacher S sent me a long message on WeChat: "Fan Qi, after reading your book, I can't be calm for a long time. You and the characters in your book have shown me a whole new world. I can't imagine you are much younger than me, but have so many difficult experiences. You guys are so tough, like little grass under a boulder. If it were someone else, it might have been crushed and sunk into the quagmire, making it difficult to get up again. I am deeply moved by you and admire you very much..."

In the process of chatting with her, I learned that she settled in Hefei after she came to the provincial capital to go to school at the age of 18. Her family has been teachers for four generations, and her great-grandfather was a private schoolmaster who enjoyed a high reputation in the local area.

Her husband, a former doctoral supervisor, was received by our country's top leaders in 2019 due to his participation in an important project.

Compared with teacher S, I feel very emotional. I am about 20 years younger than her, but the knowledge and starting point of her family's four or five generations have far exceeded my current achievements. My goal may not be as good as her starting point.

This makes me deeply realize that there is no comparability between people, only relatively speaking, there is no absolute standard.

If it weren't for attending offline meetings in Hefei, not for writing and publishing books, if I were still working in a factory, I might never have met with Teacher S. We are not in the same social circle and have no chance to know each other.

However, after getting acquainted, we gave each other signed books and agreed to meet again in other learning activities. On one occasion, I went to work in a community near her home. Teacher S warmly invited our sisters and other literary friends to have dinner together and had a pleasant gathering.

We are all people who love learning and growth. We often participate in reading clubs, speech contests and other activities, and we will soon become one.

Although she has already achieved financial freedom, she still challenges herself, actively integrates with young people and learns new things.

We are all on our own life track, practicing our own life topics and experiencing our own joys and sorrows.

# A treasure mother with a junior high school education has become a small town slash youth with a monthly income of 13000 +.

My second sister, Qi Mezi, is the most similar person to me in the world. Countless people have said that we can hardly distinguish. She is a junior high school educated mother after 85. She currently lives in a small town on the 18th line. Her monthly income is more than 13000 yuan. She enjoys 5 insurance and one fund. She works from nine to five and takes weekends off. (She is taking a college degree from Shucheng County, Anhui Province)

Second sister only officially entered the third year of the workplace this year. In the past February, her guaranteed salary for her main business was 2200 yuan, her bid commission was 4010 yuan, her sideline editing video income was 4575 yuan, her corporate human resources manager subsidized 900 yuan, plus the fast group group purchase commission and circle of friends distribution commission, etc. Her accumulated monthly income exceeded 13000 yuan, and she was entitled to 5 insurance and one fund. For others, such a monthly income may not be unusual, but for my sister, it is an achievement worth recording.

Recalling the youth of the second sister Qi Meiqi:

When I was a child, people around me said that she was the most neat of the three of our sisters, and she was also the object of praise by relatives. She was sweet and diligent. In contrast, we looked gloomy and had no bright spots. In my young and ignorant years, I was full of disdain and disgust for her. I always felt that she was deliberately beguile and pleasing. And I am the most mischievous one, always love and adults against work.

She always goes all out to play every role, no matter how tired or trivial, she enjoys it and enjoys it. My sister has been a very meticulous person since she was a child. This may be due to nature or her Virgo pursuit of perfection.

When we worked together in a clothing factory in Fujian, the factory leaders often took the clothes made by my second sister and pointed them to the old masters: "Let's take a look. This is the clothes made by the new apprentice. It is so flat and has no thread ends at all..."

There is a small scar on the back of my second sister's hand. She said it was when she was learning to make clothes with me, because I lost my temper and poked the back of her hand with small scissors that cut the thread. I myself have forgotten that in my youth I was so violent and rude to the people closest to me. I don't even remember poking her hand with the little scissors. Maybe she accidentally poked her when she was angry. She didn't withdraw her hand in time and really hurt the back of her hand.

As I grew older, I became more and more peaceful.

Earlier, when we were students, we would work in the village cousin's factory on weekends and holidays, and we would bake beer sets in the team factory next door during the summer vacation. The quality of the beer cover baked by the second sister is always better than that of others. She is also the object of praise by the wife of shop-owner. The things she makes are flat, neat and comfortable to look.

The same 1 pair of white shoes, my second sister wore them for three months, and they still looked white and clean.

Second Sister has worked as a garment factory worker for several years, and has also served as a shopping guide, waiter, and salesperson.

How did she become the 1 slash youth in her middle age and still make more than 10,000 yuan a month in a small town on the 18th line? Although Second Sister started from a low level and did not enter Senior high school school, she insisted on studying while being a precious mother. She takes care of the children, does housework, and at the same time receives photography business, does bidding documents, edits videos, works as a self-media person, etc., with a cumulative monthly income of at least 1 million yuan, which is likely to be more in the future.

As a bystander, but also her sister, looking back on her growth in recent years, I can vividly remember.

1. The first is to soak in the network to learn positive circle

I came into contact with the self-media in 2016 and tried to write from scratch. Later, I signed a contract with Jianshu and Baidu platform, and did community writing. I have become a free worker so far. After writing for more than half a year, I set up some WeChat communities. Second sister is also in several of my groups. Although she takes care of two children by herself and is dizzy every day, she still takes time to look at the developments in the group and read some good articles every day. In addition, seeing my growth all the way, I have virtually seen the opportunities of the Internet and have a little understanding of network operation knowledge.

In those years, the old family's evaluation of her was: "How many families complain about two people with one child, Qi Meiqi has two children alone, and he is so neat and delicate, never complains, and he can read books when he takes time. It's amazing."

2. Their own internal drive

Although her family has never said that her daughter-in-law has been at home for many years and spent money at home, the second sister still has to do something she likes to realize her self-worth and don't want to live a life with her hands up. She also tried to write tens of thousands of words and produced an e-book. She said that without my natural love for words, she thought she preferred photography. So she looked at beautiful pictures every day from various websites to improve her aesthetic feeling. Later, she saved money to buy a camera and taught herself how to make pictures, how to find a suitable shooting angle, etc.

She photographed the child's grandfather, photographed the trees on the mountain, and made all kinds of delicious food by herself. The egg photos she took were published in a photography magazine, and she uploaded the pictures to the visual China website and the map worm website, becoming the contracted author of the two platforms. These are all the small fortunes of her amateur self-study, which also brought her confidence and motivation.

In those years, when she was studying self-media or working on photos, she had to get up immediately 1 the alarm clock rang to pick up her for cooking. The alarm clock rang many times a day, and the children had to take some special classes on weekends, with eight trips a day. She has no regrets and enjoys it. Even in a life of chicken feathers and chaos, the second sister still race against time to learn to explore her love and find more possibilities for her future.

### 3. Constantly explore cognitive boundaries

The year before last, the two children were a little older, and the second sister had more time. She took the second construction examination, took photos, made video clips, made bids, etc. The company that made the tender is in her residential area and is relatively free. The tender is settled according to the commission.

At present, the second sister's monthly income in a small town can also break ten thousand yuan, which is no worse than that of college students. Once upon a time, we all envied the people who went to college and felt that they were unattainable and favored by heaven. At present, there are also many people from key universities who admire us very much and feel that we have strong learning ability, tenacity and energy.

Sure enough, learning ability is more important than academic qualifications, and growth is more important than success. Second sister Qi Meiqi became a middle-aged slash, and she could receive so many jobs at home, which could not be separated from her previous accumulation. Because of the practice of photography, it is relatively convenient to learn editing, and because of these comprehensive abilities, she can get started quickly in network-related work.

She applied for a part-time live broadcast job in the county with several friends, and she was passed smoothly. After work in the afternoon, she rode a battery car to the live broadcast base near the community, part-time live broadcast for two hours, selling home textile products, 30 yuan for one hour plus commission, and earning more than 70 to 100 yuan for two hours.

Later, the boss's family saw that her circle of friends could take photos and edit, so they outsourced several videos of the tremolo account to my second sister to do, shoot and edit, and released 6 videos every day, each with about 10 seconds of tremolo. My second sister spends more than 3 hours a day, and her sideline video clips make a monthly income in 4000 or 5000 yuan. (Since last month was on the edge of the Chinese New Year, there are usually more points)

Second Sister did not have a part-time live broadcast since then. Since shooting and editing videos, the time freedom has been higher. She has also participated in several public welfare photography work in Gesanghua, Hefei, Anhui Province, helping left-behind children and public welfare undertakings, and getting to know some fellow villagers in the photography industry. She is also a member of our local photographic association.

Now, she often takes some still life shots in the county and e-commerce products. The seller delivered the products by express, asked her to shoot and send the original pictures in the past, and then settled the commission. The products were all given away. She also took over the whole business of taking photos and video production in her hometown noodle factory and chicken farm.

When Second Sister first undertook the video production of the chicken farm in her hometown, she never made the video herself. She relied entirely on the steps of the online search process and groped step by step to edit successfully. A person's success or not is closely related to his action and determination.

She also worked as a food blogger. Second Sister can cook Japanese eel rice, abalone braised pork, Thai pineapple rice, pearl meatballs, etc. Chinese and western food all like to study. In fact, she also observed and taught herself on various media platforms. She posted her own delicious food on a kitchen APP, and soon there were tens of thousands of fans and Little Red Riding Book had thousands of fans. Sometimes she can also receive cooperation from some businesses. She has multi-dimensional ability by self-study for several years. Even if she does not rely on a company organization and works freely from home, she can do the work she likes, live a rich and elegant life, and have more imagination space in the future.

From the growth story of my second sister, we can see that even if you are in a remote town, even if you are a person with a very low starting point, even if you have two children in your middle age, as long as you learn to embrace the Internet, have the ability to learn by yourself, and find your inner love, you can also use the leverage of the Internet to spread your life to the fullest.

Their company's bidding documents are based on commission, and their interpersonal relationships are simple. When there is no bidding document, they study self-media and some software. There is no internal friction in the workplace, no complicated interpersonal relationships, just a favorite thing to study, and the ability to have a higher average salary than the local average is already the icing on the cake.

The current self-media is enough to carry any 1 forms of talent. In this era, there is no such thing as talent. Now the network provides countless ways to learn, as long as you are willing, as long as you want to learn. Even if you really don't have any expertise and love, you can learn and share, improve your ability, expand your network, and then make money by receiving orders, or register your own media account, continuously output content, accumulate fan readers and users, form a snowball effect, and create a personal brand. These are all priceless wealth.

Life is not limited, the future is infinite! The world kisses me with pain, but also with songs. Even in the tired and trivial life, some people are still pursuing the dream of heroes! In the final analysis, a person's growth is ultimately to enrich his spiritual world by improving his objective conditions, so that he can have more freedom of life and realize the value of life.

## Rural women learn writing from 0 to more than one book, and enter the of 30000 + growth path every month.

Time flies like an arrow, and the sun and moon are running fast. It has been the 9th year since I started writing from 0 in a twinkling of an eye. I started with 0 fans, 0 praise and 0 attention, and I didn't have any saved manuscripts. At that time, I especially envied those who had saved manuscripts, and felt that it was like a rich "family". I completely rely on temporary "squeeze toothpaste" to write articles, often the public number has no content to send.

It was very difficult for me to write 800 words a week from the beginning, but now I can continue to output 3,000 words a day, which is also very easy. As long as I can write it, I can publish it at any time. Many years ago, I imagined that there would be a shelf with all my books on it in the future. Now, the dream seems to be in sight.

It says that after so many years, time is 1 a high wall. If you cross over difficulties and obstacles, you can defeat many fellow travelers. The literary friends who wrote with me in those days have persisted to the present. And I, the lucky one who stuck to the end and got some dividends.

I am based on 1 kind of spirit of fighting to the end. As long as I can't write to death, I will write to death. No tangle, no internal friction, not afraid of ridicule, not afraid of blow. Others say that I haven't read for several years, don't I know many words? I was silent. At that time, I posted many idioms and uncommon words at the head of my bed every week, reading and reciting them repeatedly every morning and evening. Change another batch in a week, and so on.

I will be an undead Xiaoqiang, the grass under the rock, I believe that heaven will treat me well after all. I used to dream of becoming a free worker, but my fate finally came true. I didn't have to clock in, work or be bound by regional space. I often laugh and say that my daily work is reading, writing, selling and playing with mobile phones.

That's because I continue to write and live in a good age of self-media. After writing for more than a year, I finally signed two platforms. A year and a half later, I was a full-time freelance worker and signed a book contract.

So, my first 1 book, "On the Road to Dreams, Let the Soul Shines" was published, printed, and had the honor to display it at the New Jersey Library in the United States. Later, I registered a cultural media company and operated multiple platforms. The articles were published on People's Daily Online, "Philosophy", "Young Writer", "Writer Wenyuan", "Girlfriend", Learning Power and other magazines, newspapers and online platforms.

I published "A Guide to Writing and Realization that Everyone Can Learn", because this book is all about sharing practical experience, there are a lot of dry goods, and what I write is what I do. I am not an academic, I am a wild road Jianghu author, completely groping all the way to practice growth. This book is at the top of the list of search keywords on various platforms. Readers contact me almost every day because of this book. Seeing that so many people have been inspired by this book and started the road of dreams, I think this is a supreme honor, even beyond money.

There is also a book "only be the only me, not the second who" has also participated in many large-scale offline book fairs in Beijing. The book "Left Hand Moon, Right Hand Sixpence" mainly writes about the living conditions of some digital vagrant in this Internet age. Between the inner roll and lying flat, what kind of 1 life should there be? Much of this book will give us some inspiration and thought.

There is only 1 kind of success in this world, and that is to live your life the way you like. My favorite, of course, is writing. Because of writing, I got rid of the monotonous and boring sewing life in the factory day after day. I also jumped out of the stall owner's life of getting up early and selling breakfast in the village in the city.

Nowadays, you only need to hold your mobile phone and notebook at home, read books, write articles, receive business manuscripts, be a community, etc. every day, and you can achieve a monthly income of 50000 +. Everyone has an ability that is more than 10000 people, digging to find their own advantages. Hobbies and persistence are equal to talent. Useless means great use. The things you love will give you rich rewards one day.

Sit down and polish your writing skills, plus some business thinking to take full advantage of the Internet. The Internet can magnify the ability of an ordinary person by 100 times or 1000 times. For example, I have such a group of 1 people around me. They come from ordinary backgrounds, but they have 1 unwillingness to be mediocre.

Some of them like to chase stars. They stayed in Hengdian for more than a month. Later, they wrote a book and sold more than 300,000 copies 1 it went on the market. They realized the first pot of gold in their lives with this book. There is also the abandonment of enviable work within the system, but through the Internet from the media to achieve annual 500000 +. Some like to collect Thuja, relying on their own in-depth research and study, become experts in the field. Thuja has a 9-digit asset, teaches people to appreciate, sells handmade works, and has also published professional books.

These people, regardless of age, gender, and occupation, rely entirely on their own interest in a certain field, down-to-earth improvement, coupled with a certain degree of business awareness, actively and bravely show themselves on the Internet, build a personal brand, and achieve The rise of individuals has realized a free life with one hand, white moonlight, bread fragrance, and a free life.

The Internet has enabled many ordinary people at the bottom to achieve breakthrough growth, recording more, displaying more, and actively using the power of self-media to build personal brands. Be brave to be yourself and live your life the way you like. You can refer to "Left Hand Moon, Right Hand Sixpence".

# My best friend

My best friend, Yun Er, is thin, fair-skinned, talented, quick-witted, and very honest and enthusiastic about people.

As of this year, it has been 6 years since her death, and her life will always be fixed on her birthday at the age of 36.

## 01

In our beautiful youth, we made clothes in the same workshop. The parking space for making clothes is face to face. We live in the same dormitory, cook together, choose dishes and clean dishes together. It can be said that we are inseparable for 24 hours and have spent happy years together.

In his spare time, Yuner can cut carrots into petals and carve onions into roses. She does things well and fast. The same is to buy a bowl, she will choose very delicate. I have no idea. In my heart, material benefit is the first, but she said that she would feel happy when she was eating every day. The pair of bowls we used to leave the factory did make people feel good.

Yuner can always tidy up as delicately as possible under limited conditions, has his own taste of life, and will enjoy every bit of life. Every time I think that she loves life so much, is enthusiastic and atmospheric, and always puts a happy smile on her face, such a beautiful person is gone so early, and the feeling of heartache lingers in my heart.

I have experienced the premature death of people around me several times in my life. I often feel whether I have some kind of past sin and ominous mysterious force, or 1 other cruel way of God to me? Is there an unfathomable power hidden in the map of fate? I want to ask God why is this? Who can help me to answer?

I still remember one day in July 2018, I received a WeChat from Mr. Yuner, saying that Yuner was hospitalized in Hefei. The doctors estimated that it was not optimistic and the high probability was advanced lung cancer. She also posted a picture of her sleeping in a hospital bed. I suddenly brain 1 meng, heart 1 acid, suffering from advanced lung cancer? Didn't we meet not long ago and have a party? What's with cancer? I feel incredible, tears can not help but flow down.

Isn't it possible for an old man who loves to smoke? Is there a mistake? Yuner is still so young, never smokes, and has no bad habits. Is fate joking? There must be some mistake?

The next day, I went to Hefei Cancer Hospital from my hometown to see my best friend Yuner. She was scrawny and sallow, really skin and bone. She saw me say hello and motioned for me to sit down. After a few words, she 1 to the bed and immediately fell asleep. She seemed very tired and had no energy. I haven't seen you for only two months. How did this suddenly happen? Waiting for the final results of the puncture examination that day.

## 02

Yuner, and I are not from the same village. Her family is a production team across the river from my rice field. She is a little older than me, one year older, but I have known since I was a child that there is such a person in the village below, and sometimes I often see her on my way to and from school. Everyone knows that she studies very well and is very smart. The school principal and teachers like her very much. Every time others are still immersed in exams, she can always be the first to finish the paper. She and her teachers were playing badminton on the playground, and the test papers were full marks.

Since I worked as a temporary worker in my cousin's factory next door, I have had more contact with Yuner. She also came to work in our village after taking the exam that year. I still remember that she received the Senior high school admission notice, but her family had no money for her to study, so she put the notice in the water and floated away.

She is the 5 sister in her family, she is the youngest one, and her elder sister's son (Yuner's nephew) is older than her. Her second sister recruited relatives at home and had two children, both honest farmers, and living conditions were relatively difficult at that time. She has a third sister who went to a nunnery with two other girls in our village when she was a little girl. It is said that their idea is that there is no good life in this life, in order to practice the afterlife well.

When I was in primary school, I heard the news about this village. Three girls met together to go to a nunnery. One is the daughter of a firecracker processing factory near our primary school, and she is also a very beautiful beauty. I have seen her before. One of the remaining two is Yuner's third sister. It seems that the last time Yuner talked to me about her third sister, her third sister was in Wutai Mountain and told me her third sister's legal number. Now I can't remember it clearly.

Although my best friend Yuner is the youngest in the family, she cannot enjoy any better care because her parents are old and frail, and her sisters are busy with their own lives and have no time to take care of her. The family does not have any resources and means of production to benefit her young and old. When she was in junior high school, she knew that her family had no money to study. Every time she asked for pocket money and tuition fees, she was very painful, so she didn't care about reading. The main reason was that no one guided and emphasized the importance of reading.

But even if she went to school in such an indifferent state of mind, she also received a Senior high school admission letter. If she was born in a slightly better family, her talent would be a completely different scene. In the junior high school I attended, there were 72 students in the third grade class. Later, it was said that only three students did the best in the exam and entered the general high school. The others either resumed their studies, went to vocational schools, or dropped out of school as early as I did. Come back...

## 03

As a girl, we spent more than two months together in the factory at the gate of our village. During the summer vacation, the factory was full of students of our age. It was a factory that made beer sets. It was closed in the second half of the year, so Yuner went to other places and heard that it was to Guangdong.

In the twelfth month of 2001, Yuner suddenly came to my house and brought fruits and snacks. The sisters ate happily. After seeing me enter the door, she said that she hoped to learn how to make clothes with me, or to learn how to be practical. At that time, I just started to make clothes on my own. It was still the first year. I didn't have the confidence to take her by myself. I also blamed myself for being timid, so I introduced her to my master as an apprentice.

She is very clever and gets up to speed quickly when she is learning to make clothes. After eight months of apprenticeship with her master, she picked up her own clothes and began to do it independently. We cook together, occasionally take a break from our busy schedule, and go to the seaside together. Colleagues like to gossip about some things. We are both people who don't like to mix in. We are more independent.

She also loves reading and writing. In fact, she has a good foundation in all aspects, but she lacks a good soil environment. I remember she once said a word when chatting with me. When she was a child, her father gave her a life. The fortune teller said that Yuner "was originally a young lady, but unfortunately she gave birth to a maid's life".

She has such a good talent for reading, but she did not take the road of reading. This is the first time that fate has played a trick on her. She was so young that she died of a terrible and serious illness, which was the extreme ruthlessness of fate.

She is kind and generous to others. She would rather suffer losses than others. She once joked with me that I would rather be carried down by the world than by anyone. She really did this. She had to be generous and enthusiastic about people when she was frugal.

If there is God, why is God so blind and why should he treat her like this?

## 04

In 2018, when Yuner was examined in Hefei, all the expenses were collected on a temporary basis. At that time, her business has been losing money, there is no extra funds, even the registration fee is borrowed. When she first entered Hefei Cancer Hospital, she could only live in the corridor. Because the hospital is overcrowded, if you want to live in a regular ward, you have to find someone to spend money.

After she fell into a coma, her family launched a drip to raise donations. I and a few of my colleagues and friends donated a lot. Colleagues generously donated 400 yuan, 600 yuan and 800 yuan. We also forwarded them to many acquaintances and friends. I remember raising more than 80000 yuan in more than a day.

Another colleague told me that if Yuner was awake, she would never let us do it. Indeed, her character is certainly not willing. No matter how hard it is, she will not ask for help. She regards dignity and face as more important than life.

After seeing her on the first day of my visit to Hefei Cancer Hospital, on the third day, another colleague went to see Yuner. 1 colleague sent me a message telling me that Yuner was not in good condition. She began to call my name and then asked me who I was. My memory declined badly.

The day after the colleague saw it, Yuner had a head hemorrhage and was transferred to the intensive care unit. We went to the hospital again that day and several good friends were there as well as her sister and family. The third day of entering the intensive care unit happened to be Yuner's 36th birthday. Her life was fixed on this day, and she was separated from us forever.

From the Hefei Cancer Hospital to her death, only a week's time. One week time! How cruel is fate!

I often wonder why human life is so fragile. A big living person says no, it's gone. Not long ago, we were still discussing what to do and live together in the future. Death is closing in on her mercilessly, but we have no idea that life is so impermanent.

Two months before she came to Hefei Hospital, we had a brief meeting together. At that time, she said that she had a bad waist and thought it was a gynecological problem. Later, she said it was sciatic nerve. She was looking for a folk prescription and had been drinking traditional Chinese medicine at home. No one thought it had anything to do with cancer.

Maybe she has a strong personality, maybe she shields herself, doesn't think too bad, and doesn't go to the provincial hospital for a good examination. It was not until one day that she got up in the morning and found a big pimple on her neck that she went to our Tongcheng Hospital for examination and checked the blood sample and electrocardiogram. After the results came out, the doctor said that the situation was very bad, not sure whether it was tuberculosis or lung cancer, and asked her to go to Hefei Hospital for examination as soon as possible.

She was in the intensive care unit for the next few days, making an appointment to apply for a doctor to wear protective clothing to line up to see. I stood in front of her and talked to her. I saw her tears flowing with a little bloodshot in her tears, but she couldn't move or speak. She was much thinner than when I came to see her on the first day, and her lips didn't have a trace of blood...

After several old colleagues and I took turns to see it, we began to cry in the corridor. Before we could say a few words, everyone continued to cry. Everyone said that Yuner was no longer like a human being. It was only a few days ago.

Two of their colleagues had just had a party with Yuner not long ago and were having dinner and taking photos together. Fenger said that at that time, 3 of them were eating together alone. Everyone was talking and laughing. When Yuner laughed, he instinctively put his hand on his waist and said that his waist was a little painful. (The morning before I went to Hefei Cancer Hospital, I suddenly had a big pimple on my neck, which was already cancer cell metastasis)

Later that day, when I was watching Yuner in the hospital, I met several of her sisters. Her little sister said Yuner was reluctant to give up money, so she didn't go to the examination earlier. Why didn't she tell me and some friends? I will try my best to gather together the major events of checking and seeing a doctor! We have always had WeChat and QQ, but she never said anything.

Her sister also said something about Yuner's husband in those few months, which may have contributed to one of the main causes of the illness. Emotions are really important. Economic pressure, emotional discomfort, and her heart has been so strong, maybe she is really too tired and tired.

Yuner has a sister who said that women are afraid of birthdays when they are sick. Birthdays are a big node and a snag. Unexpectedly, it happened to be Yuner's 36th birthday and completely stopped breathing. Is this the established destiny?

05

In the second half of 2015, I went to Shanghai Xiaomei, a large Internet company. I live in Dongfang Road, Pudong New Area. It is a house shared by my sister. The outside environment of the community is very good, but the inside is simple, but it is very spacious, more than 110 square meters, and the price is 1 half cheaper than the market price. Colleagues are envious because we are very close to the company.

Every time the landlord elder sister comes, she brings us something to eat instead. She also gave me a Bible before I left Shanghai. I remember when I first wrote, I also wrote the landlord elder sister in the article.

My little sister once complained that everything was ready wherever the elder sister went. She said that she relied on herself to toss every place she went to for so many years. She also said that there was 3 one of our sisters. If she were the boss, she might have changed her fate long ago.

All right! Everyone's personality has his inherent limitations.

In 2015, I didn't expect Yuner to also go to Shanghai. More coincidentally, she lived only a few stops away from my bus stop. She arrived in Shanghai a few months before me.

The place where she lives can only have a narrow bed, and the table is next to the bed. It is the kind of partition made by the second-hand landlord.

It is difficult for people to stand and turn around, and the rent is more than 1500 yuan.

Yuner started out with a courier company, which cost more than 4000 yuan a month. Her husband sent express delivery, and later she went to work in a supermarket chain. The supermarket also bought her 5 insurance and one gold, which was actually quite good.

I will go to her side at the weekend. She, like me, is very good at taking care of people and doing food and housework.

I have persuaded her to go to our company to do sales! If the performance is good, the salary is still quite high. Your salary in the supermarket is too rigid.

Our company contacts are all college students, contact with network knowledge, can also exercise us, and can do easier work when we go home. If an acquaintance introduces you internally, you can definitely apply directly.

In mid -2016, I was already writing on the Internet, and I also advised her. I said that you were a student bully and had good literary talent. You should also write! Unfortunately, no matter what kind of advice, she will not do. I don't know whether she feels inferior, worries about not doing well, or is afraid of bothering me.

In the summer vacation of 2016, our two families also brought our children together to play in many places in Shanghai. Before leaving in the morning, she marinated chicken feet, eggs and dried bean curd, and made a lot of food to take with her own hands, which was like a family picnic, while I only took the 1 I bought in the supermarket. Everyone had a great time that day.

She returned home one step ahead of me. Their idea at that time was to go home and open a processing factory by themselves, but the reality was very cruel, everything was not as good as imagined, and it was even better to work for others simply and happily. This was also one of the reasons for her subsequent illness.

I often think of her for some time. If she leaves Shanghai later, it may be better. If they did not go back to the processing factory to start a business and simply went to work, they might be better off. If she had separated her family earlier, it might have been better, even if she got sick more than 10 years later.

How does God's invisible hand control everything in the world?

After Yuner died, I looked through her circle of friends for a long time. It turned out that she had also written in simple books, but she never told me which account was her.

# Li Juan's "My Altay" once again ignited my enthusiasm for writing

Writing is an extremely brain-consuming work, which consumes a large number of brain cells invisibly. Although it does not seem tiring on the surface, in fact, it hurts like a soft knife, especially for people who write for a long time, it is particularly important to exercise every day.

Writing tests not only brain power, but also physical strength. There is no 1 thing in the world that is easy. It is not physical hardship, but energy and mental effort, and the latter is often more hurtful. Sometimes, I really want to just read a book every day, a daze is enough. Who doesn't want to be able to retire and enjoy a quiet life?

But most of us are in an awkward state where we can neither fully engage in competition nor lie flat. I had promised the editor to hand in a few articles, but unfortunately I was at an impasse and time passed by inadvertently. I really don't like propositional compositions. I prefer to write whatever I want and write whatever I think.

On the way to writing, I always insist on writing freely and not rigidly adhere to skills. Although I understand some writing methods and frameworks, I still write willfully.

Recalling that I started writing from scratch, it took me just over a year to achieve a 5-digit monthly income. Thanks to the advent of the media age. I registered my own account, published and operated it myself, and I felt 1 "I am in charge of my territory. If in the era of paper media, like me, willfully only according to their own mind to write, I am afraid it will be difficult to stand out.

At the moment, I wear anti-noise headphones, in the study on the balcony tapping the text. The earphone played Li Yijun's "Promise" in a loop, which reminded me that when I first listened to this song, I was working as a salesperson in a store. At that time, my salary was only 300 yuan a month. It was 2004. After a few months of recuperation from a clothing factory in Fujian, I worked as a salesperson on the streets of Tongcheng for several months.

The two colleagues in the store are very good at singing, which makes me envious of this tone-deaf person. One of them likes to sing Li Yijun's "Promise", while the other prefers Zhang Huimei's "So you don't want anything". It is because of them that I am familiar with these two songs and can even recite them backwards.

The original version of "Promise" was released as early as 1995 and became very popular that year. The theme song "Rain Butterfly" of "Huanzhu Gege" and "Pingju", which was popular in the early years, are all works of Li Yijun. I only learned about the song "Promise" in 2004. Today, many years later, because 1 singer born in 1999 sang a cover on Douyin, the song exploded again, and its fans increased by more than 1000 million in a week.

Such is the power of the art of music, coupled with the astonishing speed of web traffic. In the vast Internet world, there will always be people selected by the platform and traffic, they seem to be the son of heaven.

Think about me and the countless writers around me, who have been writing for seven or eight years or more, with only a few hundred thousand fans on the whole network, which is already a good result in the writing world. However, it is still slightly inferior compared to the video, live broadcast and tremolo algorithms.

In recent years, the rise of online digital media, especially the turbulent traffic of Douyin and the huge influence of Internet celebrities, has made many outstanding works popular again. For example, Chi Zijian's "The Right Bank of the Erguna River" quickly sold 1 millions or 2 millions copies due to Dong Yuhui's recommend. In the past ten years, the sales volume was only 50000 copies.

In fact, this is a novel written by Chi Zijian as early as 2005. It was first published in the 6th issue of Harvest magazine in 2005 and published in December 2005.

Recently, CCTV launched "my Altay" is a small number of prose adapted from the TV series. The brand influence of the CCTV platform, coupled with the reports and reposts of the major self-media, has once again set off an upsurge of 1 shares pursuing Li Juan's works. Now, whether it is a circle of friends, public numbers or major video platforms, the introduction and recommend of Li Juan and his works can be seen everywhere.

My Altay is a collection of essays first published by writer Li Juan in July 2010, which mainly depicts her rural life in Altay. This collection of prose successfully reproduces the local conditions and customs of northern Xinjiang, full of fresh breath, and is one of Li Juan's famous and representative works.

Li Juan, born in 1979, has been writing since 1999. In January 2003, she published her first work, "Nine Snow". In 2004, Li Juan was admitted into the system by virtue of her excellent writing ability. Today, she has once again become the focus of the country, which is undoubtedly the crystallization of right time, right place, with right people. Opportunities are always reserved for those who are prepared.

Her works have obvious non fiction, regional and daily characteristics, to eat the regional dividend. Her writing is very healing and durable, and it also satisfies people's curiosity about this mysterious land of Xinjiang.

When "My Altay" was published in 2010, Li Juan had already gained a certain popularity in Xinjiang and even the whole country. Today, some students in our group talked about that when Li Juan first started writing, some people laughed at her for not even finishing high school and wanted to be a writer. Some people even read her words in public to laugh at her. This is very similar to my original writing experience.

When we write, we become what we like. Although I can't compare with Li Juan, I saw in her the infinite possibilities of continuing to write, and once again inspired my enthusiasm for writing.

In those days, many people said to me, "do you not know many words? How dare you have such a big dream? You're so naive, you want to be a writer? Do you know how many people graduate from the Chinese Department of our school in a year? "Even a former colleague from a garment factory said to me," You don't go to bed early after work and still read books? Reading cannot be used as food or food. A few years later, everyone is still a village woman?"

I silently thought, even if it is a village woman, I also want to be a thoughtful village woman. (They also said this out of kindness)

No matter when, men and women, old and young, as long as they have leisure time, they should read more books. Books can nourish your soul, enrich your spirit, and benefit you for life.

(PS: In the winter of 2004, I still chose to make clothes in a store and customize down jackets for customers. After all, technical work is better paid than being a salesperson. Wife of shop-owner is responsible for cutting, I am responsible for making, others are responsible for weighing velvet, loading velvet, I then set the lining, collar and other processes.)

# The past is like smoke, the past of selling vegetables

I remember that the famous writer Tie Ning once said that she likes to visit the vegetable market the most. There is a strong atmosphere of fireworks here. It is the real smell of fireworks and the most grounded place. You can see all kinds of things in the world.

When I was very young, the vegetable market was an unfamiliar concept to me. My family only ate vegetables or pickles grown in the vegetable garden, and never bought outside vegetables. After growing up, I learned that the vegetable market is a place to make money.

When I can ride a bicycle, I often go to Tongcheng Street with my mother to sell vegetables. I tied a vegetable basket to the back of the car. My mother followed me because she couldn't ride a bicycle. I tried to let my mother sit in the back seat of the car with a basket, but she was always worried that I would be exhausted and refused to sit again.

What impressed me most was that after a rain, the cowpeas in the field at home grew a lot. My mother said proudly that cowpeas in the field are like dried noodles. We will go to the street to sell them early tomorrow morning. I heard that they can sell for 1 yuan recently. At three o'clock that morning, my mother called me up. We pushed the cart into the street in the dark. It was just dawn. But 1 to the market, I heard that the price of cowpea fell to thirty cents. It turned out that after a rain, the vegetables of the vegetable farmers grew out, and the price of the vegetables soon fell. I saw the disappointment in my mother's eyes.

As soon as we set up the vegetable basket, the market manager came to collect the fee and paid a booth fee of 30 cents. Since we only brought a few old food bags and no new food bags, I went to the side and bought some more, which cost 5 cents. After waiting for half a day, no one bought it. My mother and I had to push carts along the street. The basket of cowpeas ended up being sold to a restaurant for 5 cents a catty. I also clamored for hunger and spent one yuan to buy four steamed buns. My mother could not bear to eat any of them. When I got home that day, I only made four or five dollars.

My mother can't read. She likes to take me with her and rely on me for many things, such as selling vegetables, paying public food, and keeping accounts. She seems to feel insecure. As for me, I often talk back in front of my mother, even being unreasonable. I don't listen to her at all. I always feel that I have such a useless mother and feel inferior and sulking.

Before, when my mother was selling vegetables alone, several people easily fainted when they asked questions. They were also cheated by others and were busy 1. Every catty of food costs a lot of energy and effort, so grandma persuaded her mother not to sell things alone.

My mother was a little slurred when she spoke. I especially didn't want her to go to school when I was studying, and I didn't want any classmates to know about her. Other children are bullied and always like to go home and talk to their mother, but I never talk about it, because even if it is useless, my mother will only persuade me to let them, and those older children are not afraid of my mother.

In the 1998 financial crisis, all crops were worthless. The prices of eggs, soybeans, and vegetables all fell sharply. 100 catties of rice could only be sold in 35 yuan, and half of the public grain had to be handed over. That year was really difficult. The day before New Year's Eve, my mother and I were selling rice and vegetables in the street. The cold wind made people shiver, but the family was waiting for the money for the New Year. There was also a flood that year, and many places were affected by disasters. The village sent relief clothes to my house. Our sisters were very happy to try them on, but my mother asked us to keep them for school or relatives.

When I went to school in the third year of junior high school, it was popular to go south to work. It was said that working in the south could make a lot of money. But there were very few ways to go out at that time, far less developed than the current network, and there were many opportunities to choose from, and we had to ask for help everywhere at that time. My child and I went out to work in the same year. Her father found a good candidate in the twelfth month and asked them to take her to work. For this reason, her parents helped others do a lot of farm work that year and treated the family like a benefactor, just thinking that their daughter would be better outside. That's what happened in those years.

When I was young enough to confirm the date of going out, I was still at home and didn't know who to go out with. I was very anxious. Until I went to my relatives' house to pay New Year's greetings in the first month, my relatives introduced me to 1 teachers. It was 1 woman who was 12 years older than me. She seemed very satisfied when she saw me. In those years, many people in coastal factories specialized in taking apprentices. They earned a 1 income from their own work, and then took a few apprentices to do chores. They could earn 20 thousands or 30 thousands a year (1999-2000), some more. There is a fellow-townsman couple with 12 apprentices, which is equivalent to 12 apprentices helping them make money.

When the master naturally likes the apprentice to endure hardship, the more honest he looks and the poorer he comes from, the more the master likes it. Because you want to make money, you won't stand the pain, you won't give up halfway, you won't run home. I stayed at the master's house one day in advance, because her house was not too far from the railway station, and there was another female apprentice with me. Early the next morning, my mother suddenly appeared at the door of the master's house. I was very surprised. My mother sent me an ID card. She only received the ID card the night before. She had not done it before. Mom said she left home at four o'clock. In this way, I started my career as a female worker in a clothing factory in my life. The traveling expenses were paid by my master. I have in my pocket the money of 20 yuan that my mother sold her hair a few days ago. My mother's beloved long hair has been kept for several years. For me, I have no choice but to cut it. My grandmother also gave me five dollars. Grandma's pocket money was given to her by her uncle, who ate commercial grain, because she was a soldier for two years when she was young and later assigned to work in Anqing Chemical Fertilizer Factory. Uncle directly converted the subsidized daily necessities into cash and gave it to grandma. My family was so poor that sometimes they couldn't even get the electricity bill 3 4 yuan a month. Grandma knew that my family was pitifully poor. She used her pocket money and posted most of it to my family. She often didn't buy meat for months. I remember she once nagged that your mother ran to a village and couldn't borrow 5 yuan for electricity. It was chilling to think about it. In the end, grandma found out about this and paid my mother all her pocket money and paid the electricity bill.

When I was a child, my family's electricity bill was the lowest in the village. I used a 20-watt bulb with tungsten wire, which was dim yellow and weak light. In order to save electricity, two rooms with a light bulb, hanging between the two rooms of the door frame.

When I went home in the twelfth month of my first year, my master, who took a small part-time job, gave her 2000 yuan. Her parents were very satisfied and even wanted to return 500 yuan. In fact, we have all learned sewing machines at home, just to find a reliable factory and learn flat cars for a few days. My master gave me 1000 yuan. We are all in Fujian, but we are not in the same town. Their factory makes jackets, and our factory makes beach shorts worn by Africans. The prices are different, the master's income is different, and the working hours are more than 16 or 17 hours a day, and there are more than 16 or 7 hours when the goods are rushed. In the factory where I work, my master is very kind to me. He never talks about me loudly, let alone is as fierce as other masters, or even hit people. I work fast and she is content. The teacher will give me 45 yuan every month, and 1000 yuan's salary will not be paid until the end of the year. 45 yuan is the cost of my monthly breakfast and daily necessities. I often don't eat breakfast, and washing powder is also saved. I saved more than half of 45 yuan's pocket money and sent it home in a letter.

When working in Fujian, there are very few rest days, unless it is the Dragon Boat Festival and Mid-Autumn Festival, or the occasional power outage. It is rare to have a rest day. I will go to the vegetable market with my hometown. There are all kinds of seafood, clothing, snacks, pop songs are sung in the stereo, and the streets are full of wage earners and working girls who speak various dialects, collectively referred to as "migrant workers". Those who worked in Fujian in those years were mainly from Anhui, Jiangxi, Sichuan and Guizhou.

Every time I pass by the vegetable market, I think of my mother. I wonder if she will sell vegetables alone? Will someone cheat her again because she can't read? Or is she going with her sister? Even if I go to the vegetable market now, I don't know why, my mother always appears in my mind.

The world is fickle and fate plays tricks on people. My mother unfortunately left us forever in 2002. That year, my family built a building with three or 3 floors. My little sister was about to graduate from junior high school. The second year I started to make clothes by myself. I could earn more than 6000 yuan a year, and my second sister had already come out to work. Life at home has gradually improved, and there is no need to talk about "people who die and are not poor" as in the past, and there is no need for heavy rain outside and light rain at home. The bright fluorescent lamps were used in the home, and the land became concrete. When killing pigs during the New Year, you can marinate more bacon. You don't have to do the same as in the past: after the 15th of the first month, there is no meat in the home, and all of them are sold for tuition.

These are my mother's wishes. When all of my mother's wishes were almost fulfilled, she suddenly left us forever due to acute meningitis. Fate is really as merciless as it is... In those days, I was in a trance, unable to tell whether it was a dream or a reality. I was so sad and speechless that I didn't cry much. It's just that over the years, 1 I think of my mother, I even burst into tears in the dark.

Mom's short life, is it just to bring our sisters to the world and bring them up? After 2003, our kind of land no longer had to pay public grain, agricultural tax and water charges. Later, when the land was transferred, every family no longer had to work hard to farm. In the past, paying public grain every year was the hardest and number one event in my family. Such a good dividend of the times, the mother did not have time to see.

What's more, we are all grown up and don't need to humbly borrow money everywhere to live. Especially after being a mother, I realize that it is not easy to be a mother. If my mother were still there, I would definitely never talk back to her again, never say why she is not as good as other people's mothers, never learn to speak like her, and laugh at her for not speaking well. However, life has no if.

When we understand this, my mother has left us forever, leaving the world she has not yet understood. The saddest thing in the world is nothing more than this. The child wants to be raised but the relatives do not wait. heartache, heartache, heartache...

I envy those who are in their fifties and sixties, whose parents are still alive, whose children and grandchildren are full, and who are enjoying family happiness.

Every head of white hair is not a gift of fate?

In my life, because I lost my mother who lived a strong life in suffering, even if the future develops well, my happiness will be greatly reduced from the beginning, and my life will never be complete.

Bless the world all mothers, every day can be happy!

Mom, if I can choose the next life, I must be your daughter again and repay the kindness of nurturing that I have not had time to repay in this life.

Mom, if there is an afterlife, I will be a daughter who makes you proud. Mom, can you hear me?

I think of my mother's words every night.
Shining tears Lu Binghua
The stars in the sky don't talk
The doll on the ground wants to mother
The eyes of heaven blink and blink
Mother's Heart, Lu Binghua
The tea garden in my hometown is full of flowers
Mother's heart and liver in the end of the world
I think of my mother's words every night.
Shining tears Lu Binghua
Ah ~ ah ~
I think of my mother's words every night.
Shining tears Lu Binghua

# That year, my family borrowed money to buy sewing machine

Every time I see the sewing machine at home, it reminds me of many past events, like a movie lens, scenes emerge in front of me.

In the 1970 s and 1980 s, sewing machines, watches and bicycles were called the "three big pieces", and owning one of them would feel very honorable and decent. At that time, people took the three major items as the standard when they got married, just as they now had to have a house and a car.

I came into contact with sewing machines when I was 15 years old. Before the third grade pre-election, I dropped out of school and went home to make beer sets in my cousin's factory. At that time, I felt very happy and satisfied that I could earn about 8 yuan a day. However, the good times did not last long. Later, cousin's factory was closed, and the little sisters all went to the street to learn sewing skills.

In those years, little girls learned sewing and hairdressing, boys learned painting and carpenter decorating skills, and old people all said that "craftsmen will never die of hunger in a famine year".

Seeing that all my friends went to learn sewing, everyone talked about how to make money by making clothes outside. After I came back from my cousin's factory, I didn't know what to do, because my family didn't have the money to buy sewing machines, and I had to pay a deposit to find the master.

I heard from my friends that a butterfly sewing machine costs 420 yuan, a pair of big scissors and 22 yuan, a total of nearly 450 yuan, plus a deposit, which is a big expense for my family. Looking at my friends riding bicycles every day, I am very envious. At that time, I didn't know much about it either. I clamored for my mother to buy a sewing machine every day. My mother said there was no money in the family, so I let her borrow it. I said so-

and-so family is very rich, you can borrow it for me. I have been quarrelling and crying all the time. Mom actually doesn't want to go. Who would like to borrow money in a low voice? I really couldn't help it. My mother went out to borrow money that night and looked for the family behind the house. Those who didn't go to school were already working, but they still didn't borrow money. The next night, I changed to another one to borrow money, but I still didn't borrow it... Later, my mother decided to go to my aunt's house by car to borrow money, and the aunt's house was in another county. My little uncle has been working as a teacher in a mountain primary school. In the environment at that time, his income was relatively stable. When my sister-in-law saw that my mother had come all the way to borrow money, she knew that the surrounding area would definitely not be able to borrow it. She gave my mother the 500 yuan she had accumulated for a long time, gave her some small benches, and bought tickets to send my mother on the bus.

My sister-in-law also told my mother not to worry. The money will be paid back after Faner works to earn money. My mother is happy to come back. She keeps nagging that it is better to be her own sister. After running so many times, she can't borrow any money. When she was a child, she didn't have leucorrhea.

I still remember that we went to Tongcheng Street to buy sewing machines that day. We chose a butterfly sewing machine and a pair of Zhang Xiaoquan's No.21 scissors. We made a counter-offer, totaling 420 yuan. That's a big, decent thing for our house. I wipe it carefully every day, like a treasure in my heart, and cover it carefully with a cloth, lest it should be soiled.

I was introduced to a tailor shop in the town to study. On that day, my mother took me to the tailor shop with a sewing machine. The store also sells cloth, bed sheets, curtains, etc. There are already six sisters in the store. The master is about 30 years old and graceful. He is known as one of the four beauties in the town. She is mainly responsible for cutting, receiving customers, making clothes and other chores are done by several senior sisters.

As soon as I arrived at the tailor's shop, I just picked out the rim of my pants, locked the buttonhole, or dismantled them wherever I needed to dismantle them. I had to help take care of the children of the master's family, wash and mop the floor for her family every day. These were all my main jobs at that time. That year, I didn't make any whole clothes, at most I put on a few waistband heads. Later, the master was keen on the curtain business, because he could earn 7000 or 8000 yuan if he took over the curtains of a unit. At that time, we all admired the master. She was not only beautiful, but also very intelligent. She was the first tailor in our town to sell cloth on behalf of others, and the first tailor's shop to start a curtain business.

I clamored to buy a sewing machine, but I didn't feel that I had learned anything. I heard people working in the south say that the factory in the south uses motors, called "flat cars", and I still have to learn after going to the factory. 1 years later, I finally found a master willing to take me out. I agreed at home that she would pay the fare and give me 1000 yuan after working with her for one year, which is equivalent to her bringing me a way out and learning the clothing technology in the motor and factory.

Except for five or six hours of sleep, I work all the time. People are like machines, boring and numb. Another fellow-townsman couple in the factory has 12 apprentices, who can earn them tens of thousands of yuan a year. The masters envy each other whose disciples are quick. Ironically, our sisters who studied sewing machines and went out to learn flat cars spent so much time and cost, but now they are no longer in the business of making clothes. Perhaps they are all afraid of doing it.

If I knew that there were so many changes in my family later, after I left school, I should go directly to work in the town's brush factory or bristle factory instead of wasting more than two years learning the so-called sewing technology. If you calculate it carefully, the salary of working outside is not much higher than that of working in your hometown. Only later, for the sake of poor face, everyone did not want to go back to their hometown to work. It is rumored that how much others have earned outside is, after all, a very small number. I only go home once in the first month until the Chinese New Year. How many family members do I miss and how much pain I can't get back.

How come I don't have my own idea! Always follow the advice of others, how to understand so late!

The butterfly sewing machine at home has been put on hold for many years. Every time I see it, I think of the youth and helplessness of the 15-year-old, and the sewing machine that I dreamed of owning at that time. At that time, naively I thought that owning this sewing machine would become very powerful. I thought that if I went out to work for 3 years, I could build a spacious and magnificent building for my family. This was all my dream in my youth.

Later, these dreams did come true, but it took more than 3 years, and I lost more and more...

# Only learn from others, only compare with yourself

In the world, there are many people who like to care about and compare. They like to stare at the people around them and compare with others. It seems that they can't see the wider sea of stars. Proper comparison is conducive to their own progress, but excessive comparison will only make their physical and mental exhaustion.

There are several business owners in the town. They like to go to the beauty shop, go shopping and go to the gym together. On the surface, it is peaceful, but in fact, it is secretly competing with each other. Behind the scenes, no one agrees with who looks good. They all feel that they have an advantage over each other. Their children are cuter and smarter, and their clothes show their figure more. Everyone even feels younger.

In fact, everyone has an illusion that two people, both 40 years old, always feel that each other is older than themselves when they meet every few years. Just like every parent thinks that their children are the best and cutest, no one will think that their children are worse than other people's children. Even if their children's IQ is not high, they also think that their children's cerebellum is more developed and more promising.

People like to unconsciously magnify the advantages of themselves and the people and things related to themselves, and expand the shortcomings of the other party. This is a human commonality.

Some women like to compare their husbands and children, depending on the income of each other's husbands and whether they love themselves more than their husbands. Once you find that the other party is better than yourself in everything, your heart will be unbalanced and you will begin to complain about life, husband and fate. They never think that there are many things that cannot be compared, and everyone expresses love in different ways. Since two people can walk together, there is always something in common.

Moreover, what others describe is not necessarily how she really feels. Every family has a difficult book to read, life is mixed, such as fish drinking water, cold and warm self-knowledge.

Many sisters-in-law like to compete secretly. You bought silver earrings and I have to buy a silver bracelet. You bought a new coat, I'll buy a new pair of trousers. Some people say that there are only two feelings between women and women, sympathy and jealousy. Of course, this sentence is exaggerated, but also said some phenomena. Mi Yue and Mi Shu in the TV series "legend of miyue" started out as a pair of good sisters. Mi Shu took good care of Mi Yue and dug out their hearts and lungs. However, with Mi Yue's step-by-step popularity, the good sisters finally turned into enemies, which is embarrassing.

Comparison and jealousy, let Mi Shu step by step into the abyss.

Some people who write words also like to compare with others, comparing how many books are published, what newspapers are published in, how many tens of thousands of copies are published than published books, and even more popular than fans. The so-called literati are lighter than others. What's the comparison!

Everyone has different writing styles and different writing motives. Some people are purely writing what I think. The long road of writing is unknown, and no one can see the end. Optimistic and open to write their own works is the right approach. If you don't write something now, you may not be able to do it in the future. Now that it is very popular in the industry and on a certain platform, it may not be able to keep going. Those who are unknown on platform a may flourish on platform B. Writing this road has unlimited imagination space.

It is the absolute principle to compare who is healthier in the end.

"Love comparison, love jealousy" is everywhere in life. It can give people pressure and motivation, but how to grasp that degree needs us to grasp it correctly. Life is too short, less focus on others, more care for their own soul, pay more attention to their own growth, only learn from others, only compare with themselves.

Exercise more, go to bed early and get up early, keep a good attitude, work happily and live happily. This is the most correct attitude towards life.

Wozkisud said: No matter who you are, at least you have three-point ambition. There is nothing to hide. Ambition itself 1 a willingness to pursue a better life. But being too competitive is also 1 kind of sickness. It is to build all happiness on winning or losing. A strong life does not fight for strength, struggle and compromise are the same. Life is like this, half to fight, half to retreat. Which half is missing, it is difficult to be satisfactory.

In life, some people like to evaluate and point fingers at others, like to grasp the shortcomings of others to satisfy their vanity, like to use the comparison heart to cover up the inner emptiness and lack of confidence. But we have to distinguish between comparison and benign competition. Healthy competition to promote development, the starting point is not the same, to meet the needs are not the same.

Healthy competition is the highlight of learning from others with an appreciative attitude and eventually becoming a better self.

All living beings, the vast sea of people, compared to when to go? A little less comparison heart, a little more self-improvement heart. Improve the pattern, broaden your horizons, devote more attention to self-cultivation and concentrate on being yourself.

# The Old Past of Accompanying Mother to Hand in Public Grain

In the past, grain had to be turned over to the state treasury. In feudal society, this was called the imperial grain; after the founding of New China, it was renamed public grain and grain purchase. This is a system in which every farmer hands over to the state for grain reserves in accordance with the required proportion, which has lasted for thousands of years. It was not until 2003 that public grain, grain purchases, agricultural taxes and water charges were officially abolished. Public grain is usually 50kg per mu, which must be free of impurities, dry and full. Half of it is used to offset agricultural taxes and the other half is handed over to the state free of charge.

There are also 1 kinds of grain purchases, which need to be handed in 140 catties per mu, and my family has to hand in a total of more than 600 catties. There is a certain reward for purchasing grain, about 17 yuan for 100 catties. As prices fluctuate, compensation varies, but is usually below the market price, about half the market price.

When the captain notified the public grain to be delivered, every household would use snakeskin bags or sacks to pack the rice that they thought was the best, the fullest and the driest. Each family has more than a dozen to 20 bags, large and small. As soon as the sky is dawn, everyone uses scooters, tricycles or tractors to pull food to the town's grain depot 8 kilometers away from home.

My mother can't pull a scooter, doesn't have any cars at home, and she can't read. Every time she pays public food, she has to say a good word and beg the people in the same village to let us ride there. This is the same as paying tuition. It is a huge challenge for my mother and our whole family. At that time, farmers actively handed in grain and lined up in long lines. Whether the grain can be received depends on the face of the grain station staff. The quality inspector said it was good, but said it was bad. The so-called good, is full grain, good color, sun dry, no other impurities.

When the public grain was delivered, the village teams rushed to the town grain station one after another. After arriving at the grain depot, we need to register the number. When we arrived at the grain depot, the compound was crowded with scooters, tractors and people from various villages. It was the hot summer, and everyone was sweating. I still remember that one of the staff of the grain station was a very fat woman, who was said to weigh more than 200 jin. She was responsible for registration and weighing. Some of the other staff members are responsible for settling accounts, and the abacus is loud. Others are responsible for invoicing and keeping accounts.

The staff are all people who eat commercial food, and individual people seem to be high above, enjoying everyone's tea, water and admiring eyes. The farmers spoke to them carefully, and my mother was even more so.

That year, I was still a primary school student, ignorant and ignorant, followed my mother to the town to pay public food. The sun was hot, we were sweating, and everyone wanted to finish it early and go home. Although the honest mother got up very early and was in front of the queue, she was always cut in by the people coming from behind, but the mother had no choice. People in the same village handed in food one after another and went home with empty bags. Some of them came later than us.

Seeing that there were still so many people in front of us, we waited anxiously until it was getting dark. My mother and I struggled to move the food forward in bags 1 bags, and occasionally some kind-hearted people came up to help us carry 1 bags. We anxiously watched the quality inspector poke the grain bag 1 with 1 hollow iron bars, then listened to him crack skillfully in his mouth, then threw the rest 1 on the rice bed, and said indifferently: "This rice is not good, it will be dried for another day." My mother and I had to move the rice bags aside, sweating profusely. I hated the quality inspector in my heart and prepared to bask in the sun the next day. That night we spent the night in a makeshift hut at the grain depot.

In the evening, several people who had not yet handed over their public grain sighed. They said that many of them were handed over smoothly at one time, which did not necessarily mean that their food was good. Some of them stuffed the inspectors with cigarettes, and some of them would flatter and be flexible. The few of us who failed to hand over the food must be honest people in various villages. The staff always have to do something to show the leaders. So-and-so rice was obviously one day less than ours, and it was all weighed and handed over. Let's just say we can hand it over tomorrow afternoon. On this hot day, there are still so many jobs waiting to be done at home!

My mother also said that she specially chose the best and fullest rice in the family, and it was drier than anyone in Zhuangzi. So what? They have already handed it in, and it is estimated that they will all be home by now. A cigarette? The family has to save a long time to buy 1 bags of salt. Fortunately, the next day was a sunny day, and my mother dragged bags of rice to the yard of the grain depot to spread out for drying. Until more than five o'clock in the afternoon, we took them for inspection. This time, we finally handed them over smoothly. Unfortunately, others stole 1 bags of rice.

On the way home, my mother said, "I brought you here because you can read. What you are looking in all directions must be that when I was holding the rice, the people behind or on the side stole 1 bag, which can weigh more than 70kg and how many bags of salt can I exchange." Then my mother comforted herself again and said, "if you steal it, you will steal it. let's be a broken fortune and avoid disaster! Next time, watch more closely. Fortunately, we were not allowed to stay for another day to bask in the rice. We also brought enough rice. There were many fewer people jumping the queue this afternoon than yesterday..."

Later, when I grew up, I thought to myself countless times, why didn't my grandmother let her mother study among her seven children? And why did you marry your mother so far from Shucheng? If you have uncles and aunts to take care of you in your local town and village, you will always suffer a lot less injustice. Things like being cut in line, stolen rice and bullied are numerous in my memory. Sometimes I hate myself even more for being sensible so late and not strong enough. I only know how to play and be curious. I never stare at my own rice. I hate myself even more for not being a man and not being able to protect my mother.

At that time, the farmers, especially in the central area of Anhui where I was located, harvested early rice and sowed late rice during the "double snatching" season in the countryside every year, which could make people exhausted. They had to obediently hand in public grain and send it to the grain depot in person. It seemed that they had to beg those who ate the imperial grain, looking at their faces, for fear that they would not want it.

Today's farmers not only do not have to pay public grain, water charges and agricultural taxes, but the state also subsidizes farmers. moreover, now all the old people are holding land rent and do not have to go to the fields any more. this is really a good time!

# I was so eager to be away from home

I guess that everyone wanted to stay away from home when they were young. This is due to rebellion in their bones, or the necessary process of growth.

Ever since I learned that girls can get away from their hometowns by marrying far away, I 've been looking forward to growing up. When I was 17 years old, I went to work in Jinjiang, Fujian, a 3000 away from home. This was forced by life. At that time, I only knew the master who worked in Jinjiang, and I couldn't find anyone else to take me out, so Jinjiang became the first stop in my working career. At that time, I was very happy because I could work so far away from home.

I only go back to my hometown once after working for several years. Every time I go back to my hometown, my neighbors introduce my blind date one after another. Because of my dislike of my hometown when I was young, I think many people in my hometown are too snobbish and look down on my family, so I don't want to find someone in my hometown, and I don't even want to see them. These are all "seeds of disgust" planted from a young age. At that time, I felt that any part of the country would be better than my hometown.

Now none of our sisters have settled in their hometown. I left Anqing and went to Chizhou. My younger sister settled in Hefei, the provincial capital. My second sister followed her sister-in-law and her boyfriend to settle down in Shucheng County, Lu'an. Both of them realized their childhood "wishes" and left the county where their hometown was located.

In fact, Tongcheng is really bad? Tongcheng, Anhui, is a county-level city under the jurisdiction of Anqing City, has been known as the "cultural capital" since ancient times. Emperor Qianlong of the Qing Dynasty once said that "all articles in the world come from Tongcheng", the "Tongcheng School" culture once dominated the literary world for more than 200 years, and the "Tongcheng Three Heroes" were written into Senior high school history textbooks...

Only when I really grow up can I understand that it is the root of human inferiority and nature to dislike the poor and love the rich. A small village is like a small kingdom, the local bully is more terrible, the sky is high and the emperor is far away, the weak and poor people are naturally bullied.

Nowadays, I am often proud of being born in Tongcheng, the "capital of literature. Every time I go back to Tongcheng, I can't hide my excitement. I told my daughter about the history of Tongcheng, showed her around the famous "six-foot lane", and explained to her the story behind the poem of the same name, as well as the history and famous figures of Tongcheng, such as "two prime ministers in a 3, five li Jinshi, and two top scholars across the river.

I even secretly thought that if one day some of my children or nieces have made some achievements, I must ask them to talk more about their experiences of being influenced by the "Tongcheng School" culture. Over the years, I have seen and heard many other people and things from my hometown in rural areas, and I feel that the overall quality of the people in my hometown is very good, and the living conditions are relatively good. And the hometown of private enterprises, private enterprises developed, the town is full of brush factory, known as the "Chinese brush town". My hometown is also known as the "hometown of plastic bags". 70% of the plastic bags in the country are produced there. Geographical location in the middle of Anqing and Hefei, traffic developed, outstanding people, Wuhua Tianbao. I really don't understand why I hate my hometown so much.

I once heard an older sister say that at the age of 15, she determined to grow up far away from home: the farther the better. I always feel that my parents are too nagging, and I also feel that some people in my hometown don't like their faces. At the age of 19 at the beginning of her youth, she went to other provinces and came back 1 every two years. Many years later, she told me that the most regretful thing in her life was that she got married too early and married so far...

I understand that she is using this rebellious way to leave home, in fact, the mind is not really mature. There should be many others who think like her. For our hometown, from loving to wanting to escape, and then to loving more deeply, this is the process of our continuous growth and the result of our mentality becoming more mature.

No matter how many cities we have traveled, how many footprints we have traveled, and where we finally settled, in our dreams, the most common place must be our hometown, the place where we were born and grew up.

Have you ever had the idea of escaping from your hometown?

# We all don't know how high the sky is.

Think of the personal experiences shared by 1 colleagues. He said that one summer vacation when he was at school, the school introduced the students to Shanghai for internship, and the working place was Jiading, Shanghai. Only later did I find out that it was a liar factory, not including food and housing, the salary was pitifully low, and the rent was very expensive, so it was better not to do it.

He and several classmates plan to take a look around the 1 circle in the Oriental Pearl and leave Shanghai to return to their hometown. The day before they left, they wanted to find a hotel nearby. Every family was so expensive that all the money on several people was not enough to stay 1. Several boys who had just tried to enter society had no choice but to sleep in the open air at the Bund for a night. Pointing to the Oriental Pearl, they said, "In 10 years, each of us will buy a house there to use as a toilet!" What a grandiloquence! Laughed all our colleagues back and forth. Did everyone do that when they were young?

I remember a passage in Zhang Xiaoxian's book: "A 20-year-old man always thinks that the world can step under his feet and that he will be omnipotent in the future. After the age of 35, he never dared to say this again. Life has given him a cruel reality. Where is he still confident to make public."

When I was young, everyone had a face that had not been bullied by life, the edges and corners had not been smoothed, and the self-confidence and narcissism of winning the future. When working in Wenzhou that year, the two post -85 boys on the opposite side of the assembly line were full of pride when they talked about their dreams for the future. A boy said, "I will have a BMW sooner or later. My girlfriend broke up with me. Her mother just thinks my family is too poor. I will drive the BMW to her door to make them regret it and make her angry." Another boy said, "I'll definitely buy a Land Rover if I want." The two men clapped their hands and cheered, feeling that it was not a dream to enter millions in the future.

They said this in a tone as if BMW and Land Rover had already paid a deposit and were waiting for them. In fact, at that time, when working on the assembly line of the factory, the workers' monthly salary was only 1000 or 2000 yuan. Boys could only spend their own money, and some people even borrowed money every month. Because young, so fearless, dare to say any wild words. A child from the countryside, without any help, the probability of buying a BMW or Land Rover by his personal ability is extremely low. If the family has a very thick family background, it will not let his son go to the factory to work as an assembly line worker early without studying. When boys work in factories for a few years, most people will not have any savings, and there is limited room for growth. They have to face the tremendous pressure of buying a house, getting married and starting a family. It is not easy to achieve an annual income of one million. All the high expectations for the future, just because they are too young.

Last year, I was drawn into the former Wenzhou colleague group, and the two boys opposite were also in the group. One is married and the couple are making costumes together. The other is not married, runs a garment factory, and then goes to work after failure. The profit of the processing plant is extremely meager, and it has to be very good at arranging calculations. Each link is very testing. Even if it succeeds, it can only be a little better than being an assembly line worker. The total added value is there and there will not be too high huge profits. His elderly parents broke their hearts about his marriage and asked people everywhere to introduce their son to him and help him pay his debts frugally. Nearly ten years have passed, and they find that they no longer have the confidence they used to speak. I think they 've seen life for what it is.

In such an era of talent saturation, people from rural backgrounds, no education, and working in factories, no matter how hard they try, it is difficult to make more waves. It is good to be able to get married and start a family, not to let parents worry about themselves, and to live a stable and well-off life. This is not at the beginning of reform and opening up, people who did not read books will achieve something as long as they have courage and ideas.

Now, looking around, there are very few successful people without academic qualifications. Some rich and powerful people in China are basically from famous universities: Lei Jun is from Wuhan University; Liu Qiangdong graduated from Renmin University of China and was the top student in the college entrance examination. Ma Yun spoke English well when he was 12 years old, could talk with foreign friends easily and freely, run magazines and do his 5 job when he was in college. Baidu's Robin Li is a proud son of Peking University and studied in the United States. He is a computer genius...

The society has basically been stereotyped. Your environment, your knowledge, your family and your vision have already determined the development space you may reach in the future. You can only toss in a small area at most, and the ceiling is limited there.

Besides, most of the students who said they would buy 1 Oriental Pearl house as a toilet in ten years did not set foot on the land of Shanghai, let alone buy a house in Shanghai. There should be many, many people who say such heroic words, but they are just nonsense when they are young and frivolous, bragging between men, and a mouth addiction. Or did you come to Shanghai hopefully and end up sleeping on the floor outside, saying some bold words to comfort the injured heart.

The boy who took the lead in buying a 1 room in the Oriental Pearl Tower later came to Shanghai. Now he works in sales in Shanghai, and his salary fluctuates. Now the competition in various industries is getting bigger and bigger, with good jobs and good money. In the future, maybe he can realize the dream he once had, maybe forever just a dream. When I was a teenager, I also secretly thought that I must stand on a high stage and speak to many people in a radiant manner. It must be very beautiful and attractive. I once fantasized that I would become the top ten rich people in our village in the future, so that no one dared to look down on me. Now I think that I am really childish and ridiculous.

Some people will say that starting a business from a factory may realize the dream of youth. Entrepreneurship? The capital is not as much as others, and the natural confidence is not enough. Will good projects or shops in prime locations wait for us? How many resources do we have? Can you get good information earlier than others? Or have a superior talent for doing business?

Successful people are closely related to the opportunities of the times, their own efforts, their level of life and their knowledge and vision, the so-called right time, right place, with right people. Yesterday, a student talked to me. She said that she wanted to change her fate. She was originally working in graphic design and had a salary of 6000 yuan a month. However, she was unwilling to do something for herself and chose to open a Taobao store to start a business. I told her that the starting point is good, but the reality is too cruel, or it is more reliable to move forward step by step. At the beginning of my current work, when I talked with her, I felt that she was full of sorrow. I was worried that she would be depressed. I enlighten her over and over again, hoping that she could adjust her state. Taobao platform has been developed for more than ten years, and anyone who does Taobao before 2010 should be able to do it. It is naturally difficult to start now. Fortunately, the investment is not much. If there is really no hope, you can stop loss in time. I said, you'd better do your old job design. If you do it well, you can also take over private jobs. It's also a lot of income. It's better to write words in your spare time than to change your industry rashly. We are all born in the 1980 s, and the effective working time of our life has passed 1/2 and we can't afford it.

See: This is the truth of life. How many people can realize the dreams they had when they were young?

We have all known that the sky is high and the earth is thick. We all don't want to live a life of mediocrity.

# Impression of the village in the city where I once lived

In 2008, we took our 1-year-old daughter to run a snack business in Lucheng District, Wenzhou, Zhejiang Province. Our store is located at the gate of Liming Industrial Park. It is a mobile board room. Almost all the 1 rows are snack bars, including pancakes, noodles, malatang, milk tea and occasionally telephone booths.

For people who do small businesses, the accommodation conditions are usually not very good. Most of them choose to live on the 1 floor, because things that cannot be put in the store can be temporarily stored, and inventory and pick-up are very convenient, and time can be saved. There are many small private processing plants near our housing, producing ballpoint pens and hairpins. Those Wenzhou natives can live a comfortable life just by collecting rent. We live in two old-fashioned buildings on the 1 floor. As the locals want to charge more rent, the houses are built very densely and the lighting is very poor. We must turn on the lights when entering in broad daylight. The rent at that time was 280 yuan per room. Wenzhou locals are indeed very business-minded, active in thinking, rich in life, and are known as "Chinese Jews. But in Wenzhou, the vast majority of outsiders do small businesses, mainly from Anhui, Henan, Jiangxi, Sichuan, Hubei and other places. Wenzhou belongs to the edge of Zhejiang, sometimes referred to as the "three regardless" area, there will naturally be people of all colors, public security is more chaotic. Petty theft and robbery occur from time to time. One day at noon, when I returned to the rental room, I found the door open and the TV was gone. It turned out that there were thieves in broad daylight, and the thieves dared to move the TV blatantly, which was really infuriating and helpless. On another occasion, the thousands of dollars we were going to purchase next quarter were also stolen, and even wallets were thrown at the door of the rental house. What is even more frightening is that my mother-in-law's 1 pair of gold earrings were dragged away alive on the road. There are also pedestrians on the road with mobile phones to talk, robbers riding motorcycles directly to the mobile phone snatched...

At that time, the village in the city, such a situation abound. Losing 5 bicycles and 3 battery cars a year is normal. Thieves, whether they break into a house or steal a car, are more professional than the secret agents in the movie.

Most of the residents of the villages in the city are people of all kinds at the bottom. There are small businesses, scavengers, and motorists, as well as tricycle drivers, cleaners, porters, etc. The public security situation is particularly poor.

That year, the resident next door to me was an old couple cleaning at Wenzhou bus station. They had a monthly income of 900 yuan. They bring back many bottles and jars every day. Due to the large number of things, their daughter-in-law takes her two children to the intersection to pick them up every day. The son of the family is too lazy, like an ignorant child, fond of playing, not good work, love to play cards and gambling. His wife is the same age as me and is very beautiful and virtuous. At that time, she was pregnant with her third child. Some locals in Wenzhou wanted to book the adoption, but she was reluctant and did not agree.

All expenses are dependent on the old couple. Every evening, I can always see the wife dragging her two children to pick up her parents-in-law. The old man will not let them down. He will buy some fruits and vegetables at a discount and pick up some clothes that others have discarded but can still be used.

When I write these words, I think of the neighbor who has a beautiful face in my mind. I don't know what happened to her. Why did such a good woman marry an irresponsible man? Beauty and happiness are often not necessarily proportional.

At the door of my house, there are often some housewives who take their babies at home. They sometimes take home some manual work from the factory. When I came back from the stall, I often saw them sitting together doing handicrafts. Although they had very little income, they were also very happy and seemed to have no worries. They gathered together to do handwork, talking and laughing. They often eat tomato noodles, and they often wait until the supermarket discounts in the evening to buy vegetables, but this does not affect their happiness index.

Opposite the house we live in is a small clinic run by Sichuan people. The owner is a woman about 40 years old. Her husband has his own job and occasionally comes to help. The headache and brain fever in the village in the city all go to this small clinic. There are several beds in the room, and the infusion often has to queue up.

That year was during the financial crisis. In the second half of the year, many people moved away, some went back to their hometown, and some went to other places. The industrial park is also rumored to be relocated elsewhere. We also left the village in the city in 2009.

In 2011, we went to Yanta District of Xi'an again and lived in a village called Cao Jiamiao. At that time, demolition and reconstruction were everywhere. When we went to the shop, everyone said that it would never be demolished. They have been shouting for several years. It is not so easy to demolish. Don't worry!

We rented a large access to the door, people live upstairs, a total of five floors. On one side of the passage, we built a 4-square-meter cabin with wooden boards, where we pressed noodles to make steamed buns and steamed buns. After the end is finished, the stairs will be sold under the slope of the stairs. Two tables and steam stoves will be put on the steamer and soya-bean milk will be beaten.

Because it is a village in the city, the rent is still cheap. Stairway 600 yuan per month, upstairs housing 300 yuan per month. Every month, all expenses are removed and 8000 yuan can be saved. It was very satisfying then. After cutting the dishes in the afternoon and preparing the ingredients for the next day, I went to the nearby second-hand bookstore to find a lot of books to read, and the days were quiet and quiet.

It's just that the good times didn't last long. One morning when I got up, I saw red banners hanging all over the streets, which said, "in order to improve the living environment, we should cooperate with the demolition and build a beautiful home, and all of them should be moved out within 3 days". The news came so suddenly that even the landlord was surprised.

We made some buns from the leftover stuffing in the fridge. A little after eight o'clock, the men in uniform arrived, and the appearance was quite frightening ... with a loudspeaker shouting, that is, to persuade us to evacuate as soon as possible. Those people beat and kicked our countertops and tables and yelled at us. I said to sell this and take it away, but they refused and had to waste a lot of food.

I have to move again and go out to find a store. Those years of making some money just went away. The prosperous and good location in the city center will not be demolished, but there is no confidence and no capital to rent, so the transfer fee is prohibitive. Only in Xi 'an did I know that noodles alone can make so many varieties, such as Dandan noodles, spinach noodles, trouser belt noodles, dipped noodles, etc.

I specially ordered a pair of trouser belt noodles. In 1 large porcelain basin, there were only 1 lasagna, celery leaves, and a small bowl with seasonings for dipping. It tasted delicious.

During my four years in Xi 'an, I learned that Shaanxi is a major province of education and that Liu Qing, Lu Yao, Jia Pingwa, Chen Zhongshi and other literary giants. Making a living in the ancient capital of the thirteen dynasties for several years has had a great impact on my life. It was at that time that I read literary books such as "The Ordinary World", "Life", "White Deer Plain", "Me and The Temple of Earth", and "Eternal Regret". Thanks to an old bookstore nearby.

The shops in the villages in the city do not know how many customers they receive every day. The shouts, the collisions of pots and pans, and the ringing of tricycles from the door are also thriving. How much prosperity, how many vicissitudes of life, human fireworks, market breath, all kinds of life in this small village!

Later, I heard that the villages in the city where I lived had already been transformed into a new one, which was a far cry from the past. Once unbearable appearance is also the inevitable in the process of urbanization, everything is the story of this era.

# From a firewood cutter to a little uncle in engineering.

My little brother is only 9 years older than me, after 70, the same age as my big cousin. In those days, there were many situations like this: mothers and daughters were confinement together, and no one had time to take care of anyone. My grandmother gave birth to 9 children and 7 adults. Little brother is the youngest one, but did not get more family care, but bear more. Up to now, I don't know how to divide the family in that era. It seems that the young and old still suffer more.

When little uncle was a teenager, big uncle and 3 uncle had already married and separated. The rural living conditions in the 1980 s were generally difficult, especially in the mountainous areas where my grandmother was. The old and frail grandparents lived with their little uncle in a house built of 3 hollow bricks in the depression. The older uncles and aunts are too busy to take care of their families. That year, my grandfather died of illness, and my 13-year-old uncle dropped out of primary school and began to work as a temporary worker to make a living alone. In the absence of more network resources, my brother-in-law can only go up the mountain with the people in the village to cut wood and pick out food from the mountain. At that time, it was the only way to rely on the mountain to eat the mountain. The rest of the labor force was either cutting wood or burning charcoal to sell.

In this way, the young and thin little brother began to work hard to make a living, doing the work of adults: every day from Tianma Ma Ma Liang to get home in the evening, shuttling back and forth over 30 miles of mountain trails. Every now and then, I don't forget to buy some fresh snacks from outside the mountain for my grandmother to taste. Grandma saw the young uncle whose shoulders were red and swollen, and worried that he would not grow tall in the future. She was so distressed that she often shed tears secretly. (My brother-in-law is now 1.65 meters tall. It is estimated that he is really under the pressure of a pole.)

After more than a year like this, my uncle also met a few friends who had a good relationship and had a lot of ideas. They talked about the outside world and all kinds of business, and their hearts were surging. They felt that selling firewood was too low-end and not a long-term solution. They are going to sell clothes wholesale together.

In the early 1990 s, there were far fewer small businesses than now. Little brother and friends are wholesale clothing, hats, dragging bags to buy and sell. However, because my little brother is too young and lacks calculation, he earns much less money than others.

But compared with cutting and selling firewood, this has made a qualitative leap, at least opened the horizon and exposed to a lot of information resources. Later, my brother-in-law took my sister-in-law to sell clothes together.

Later, my brother felt that selling clothes with his bag on his back was still limited in development. It may also be young, with infinite thoughts, feeling that you can step on the world under your feet.

My brother-in-law also decided to contract a tea garden with 100 mu of mountain top and pay a deposit to sign the contract. The younger brother asked his sister-in-law and sister-in-law to help him find dozens of female workers to pick tea, which was weighed by catties. It was very easy to hire people to work in the countryside at that time. It was also in that year that my uncle met my aunt who was picking tea in the tea farm. Now my little brother often brags. When he contracted the tea garden, 1 group of girls courted him. Every time he changed clothes, he didn't know who washed them well. That was his proud time. My aunt is 5 years younger than my little brother. She is petite and exquisite. She is very elf. At that time, she was also a worshipper of my little brother. She followed him wherever he went, and slowly they came together.

Just when my little brother was in high spirit and had a bumper harvest in his love career, but the three female workers invited went to pick cucumbers from other people's fields in their spare time. Unfortunately, they were poisoned by pesticides. Two of them were rescued and one died. The young little uncle had never seen this battle before and was terrified.

He is the boss, and he has brought in all the people. Naturally, he cannot get away with it. It is not enough to lose all the savings from selling clothes and the income from contracting tea gardens. I still owe a lot of money. The incident hit him hard. The house leak happened to rain overnight, and my grandmother died of heart failure that year. My brother-in-law knelt in the mourning hall and could not even get the funeral expenses for my grandmother. It was my sister-in-law who borrowed 800 yuan to get grandma's funeral done. At that time, she was still the aunt of a young girl. No matter how down and out my uncle was, she was always with him. She has no brothers and her only sister is married. After my grandmother left, my uncle stayed at her house. My aunt only has a father, who is a deaf and honest man. She lives in a wooden house with poor conditions by collecting chestnut tea. That year, because my little brother owed too much money outside, the twelfth lunar year was over, and every day there were debtors asking my little brother for money. My aunt's father sold the two big fat pigs in the family and helped my little brother pay off the debt, which was the biggest fortune in my aunt's family.

At that time, they were not engaged yet. Those people saw an old man in Huajia who was so kind and righteous, and it was not good to continue pestering. Each of them took some money back, and the little uncle's family finally passed a peaceful year. After that, my uncle and aunt went to Wenzhou, Zhejiang Province together. He wanted to go to developed places to find more opportunities. However, they all had only primary school education and could not find a glamorous and decent job, so they had to dig earth on the construction site with the villagers in this town, that is, the foundation before the house was built. It was a very hard work. The income was calculated on the basis of square meters. Every day, yellow sweat flowed black sweat, just to save money to pay off debts. When they went to Wenzhou in the first year, they didn't go back to their hometown during the New Year. They wanted to save some back and forth expenses and help to watch the construction site to earn more income. It's just that the day failed, the cable was stolen from the construction site, and my little brother lost a lot of money to go in, and half a year's salary was for nothing. In those difficult times, fortunately, there are still aunts who will never leave.

After digging earthwork on the construction site for a year or two, my uncle became a team leader and managed more than a dozen people. He slowly did not have to do any more heavy work and just led the workers to do the work. Soon, he also sent my two cousins to Wenzhou for development.

After being the team leader for two years, my uncle has paid off all the debts owed by his hometown and started to contract the construction site by himself, bringing 3 40 workers. My aunt helped the workers cook and keep accounts at the construction site.

In 2004, my uncle took over the framework projects of several villas in Lishui, Zhejiang Province. He made a net profit of 80,000 yuan that year. He bought a van and drove back to his hometown. He had a lively wedding with his aunt. Little brother finally raised his eyebrows! My sister-in-law, sister-in-law and everyone were happy for him. Unfortunately, my grandmother, who loved my brother-in-law, did not see this day.

Over the years, my brother-in-law has been working hard in Wenzhou, following a large construction company to pick up work. My brother-in-law is sincere and kind. Even if he didn't receive the project payment in time, he tried his best to advance some wages to the workers. The workers behind him have followed him for many years, mainly from Anhui and Sichuan.

My brother-in-law once told me that he regretted that his cultural level was too low and that he was struggling to read the drawings and did not dare to expand the scale arbitrarily. In fact, after receiving the external framework of the project, there is no high profit for interior decoration. What he earns is hard-working money. He is under great pressure and often suffers from insomnia, especially worrying about the safety of workers. God treats tenacious and hardworking people kindly. Wenzhou, a magical land, has given my brother everything he wants. The two cousins who followed him to work in Wenzhou have developed well there.

Now, although my uncle is not very rich and expensive, he built a small western-style building in his hometown of Shucheng in 2009 at a cost of 550000 yuan. Last year, he bought a big house in the center of Hefei, and the car was changed from the first van to the third Buick Regal.

Two little cousins, one is 11 years old and the other is 8 years old. They are sensible and lovely and have excellent studies. My aunt is now full-time with her baby, and the years are quiet.

My brother-in-law is very homesick and attaches great importance to the education of his two cousins. People often boast of my aunt's good life. My aunt always said with a smile that there were a lot of 1 behind her who were collecting debts in those years. Everyone said that my uncle was a pickle (meaning not steadfast) and was the object of ridicule. Now it is a little better. She came slowly. She believed that she could live a good life from beginning to end.

In my heart, the little brother has been very great. After graduating from primary school, he made a living by himself, from chopping firewood to selling clothes and tea gardens, to doing hard work, and then to becoming a contractor, all the way through ups and downs.

Do not experience wind and rain, how can see the rainbow, no one can casually succeed.

# Wenzhou people in the shop of flowering rice noodles

On the street where I go to eat at noon every day, a new Huajia rice noodle shop has been opened, mainly Huajia of various sizes and the like, which is very novel. Looking at the introduction of the big billboard at the door, saying how delicious the flower armour is, high protein, low fat, and how beneficial it is to the human body, I couldn't help walking into the store.

Rice noodles, fish balls and beef balls can be added to the flower armor. The couple are operating, the storefront is about 15 square meters, and the tables and chairs are of the small and delicate type, which saves space. Listening to the accent of the hostess greeting me, I guess they are either from Fujian or Wenzhou. There weren't many customers that night. The hostess was about 30 years old. While she skillfully put the flower armour in the tin foil, she asked me if I had been in the coast. I answered truthfully that I had been in Fujian and Wenzhou.

She said she was from Ouhai, Wenzhou. Looking at her wrapping the flower armor in tin foil and putting it on the induction cooker, I think this way looks quite fresh, which may be the reason why I have not noticed such shops before. Asked how their business was, she said it had only been open for a few days. The rent for this slap-big land was more than 5,000 a month, and the transfer fee cost 100000, which made me open my mouth. This kind of shop belongs to subdivision specialty, competition should be small point.

I said that Wenzhou people are smart and have the name of "Chinese Jews. It is said that in some African countries, Wenzhou is much more famous than Beijing.

The male shopkeeper was black, thin and shrewd. Hearing our chat, he also took the initiative to join us. He said that Wenzhou people are most afraid of hardship, and there has been an old adage that "I would rather sleep on the floor than be a boss. Wenzhou people are unwilling to work for others, even if it is to set up a stall, open a small shop, no matter how hard they eat, no matter how much they suffer, no matter how much they suffer, and go in the wind and rain, they are willing to be their own bosses, preferring to be chicken heads. I don't want to be a phoenix tail. This comes from the entrepreneurial genes in their bones. I have been in Wenzhou for 3 years (Chashan Town and Lucheng District), where there are many clothing factories, shoe factories, lighter factories, razor, hairpin, ballpoint pen factories, etc. Like Metersbonwe, Semir and many other well-known clothing brands are in Wenzhou.

Among the four famous leather shoes in China, Aokang and Kangnai were born and grew up in Wenzhou and went to the world, which is also the pride of the Chinese people.

In 2007, I worked as a assembly worker in a women's clothing factory near Chashan University Town (responsible for the cuff). The women's clothing named "Snow Song" had its own specialty stores in more than 100 countries around the world, and the boss was just a 30-year-old Petite and beautiful woman. I heard that she learned to make clothing and design at the age of 17, and then registered her own trademark, constantly promoted and made her own brand. When she got married, she didn't want any machinery in the factory. She left it to her brother and only took away the trademark. However, she was still able to grow rapidly in a few years. Many central intersections in Wenzhou had her clothing advertisements. She herself has become a legendary myth, several radio media reported.

There are still many successful entrepreneurs with such a low starting point in Wenzhou. In 2008, opposite my breakfast shop was a "big tiger" lighter factory with nearly 1,000 employees and its products were exported to all parts of the world. The most remarkable thing is that their lighters can fire in the oxygen-deficient areas of the Mexican Plateau, while other lighters cannot fire, so they can survive the financial crisis.

The cultural level of their generation of entrepreneurs is not high. With the advantages of coastal geography, coupled with a strong entrepreneurial atmosphere, they are willing to endure hardships and study. The vast majority of Wenzhou people have achieved good results, which have played a role in the country's economic development and employment. An immeasurable role.

At that time, we Anhui villagers gathered together and often said that most of the middle and senior managers in Wenzhou enterprises were from Anhui. At that time, my cousin and other relatives were indeed in the management of the factory. However, some old people said that Wenzhou was not as good as Anhui in the 5 1960 s! It is both a mountainous area and a saline-alkali land, and there are no special products. At that time, Wenzhou people went to Anhui with big bags to run small businesses such as quilt beating and pot mending. After the reform and opening up, Wenzhou has developed rapidly. We all work here to make a living. This is called 30 years in Hedong and 30 years in Hexi!

Eating delicious flower armor, think of the past time. Although the competition in the real economy is becoming more and more fierce, and the operation of some traditional enterprises is deteriorating, I believe that the Wenzhou enterprises mentioned above will surely eliminate all difficulties and remain invincible.

Wenzhou people have created miracles and myths. In the future, they will still create various legends and make immeasurable contributions to the growth of national GDP.

Whether it is Wenzhou people who set up stalls, open small shops or do enterprises, their spirit of daring to work hard and bear hardships and stand hard work is always worth learning and paying tribute to them!

# About the soil

## 01

For those of us who come from the countryside, the soil is always more intimate. The fragrance and memory of the earth are buried deep in our hearts. We were born with soil. From childhood to adulthood, the houses I lived in were built of adobe. The rice farm at the door, the vegetable field and the fields beside the house were all inseparable from the nourishment of the land.

Today, many people live in high-rise buildings in big cities, as if living at high altitude. Even if they are down-to-earth, they are surrounded by concrete floors. If you want to raise some flowers and plants, you have to go to remote villages to find soil. With the development of the times, we are getting farther and farther away from the soil.

## 02

Recalling that when I was a child, my father used a brick-shaped wooden mold to put the well-made mud into it to make adobe, and then put it in the sun to dry. Once dried, the adobe is used to cover the home's kitchen, pigsty, and even build walls. At that time, clay played an extremely important role in our lives and was almost a necessity of our lives.

Over time, the adobe houses gradually disappeared and were replaced by hollow bricks. I still remember that my family once bought a batch of bricks at 30 cents each to renovate the pigsty. In addition, there are 1 kinds of black brick. Later, smaller red bricks became popular. Buildings were built with these bricks, which are still in use today. But the source of red brick, is still the soil, just after the kiln factory high temperature firing.

For us who grew up in the countryside, the soil is closely related to our life.

03

In our childhood, we 1 a group of friends who like to build pots and pans with clay and cook like adults. We will use pebbles as dishes and clay to make small pieces of various shapes for pots and cookers.

Whenever we have conflicts, we will use mud to fight with our friends. You throw it on me and I throw it on your back. In a short time, everyone is as good as before and continues to play mud together. We also like to make a radio out of mud and plug in bamboo silk as a switch button, as if we had a real radio in our hands. Sometimes, we also made the shape of a transmitter out of mud and shouted to each other, "Hey, hey, can you hear me?" and then smiled at each other as if it were real.

Now in retrospect, in that era of material poverty, how much joy the soil has brought us!

The adults are in close contact with the soil every day, going to the vegetable garden to turn the soil and fertilize, planting Chinese cabbage, beans, garlic, building cucumber shelves, etc. My mother often goes home with dirt on her trousers. The smell of dirt makes people feel at ease and at ease. This is my indelible memory.

Especially in the busy farming season, we children also have to go to the fields, mowing rice, pulling rice seedlings, transplanting rice seedlings, weeding, clothes and faces are covered with mud, and the whole person is like a big cat. The work clothes during the busy farming season 1 soaked in the pond, and the muddy water soaked the 1. At that time, my mother asked me to wash the dirt on my clothes.

## 04

For generations of us who have lived on agriculture, soil is the foundation of our survival and an existence that cannot be ignored.

The famous writer Lin Qingxuan once recalled that his old father brought sweet potato seedlings to him from his hometown in Tainan. When he saw that Lin Qingxuan was living on a high-rise building and could not even find a piece of dirt, his father shouted in great disappointment: "Son! How do you live in this unadored place!"

This is the deep love of the older generation for the clay. Another celebrity, when 1 studying in the United States, missed the motherland and was homesick. He asked people to take 1 small bags of dirt to Beijing. Whenever I miss my hometown, I take out that bag of soil to smell it to relieve my homesickness.

## 05

The Bible says that God made Adam, the ancestor of mankind, out of clay: "God made man out of the clay of the earth and blew his anger into his nostrils, and he became a living man with spirit, named Adam." God also said to Adam, "You are the clay, and you will return to the clay."

In Chinese myths and legends, Nu Wa is also made of earth: "Nu Wa kneading loess to be a man." These similar legends illustrate a profound truth: the land is the source of human life.

Human life, spiritual civilization and material pursuit are inseparable from the embrace of the earth. In the embrace of the earth, we can see the vast sky. It is the earth and the sky that give us a broad mind and allow us to appreciate all the beauty of nature.

China is a large agricultural country, and the land is the foundation of the people. But now there are fewer and fewer people farming, and even some fields are abandoned, which makes people sigh and sigh.

Today's children don't play with mud, but instead have fake sand and mud made of plastic. We humans are always relying on the earth and existence, that is the habitat of our soul. Miss the playing mud childhood, miss those years gone.

# To record life is to record history.

### 01

Many people dream of writing a grand book to reflect the development and progress of the times, but such a grand dream often makes people flinch and dare not write easily. Yesterday I said in the group of students that, in fact, we are recording our own lives, which is to record this era. Later generations will be able to get a glimpse of our current living conditions from our records.

### 02

Recently, I read the author Ding Yan's "factory girl", she also has a copy of "factory boy". Isn't what she recorded also the story of this era? She wrote electronics factory, injection molding factory, welding factory, speaker box factory workers. This book is Ding Yan's 200-day record of experiencing Dongguan Electronics Factory and Audio Box Factory in 2010. She quickly records in the toilet every day, and drags her tired body to write articles after work at night or on weekends.

I used to be a 1 member of the factory, and I feel very kind to read such stories. Although her living and working environment seems to be harsher than what I have experienced, the working time is only 11 hours, which is several hours shorter than ours, but they are supervised by the supervisor and must be highly concentrated.

At that time, we paid more for more work. No one was in charge.

Everyone worked hard consciously. When you want to rest, you will occasionally rest in the corridor, drink water, chat, and be relatively free.

In my second year in the factory, I already had a six-story new dormitory building, which was clean and spacious. At that time, we did not take a single break, nor did we contact people outside the factory. We only got along with fellow villagers. Life was just work except eating. Although it was boring, the environment was simple and safe.

## 03

In her book, some girls do welders, their hands are rough, their nails even fall off, they can't bear to look closely, their bones are thick, and their faces are extremely inconsistent. And people who do clothing work have good hand care. If the hand is a woman's second face, I think my second face is better than the first face.

Many years ago, my aunt joked that I had a pair of "artist" hands, suitable for playing the piano, but unfortunately I threw the wrong baby.

Perhaps it is because I have been away from the factory for some years and have forgotten the tiredness and hardship of the past. When I read "Factory Girl", I always felt that I was much luckier than the working girl in the book. The inferiority of my childhood and adolescence was gradually improved in the factory.

I have seen the introduction of this book on Weibo before. Before reading this book, I once thought that 1 a poet and writer, 1 a graduate of a famous school, no matter how deep he goes to the front line, he is also a bystander. But when I opened this book, I immediately lost that confidence and admired the depth of the author's writing. Although I stayed in the factory for a longer time, I could not write such delicate and profound words as her.

She wrote about the first generation of migrant workers, the second generation of migrant workers, the story of migrant girls choosing Hong Kong Taiwanese as mistresses, and migrant girls in remote mountainous areas in Guangdong. Although they have some advantages over mainlanders, they are always cheated by migrant workers.

## 04

The author links the stories of different working girls into a whole book. Some girls are in poor health and cannot do factory work. Some want to take a shortcut. But although these girls enjoyed the blessing for a while, they finally returned all the happiness of the rest of their lives to their fate, some even worse.

The book also contains the true story of a broken toe crippled by a worker in an injection molding plant. This worker has 3 children to raise in his family. He wants to fight with his boss with beer bottles all day long. Under the persuasion of others, he finally had to compromise with his fate, only to get a small amount of compensation. He who lives by strength, his feet fail. The author's language is extremely restrained, and there is not 1 worker in that factory who has not been injured.

Other factories are prone to lung disease and replace workers every 3 or four months. There are also underground black factories, arrears of wages and so on. A living story is shocking, but they are real. Usually, the workers who go to coastal factories have junior high school education and primary school education, and some have only three or four grade education, mainly in Sichuan, Hunan, Hubei, Guizhou and other places.

There is a Sichuan girl named Qinghe. She graduated from Senior high school and belongs to the second generation of working. She is tall and beautiful. She alone applied for a Japanese electronics factory with more than 2,000 people. During the summer vacation, she worked in her mother's factory. She despises the small factory where her parents work.

Her parents have also worked in Dongguan for many years, and their biggest dream is to save money to go back to their hometown to build a three-story building. Qing He was a left-behind child from an early age, lacking emotion and estranged from his parents. In the electronics factory, you can have dinner with your parents every weekend, which is a little bit superior to other migrant workers.

After working as an electronic component in an electronics factory for 3 months, Qing He turned to work as a clerk. This is the first phenomenon in the factory since its establishment 20 years ago. However, she was faced with the malicious intentions of the team leader and manager. Smart, she had her own opinions and finally chose to continue to study and study Japanese. At that time, people who could speak Japanese in the surrounding electronics factories had a great advantage in choosing jobs.

There is no doubt that Qing He is the luckiest girl among the working girls. Her parents built a three-story building at home that year, borrowed 70000 debts, and prepared to continue to work in Dongguan to pay off the debts. I heard that my daughter is going to resign to study, so I still need to borrow 30000 Japanese tuition fees for my daughter.

## 05

Writer Ding Yan records the stories of the lowest and most ordinary people, isn't it the story of this era? Factory Girl, published in 2013 and Factory Boy in 2016, is not far away.

These factory girls, factory boys, they are the screws on the production line. They are also countless screws in the process of China's industrialization and modernization, and they are the mainstay in the history of China's township economic development.

This book also enforces countless people's inquiries about the torrent of modern industry. Millions of country girls across the country went there, their youth, their blood and sweat, their dreams, their love...

## 06

I like what Zhang Ailing said, mortals can represent the total amount of this era more than heroes. Someone once satirized Zhang Ailing's novels that only wrote some small love, did not care about politics, did not care about war, and did not have family and country feelings.

Zhang Ailing's works have written all the flashy glimpses of old Shanghai, the various conditions of the market, the love of men and women, and the rise and fight of small people. She used words to record the joys and sorrows, love and hatred of a generation. She is good at portraying human nature, and human nature and love are eternal themes that never go out of style.

Hong Kong's Yi Shu and Zhang Xiaoxian, aren't their little love novels the stories of the times? There is also Anne Baby, who writes marginal emotions. Her subjective and unique words that can see the soul are still welcomed by countless people.

Any creator, his creative carrier will more or less reflect the story of the times, because he can not be separated from the era of his life. 1 a writer starts from childhood, starting from personal subjective feelings. It is impossible to control the grand narrative structure 1 the beginning. Besides, literature is full of flowers. Can all authors write the same type?

With the rapid development of science and technology, in another 20 years, artificial intelligence will become popular, and future generations will see the book "Factory Girl" again. Aren't they reading historical stories? Maybe you will sigh, maybe you will feel incredible.

## 07

I once wrote that when I was a child, I engaged in double robbery in rice fields and accompanied my mother to hand in public grain. My father used mud to make adobe in rice fields to build pigsty. My husband and I used mud to make cookers to play. In order to catch the train during the Spring Festival, I waited in line for two days to buy tickets. I had to send money to the post and telecommunications office to remit money for my family. I used the card to make a phone call and wrote the manuscript in advance. To make a long story short, in order to reduce the telephone bill...

Those true and distant stories, do we write in the article, this is not also a microcosm of the times? Although we are only small writers, just a drop in the ocean of this era, we are also recording our own "history". Our descendants can glimpse the life of the past from the words.

Wang Tuodi, a Gansu girl who I have known for many years, likes to write about the Loess Plateau of her hometown, the Qin Opera of Gansu, the surface of the pulp, the wheat straw, and some special intangible cultural heritage ... These are all very fresh and curious to me, making me full of yearning.

She is only recording the story of herself and the people around her, but this is also spreading the culture of her hometown! I once wrote in the article that if I have the opportunity to go to Gansu in my lifetime, I must look at the Tianshui Qin 'an written by Tuo Di.

She is writing the story of her hometown, but also the story of the whole Gansu Loess Plateau. She was proud to be born on the Loess Plateau, just as I was proud to be born in Tongcheng, the "capital of literature" in Anhui.

Last year, a WeChat friend passed by my hometown. She stayed for a day and sent me photos. She said, "Teacher Qi, I have come to your hometown."

This is the greatest significance of being the 1 writer!

## 08

In 2014, Marquez died at the age of 87. In his eulogy, Colombian President Santos said: "For us Colombians, Marquez is the best narrator in this country... Colombia is grateful to Marquez."

Marquez himself said that he lived to tell. He also famously said: "Life is not the day we live, but the day we record."

Because Marquez's works are great and spread widely enough, his narration and records can be known all over the world. We writers record, spread and write positive energy words, and our words are also meaningful characters.

Mo Yan, the winner of the Mao Dun Literature Prize, heard that writers can eat dumplings every day when he first started writing. In those barren years, being able to eat dumplings was the greatest temptation and motivation for Mo Yan. He couldn't have started writing for the Nobel Prize in Literature 1.

## Unforgettable childhood fun

When I was a child, I liked to wear handmade cloth shoes made by my mother, running step by step, jumping step by step, clapping my hands and singing a minor tune. I was as happy as a bird. Far away, she waved to the swallow and called her. She came over. We held hands and went to play mud behind the house. We knead the mud into square, round and long ones to make cars or houses. When you are unhappy, cut them into pieces and knead them again. With imagination, we can freely control the appearance of mud and play at will, and we can find the source of happiness from this monotonous life.

Sometimes, we also make the mud into the shape of the transmitter, pager and radio seen in the movie, plug in the bamboo silk as the antenna button, and then learn the appearance of adults, take one each, and "feed" to the top while walking, take a few more shots, laugh at each other, and laugh far, far away...

On the way to school, I wrapped a few pieces of dried pickled radish fried by my mother with newspaper every day and put them in my pocket. On the way, little friends, you take one piece, he takes one piece, puts it to his mouth, sizzles off the chili noodles outside the dried radish, and then puts the pickled radish into his mouth, biting it crunchly and crisply. Accompanied by the laughter and slapstick of my friends, eating delicious food, I unconsciously arrived at the school two kilometers away from home. At that time, there was no adult transportation. Even if we were in preschool, we would walk, kick stones, pull weeds, run if we want, and rest if we want, which did not affect our happiness at all.

In spring, in the large peach orchards not far from the school road, pink and tender peach blossoms bloom one after another, like a crimson cloud, and like 1 beautiful landscape paintings. If a person stands under a peach tree and the flowers set off against each other, he becomes a person in the painting and can make people intoxicated by looking at it. A few days later, the flowers were gone, and small peaches grew on the peach trees, and our hearts became urgent. In our expectation day after day, the peaches turned from green to red and became bigger and bigger, bending the peach trees. The peaches in the garden are pink and full of fragrance. Looking from afar, we kept swallowing.

At noon on a holiday, it is estimated that the host is eating. We 5 a child to secretly discuss and plan to steal peaches together. Along the way, both excited and nervous, see acquaintances also dare not say hello. Unexpectedly, as soon as we arrived in Taoyuan, a grandmother in her fifties 1 greeted us and said, "Don't pick your children indiscriminately. Some of them are growing up. Don't waste them. I'll pick some cooked ones and give them to you to eat..."

I remember that day when I came back with 1 big pockets of peaches in my dress hem, I was really overjoyed. We all ate with red lips and sucked the outside of the peach pit clean, finally eating a round belly. My mother washed my skirt for a long time and washed it several times before washing the hair and color on it.

The adults all said that the Taoyuan family was really good. They didn't scold or make any noise, and they gave you so many for nothing. Such people are really rare. People live on those peaches to sell money! In the future, we are all embarrassed to go to that house to steal peaches again. When we go there, our faces will turn red. Some friends with good conditions asked their parents to go to that house and buy a lot of them. At that time, it seemed that they were 5 dime 1 jin.

Now that I think about it, the Taoyuan grandmother inadvertently sowed the seeds of goodness and warmth in our young hearts, so that we can know how to give.

There is really nothing to eat. When there are cucumbers in the vegetable garden, regardless of whether they grow thick or thin, pinch them off with one hand and wipe the burrs on the outside of the cucumbers with two palms, then treat them as washing, send them to the mouth, and chew them loudly.

Take the pot, this is the common memory of many adults! At that time, we would secretly cut 1 small pieces of bacon at home, pack a handful of rice, bring a small iron pot, pickles, oil and salt seasoning, and then bring a pack of matches. The 1 group of children ran to the mountain and dug a small pot hole by the soil bank. Then they divided their work and everyone worked. Some go to wash rice, some go to wash vegetables, some are responsible for making a fire, and some cut bacon into small cubes and roast them with seasonings in the pan. Although they have a smoky flavor, they also feel very fragrant.

When the meal was cooked, we cheered and cheered. Excited, you 1 shovel my 1 spoon and even grab it with your hands. 1 was a sense of accomplishment. Now think of it, that kind of warm happiness immediately surrounded me.

In summer, the cici on the tree called Huan. We braved the scorching sun, not afraid of the heat, the little face red, running around, climbing trees, pursuit. Once caught, it is like a treasure. Cut the cicadas wings short and share them with your friends, or put them in a matchbox, beat them from time to time and listen to them squeak. A cicada can often play for a day, and then put it on a tree in the evening.

On the road to school, there are some wild trees and weeds. We often look for wild fruits to eat. There is a kind of wild fruit (dialect: wheat fruit) that grows on the thorn vine. It is small, red, and has the fragrance of the field. It tastes sour and sweet, and it is very exciting. There is also a kind of thorny fruit on the hillside. We call it thorn fruit, and we will carefully pick it and eat it. As well as the 1 grass roots on the grass, 1 1 knots, white and tender, bite, sweet. These are all of us as children, the most delicious natural snacks.

In my memory, adults never want to waste the ridge of their hometown. Only a foot wide ridge, near the edge, planted with soybeans in spring and radishes in autumn. We ran back and forth on the ridge, our trousers rustling the leaves of those plants.

In winter, we 1 a group of children to the ridge to pull out the radish, tear off the radish tassel, and peel off the radish skin three times five times two times, like rabbits, and eat happily. It's crisp and sweet, and the corners of my mouth are full of radish and foam.

In the cold winter months, nine cold days, several ponds on the way to school are covered with thick ice. We all have to walk on the ice, trembling, laughing and shouting "skating, skating!" Once I accidentally fell on the ice and smashed a big hole in the ice. The bigger friend on the side was quick-eyed and pulled me up quickly. Fortunately, the cotton-padded jacket in winter is very thick and has not been soaked in water. However, at that time, I really didn't know the word "cold". As long as I was happy, I could put everything aside.

In the winter of those years, I felt much colder than now, and the winter was boundless. The snow often falls below the knees, but our children feel very happy. They like to make snowmen and have snowball fights in the white world, and knock on the ice under the eaves with bamboo poles.

Snow, it is the most beautiful love letter from heaven to the earth. It is the spirit of the world. It once decorated our beautiful childhood and brought us pure and innocent memories.

At that time, the children did not have many toys and all had the hobby of collecting. The collected treasures were cigarette boxes, candy writs and so on. We often scrape 1 the tin foil in the cigarette case, separate it from the white paper, fold it neatly, and flatten it for collection.

In my impression, there is a kind of candy called "Little Dragon Man". Everyone likes the beautiful wrapping paper outside very much. Everyone will collect a few. Sometimes we will exchange different brands to enrich our treasures day by day. At that time, there was a TV called "Little Dragon Man". I saw it at the aunt's house next door. It mainly told the story of Little Dragon Man looking for his mother. Until now, I still remember many plots in it. The cover of candy paper is dressed up like the little dragon man on TV. Every time I see candy paper, I think of that TV play.

The world of adults has nothing to do with children. In childhood, we only care about wild flowers and weeds, bees and butterflies. We only care about everything we can eat, all the fun things, all the things we are interested in.

Childhood memories affect our habits, personalities, and emotions throughout our lives. Although we are old, but those memories will never be old.

May we keep our childlike innocence forever, pure and happy forever!

# The path in front of the memory

When it comes to my hometown, the first thing that comes to mind is the path in front of my home. It is next to my family's rice field. In the earliest memory, the path was only wide with poles, potholes and muddy in rainy days.

When I was a child, my friends and I liked to play on the roadside, picking up stones and candy paper, and collecting them as treasures. In our spare time, we put small stones in bottles and shake them jingle. Wash and tidy the candy paper, fold it into stars or pagodas, and connect it to make bracelets, not to mention how happy it is. That is our childhood, monotonous but happy.

Also one evening, I was waiting for my mother working in the fields by the side of the road, imagining: Where is the end of this road? Is it a way to the distant sky, or to heaven, connecting the clouds in the sky?

With the continuous development of the times, the path in front of the door has also widened. In order to prevent muddy rainy days, the road was gradually paved with stones. When a cyclist passes by, he can hear a thumping sound from afar, like a gust of wind passing.

I remember when I was in the fourth grade, motorcycles were still a rarity in the countryside. My friends and I like to squat on the side of the road and count the passing motorcycles. What impressed me most was that one day after passing eight motorcycles, we clapped our hands and cheered loudly, as if those motorcycles were our own.

In the summer vacation of the fifth grade, I began to learn to ride a bicycle. First learn to use the 1 foot to pedal the bicycle to slide, and then practice riding a triangle fork. Ride sweaty every day, but enjoy it. On the path, leaving only the tinkling bell and our crisp laughter.

That summer vacation, we all learned to ride a bicycle, and the path remained deeper in our memory.

Time flies and we grow up. A few years later, she was no longer a teenage girl who liked to count motorcycles, but also passed that curious age.

That year, Fa Xiaojia bought a motorcycle and she asked me to study with her. Start by learning to accelerate, brake, turn, and turn around, and make progress a little day. Although the motorcycle does not need to be stepped on, it is difficult to grasp the speed at first, especially when turning around on the path, which is much heavier than the bicycle. Whenever this happens, call on adults to come and help. After a few days, we were finally able to ride the motorcycle easily.

We are like two free fish, shuttling in the path. It was a happy time of innocence, a good time of carefree.

Later, the road in front of the door was widened again and paved into a concrete road. We all started working outside. But in the dream, the path in front of the door appeared countless times.

With the opening of the Tongqian Highway, the main road moved to the back of the village committee. It was a 20-meter-wide asphalt road with camphor trees planted on both sides, like guards. In contrast, the road in front of the house is deserted, and there are very few other villagers except the nearby residents.

The road in front of the door is no longer popular in the past, the roadside is overgrown with weeds, and the cement pavement is damaged and no one cares about it, as if it has been forgotten.

The village where I was born also looks lonely and depressed these days. With the acceleration of urbanization, many villagers have moved to towns or counties, and some have moved to Anqing or Hefei, the provincial capital, leaving behind mostly old, weak, women, children and old houses.

Whether it is the path in front of the door or the village in my hometown, they are now like an old man in the twilight, guarding an old time with few patronage.

The hustle and bustle, bustle and brilliance have passed, and the hometown is no longer what it used to be, and the warmth and joy of the past can no longer be found.

This time back to my hometown, I stood in front of the path in a state of mind. Remembering that I used to ride a bicycle to school on this road, when I fell down, the big boy in the next village laughed. I got up with pain and shouted stubbornly: "I don't have any pain, why are you laughing..."

And later learn to ride a motorcycle, from this road to travel. This road witnessed my growth, from childhood to adulthood, to become a wife and mother.

The changes of paths and villages have also witnessed the development of the times. In the face of the trend of the times, individuals can only adapt and accept.

In a trance, I saw the little me standing by the road, shaking stones, folding candy paper, holding my head high, imagining the mysterious distance and the future.

The road in front of the door carries too many memories of me: happiness, sadness, laughter, tears and yearning. Only in the dream, to find its past appearance, miss that simple quiet time.

In this life, no matter how many roads I have to take, the path in front of my hometown will always be the deepest and most beautiful nostalgia in my heart. It has been winding in my heart, stretching far away...

# We are all "diluters" of the fading taste of the year"

It is the end of another year. The small year has passed and the big year is approaching. Looking around, whether it is a city or a country, you can't feel the atmosphere of the New Year, and the taste of the New Year seems to be getting worse every year.

Due to the supervision of the environmental protection department, firecrackers and fireworks have been rarely seen, and they appear to be deserted everywhere, which is not 2 to usual. Some people say that the New Year is just a festival for rural people, and urban people no longer pay attention to it, but now even the taste of the new year in the countryside has become weak. With the continuous development of society, the New Year is no longer as lively as in the past.

In my memory, since the Laba Festival, the children count down the days of the New Year every day, and every morning they ask their mother how many days there are for the New Year, even if they know it in their hearts, they have to confirm it again.

In the past, as soon as the twelfth lunar month entered, adults began to get busy, cleaning, purchasing new year's goods and preparing all kinds of food. Killing pigs, making tofu, fried dried sweet potatoes, fried peanuts, fried popcorn, fried nuts, fried pumpkin seeds, made rice candy and sesame candy, everything can make children cheer.

Killing pigs is a big deal in the countryside. Pork is usually half preserved and half sold. Only my family left only pig water and a few kilos of meat, and sold the rest to pay for tuition.

When making tofu, soak the soybeans in advance and then pick the tofu workshop in the village. Because every family has to make tofu during the Chinese New Year, the business of tofu workshops is extremely hot, so we must make an appointment in advance. When it was my turn, my sisters and I were always dancing with excitement because we could drink fresh soybean milk.

Looking back now, I think I was ridiculous at that time, and I also lamented the rapid development of society. Nowadays, soybean milk can no longer drink the taste of childhood, not soybean milk has changed, but we have grown up.

In the twelfth month, when my mother fried peanuts, we were always impatient to grab them and eat them. The fried peanuts were packed in small iron boxes and could be eaten until the end of the first month. My mother will also fry the stored rice crust, which is fragrant, crisp and delicious. It can be stored in a bag for a period of time.

During the Spring Festival, even if the family is poor, they will buy new clothes and red rope for their children to add to the festival.

The braised fish on the New Year's Eve dinner remained intact until the fifteenth day of the first lunar month. This symbolizes "more than every year". People pay great attention to this sense of ceremony. The plate of fish is not chopsticks. This is also a 1 kind of expectation for a better life.

The Spring Festival Gala in those years was a must-see program for every family and the focus of Chinese people all over the world. Ni Ping, Cao Ying, Chen Peisi, Zhao Benshan and others have become deep memories in the hearts of our generations.

The post-70s and post-80s have a profound understanding of the flavor of the year in that era of material scarcity. What we are looking forward to is not the Chinese New Year, but the delicious food that can only be enjoyed during the Chinese New Year, the people that can only be seen, and the leisure. In the final analysis, the taste buds are the floodgates of emotion.

Now, we are all sighing that "the taste of the year is getting weaker and weaker" and feel more and more boring. In fact, each of us is a "diluter" of the new year ".

Visiting relatives for the New Year has become as hasty as sending an express. Everyone is busy, they are constantly rushing for time, but they cannot stop to enjoy life. What the hell are we up? What is the meaning of life?

Even if relatives and friends seldom get together, after exchanging pleasantries, they often play with their mobile phones. "The furthest distance in the world is not between life and death, but when I am in front of you, you are playing with your mobile phone."

The rapid development of social rhythm, the rise of electronic products and self-media platforms, as well as the popularity of small videos and diversified entertainment programs, have distracted people's attention, making it rare for a family to sit around and laugh and watch the Spring Festival Gala.

Now, people's mentality has become impetuous, what are the pursuit of efficiency. New Year's greetings can't wait to be completed in one day, and melon seeds, peanuts, rice candy and other new year goods can be delivered home with just a little on the phone.

The improvement of living standards, so that people no longer need to wait until the New Year to enjoy food. This has reduced the ritual of the New Year, and people are not so looking forward to it.

Residents of some big cities even no longer celebrate the New Year, choosing to go on family trips or book New Year's Eve dinner on their mobile phones. A mobile phone can do everything, eat, drink and have everything.

We have grown from children who received New Year's money to adults who sent New Year's money. The people who don't like the New Year the most may be middle-aged people, because the New Year means an inventory of the past year, as well as facing comparisons and comparisons, which makes people feel helpless and sad.

From childhood, adolescence to youth and middle age, our lively memories of the New Year have faded or even disappeared. This may be an inevitable trend of social development.

The once strong flavor of the New year, nostalgia, and the lively scene of doing New year goods have all become pictures in memory. Only wish the Chinese traditional festival can be passed on forever.

# Because I had no academic qualifications, it took me 18 years to live as a decent ordinary person.

## 01

When I was in primary school, my composition was used as a model essay by my teacher. When I was in junior high school, my Chinese performance ranked 3 in the top seven classes in the whole grade.

I remember once the full score for my composition was 50, and I got 45. The composition title of the examination is based on the 1 document, which tells the story of 5 million losses caused by mistakenly writing "Urumqi" as "Urumqi" in the contract, which is intended to describe careless people.

Due to family reasons, I left the campus in the third year of junior high school. In order to save the examination cost, I did not complete the third year of junior high school. At the age of 14 and a half, I started making a living. At first, I did odd jobs in the village, such as making tin foil covers on beer bottlenecks in my cousin's factory.

Later that year, I began to learn sewing. As the village could not borrow money, my mother borrowed 450 yuan from her aunt's house, of which 420 yuan bought a butterfly sewing machine and 20 yuan bought a pair of Zhang Xiaoquan scissors of size 12.

I'm not sure if I like this business, but I remember engraving the words "where there is a will, there is a way" on my sewing machine.

The next year, I went to the town to continue to learn sewing, because there was not much work in the village facade to learn anything. I 4 fifty minutes to town by bike every day. The master in the town has "Reader" magazine and books by Bi Shumin and Liang Xiaosheng. This may be my first contact with literary works.

At that time, we had seven teachers and sisters and had little spare time to read. We didn't dare to look when the master was present. Every day, I have to help the master's house mop the floor, take care of the children, wash clothes and do chores. As the last apprentice to join, removing stitches, sewing feet, ironing, buttonholes, buttonholes and other chores are all my tasks.

In addition to these two books, I read almost no other extracurricular books during my childhood and adolescence. I'm not afraid of jokes. I don't even have a Chinese dictionary and I don't have a composition book at home. Compared with many people with family cultural background, I am many years behind in reading.

## 02

After studying sewing technology in the town for a year, I went to work in the coastal area, and the destination was Nanxing Garment Factory in Panjing Village, Dongshi Town, Jinjiang, Quanzhou, Fujian.

In the factory, my best friend and I are two special existence. Other people say that we like to talk like a book, in their view, this is a derogatory term. We are all children of the rainy season. At that time, the working hours were very long, from 8 a.m. to 2 a.m., but they were often delayed until 3 4 a.m.

Every night at 10 o'clock is supper time, almost all year round. Unless a batch of goods is finished and has a half-day rest, or the Mid-Autumn Festival and Dragon Boat Festival do not go to work at night.

Sometimes when the rice was still in our mouths, we rushed back to the workshop just to step on the flat car a few more times than others. In my first year in Fujian, I was still an apprentice. I worked hard all year round and only had 900 yuan when I came home. I caught up with the end of the mentoring inheritance and studied for a total of two and a half years.

Even in busy situations, I still like to extract lyrics, such as those of Zhang Xinzhe, Andy Lau, Ren Xianqi, and later those of Adu and Dao Lang. As long as a colleague bought the tape, I immediately borrowed it and copied the lyrics.

Sometimes there will be extra pocket cloth or defective cloth in the factory. I will arrange them, look at my heart and write on the pocket cloth. When I am free, I write things on it, sometimes copy lyrics, sometimes write diaries or regrets.

In that closed environment, I knew nothing about the future. Everyone compares who is more economical, who makes clothes faster, and whose salary is higher, but no one knows what the dream is and where to go in life. People are like machines, like tools.

When I am busy, I will read magazines for 10 minutes before going to bed, such as "Nanfeng", "Huaxi", "Reader", "Yilin", "bosom friend" and "Special attention.

The villagers next door laughed at us, saying that our dormitory was still awake so late, either reading or practicing calligraphy. They thought we were still village women years later, not believing our fate would be different.

In their eyes, my best friend and I became a different kind of factory. But I think, even if it is a village woman, I also want to be a village woman with thoughts and feelings.

I have been in the factory in Fujian for 4 years. In 2007, I also worked in a women's clothing brand factory in Wenzhou Chashan University Town for one year. In addition, I also worked in the down jacket shop in my hometown twice, each for half a year.

In 2007, there were many slogans on the wall of the women's clothing factory. I excerpted them all in my notebook, such as "we should not only race against time, but also care about needles".

In retrospect, perhaps the seeds of loving words have already been planted, but they have not met the right environment to take root and sprout. For many years, I have been forced to make a living for survival, and life is numb and boring. There are too many people in society who expend all their energy just to stay alive.

The best youth in my life was spent in a closed factory, the distant flower season, rainy season and dream season!

## 03

In the next few years, I worked in an electronics factory and tried my own business, selling snacks. My footprints are all over Luohe in Henan, Kuancheng in Hebei, Wenzhou in Zhejiang and Xi'an in Shaanxi.

From 2013 to 2015, I began to learn to use QQ on my mobile phone and accidentally met many literary friends in QQ space. Jumping from one literary friend's space to another, I seem to have entered a whole new world. Their log with pictures and music, look very beautiful.

I feel very happy because I can read so many excellent articles without spending money on books.

I like to leave messages and praise for their logs seriously and cherish these works very much. Although they may not have any impression on me as a reader, I occasionally send some news in QQ space. I also buy the books mentioned in their articles to read. Fortunately, there is an old book stall next to where I work, where I read many literary classics.

At the beginning of 2016, I learned about the simplified book through QQ group and downloaded the simplified book App. For the first few months, I was just reading, and I didn't write.

It was not until the middle of that year that I officially started writing and registered the WeChat public number "Qi Fan Qi". So far, the public has updated more than 1700 articles.

At the beginning of writing, because I still need to work during the day, I can only stay up late at night to write. From writing 1 articles in the first 10 days, to one article per week, to a stable 4 articles per week.

That year, I only slept for more than 5 hours most of the time. I find as much time as I can to read, write, typeset, and study self-media. I think this may be the last chance to change our fate.

I write a lot of stories about people at the bottom of the grass, because they are myself or people around me, and their stories are real and sensible.

For the platform, these stories are very fresh and the reading is very good. I have written about couriers, breakfast villagers, noodle sellers, wonton restaurants, paint sellers, etc. These are all down-to-earth and deeply rooted character stories.

In May 2017, I applied for the publication of an e-book and put it on Douban. The book was pushed to the front page and was screened for a long time.

In July of the same year, I became a contracted author of a brief book. At the end of August, my article was published on People's Daily Online, and the number of readings exceeded 100000 within two hours. At the same time, I also signed a Baidu platform. In other words, in more than a year of formal writing, I signed two large platforms.

At that time, the platform supported contracted authors to offer courses. Each signed author has his own agent. Through WeChat public number, course income and Baidu platform income, my income has far exceeded my main business.

In November 2017, I became my 1 full-time freelance writer. In 2018, I signed a book contract. In January 2019, my book "On the Road to Dreams, Let the Soul Shines" was published. In 2021, my student collection book "Meet Dreams, Meet Flowers" went on sale.

There are now four of my books on palm reading. At the same time, I also recommend the students to write nearly 200 books, recommend them to join various writers' associations, Chinese prose society, etc., and sign contracts with various platforms.

What makes me feel the happiest is not only that I have grown up because of words, but also that many people have adhered to the road of writing because of me, realized their literary dreams and saw more possibilities in the future.

Hope that friends can find inner love, love can help us find the light of happiness. Do love, heart is full of joy, is also the most easy to produce results. We must have the determination to stick to it and make reading and writing a spiritual breath.

There is no white road in life, and there is no white word in life.

Because of the family environment, no education, no background, I have experienced 18 years of going around, wandering, floating in the torrent of fate. All the experiences have become the best material for my writing.

I am very grateful to have met a great era of self-media, so that ordinary people can be "seen" when they continue to output content. Grateful meeting the simplified book platform gave me the source of motivation to write.

Writing has no age, education, status, gender, no time and space restrictions. I hope everyone can stick to it.

# Originally there was nothing, every inch was joy.

01

The same thing, different people feel happiness is different. That day, I read an article by a friend of the same 1. There was a sentence in it: "There is nothing in the first place, and I am very happy every step further." Let me feel deeply.

The author said that he came out of the mountains and when he was a child, he thought that owning a 1 new house was the biggest dream. Later, he read a master's degree in literature. During his graduate school, his articles were published on a large platform many times and three books were published. Just graduated last year, he relied on book royalties to make a down payment on his house in a provincial capital city.

This is the story of an ordinary boy who changed his fate by reading and writing. It can be seen that he is very satisfied with his life.

I am a person who has not even participated in the high school entrance examination. Now I can work with my mobile phone every day. I can read and write at any time, walk to meet people, participate in literary friends' meetings, go where I want to go, and take advantage of the time and the youth.

All this is what I did not dare to imagine in the past. Even though there is a big gap between me and my peers, I still have a strong sense of happiness. This is determined by everyone's mentality and the height of his bounce! As the saying goes, the contentment is always happy!

I registered a cultural media company in 2019, just to get out of the way. I don't like to say that I am the founder and CEO of the company, but I prefer to say that I am a freelance writer and online writer, which makes me feel more comfortable.

It was not until this year that I slowly accepted this identity, sometimes saying that I was the founder of a cultural media company. 1 I am not used to claiming this at first, it may be the reason for my low self-esteem and slow acceptance of new things. My mood needs a process of adaptation.

Before I wrote, the longest job I did was to make clothes in the factory. I also did a small self-employed business for several years. I set up a stall, worked as a salesperson for several months, and worked in an electronics factory for a period of time.

This year is my ninth year of reading and writing. I feel that it is only a blink of an eye. Everything is like a dream. Suddenly looking back, life has reached middle age.

## 02

The year before last, my second sister bought a small house in Hefei, Anhui province. she said she was so excited that she didn't sleep well 3 night.

We chatted in a small group and said how many people in Hefei bought 4-room houses, some of which were foreign-style buildings, villas and high-end school district houses, with an area several times more than her house, but they may not have such a strong sense of happiness as she did and will certainly not be excited like this.

In fact, my second sister has a school district house in the center of the county seat, with more than 120 square meters and good decoration, but she is still very happy to have a small house in the provincial capital. This is a person's happiness!

As the younger sister said, whenever you see good weather and see flowers blooming, you want to sing with joy. This is also a manifestation of 1 a good mentality.

Some people live a very good life and do not need to work as hard as we do, but their hearts do not have such a great sense of 1 pleasure.

From this point of view, our sisters are very lucky, can eat can not sleep long meat, a strong sense of happiness, a little bit of luck has a great sense of joy.

Every day we have endless topics in small groups. A literary friend once commented that your sisters are so good that they must have the same spiritual thoughts, otherwise they would not have so much to say.

Our generation of people born in the countryside, if they don't read any books and have limited horizons, they have to spend most of their lives or even their lives from the countryside to the county to the provincial capital on their own.

The first 1 generation from the countryside to the city is destined to be sacrificed, and the next generation will be better.

Today, I saw a sentence on Weibo: "Struggle! Your efforts alone can change the fate of three generations."

## 03

Not long ago, I sent a circle of friends feeling that I am a child of God's "food? After one year of zero-based writing, I wrote People's Daily Online and signed two well-known platforms. After one and a half years of writing, I signed a book contract and joined the Anqing Writers Association. Later, I became a member of the Anhui Writers Association and got a college degree from my own examination. Wait.

I think to a large extent, it comes from the blessing of opportunities and the combined factors of the general environment. Perhaps for many fellow celebrities, this is not an achievement, but for people like me who have never really written a long article before writing, this 1 a great encouragement. Thanksgiving karma opportunity.

When I was making videos for two months, there were two explosions, 260000 + and 190000 +. When I was doing the third live broadcast, the number of viewers exceeded 1000 and more than 30 new people were paid attention to. These screenshots were posted in the circle of friends. These are all my small fortune.

I often lament that there are different opportunities in life. Before writing, I have done several different jobs. I am confused and have accomplished nothing. I think, this is the way of my life!

Since writing, everything has gone smoothly. It seems that I have found the right soil, the right track for my own development, and realized everything I could not imagine.

Now, I have a very meaningful life every day. I influence many people who are not in a good mood through words, and use my words to warm them and give them strength and confidence.

At the same time, writing gives me a sense of mission and significance. Many people say that because of me, I insist on reading and writing. My mood is bright and my mental state is getting better and better. It turns out that words can both redeem themselves and save people.

My writing community can be said to be a group that has published more books in the market and joined the writers' association. A literary friend told me that you can link resources and have strong spiritual guidance, so students have achieved more results. I always think these are my luck, many of them are better themselves.

## 04

Today, I signed a contract with a cultural company to put online classes on shelves. My fourth book is undergoing its third review and is expected to be released by the end of the year or early next year. I don't make millions a year like my peers. I am not as bold and confident as some people. I have only been doing it for a year or two but have developed very fast. I crawl like a little snail.

At least 5 people said that I was sitting on a gold mine begging for food, thinking that I was too Buddhist, could not market and build, and had a low sense of self-worth.

They said, for example, you see XXX has only been on the Internet for two years, and his current income is n times that of yours.

Everyone has his development time zone, life is 1 marathon; everyone has everyone's way of life, or step by step, step by step to move forward.

Fame and profit can never be earned. It is good to improve steadily within the scope of one's own control.

Originally there was nothing, so every inch I entered was joy. My sense of value and happiness was no less than that of them.

## Writing is ultimately a contest between insight and mental models.

Many people think that writing is out of reach and that only professionals or highly educated people can do it. However, countless facts show that if you are willing to write, you can become a writer. As Wang Xiaobo said: "As long as you can speak, you can write." Writing, like speaking, is an expression, but in a different form.

Writing is not only a contest of literary level, but also a game of mental models. Except for a few people who have real literary talents, most writers rely on a lot of practice the day after tomorrow to constantly temper their language, improve their writing power and sense of language, from quantitative change to qualitative change, and finally realize their dreams.

Some people are self-doubting, self-limiting, self-wasting, and time passes in self-denial. When they grow old, they leave behind only sadness and chagrin.

I often hear people say, "Wait until my child is older, wait until I retire, wait until I have a quiet place in a big house, wait until I change to a relaxing job..." Such people usually don't write anymore, because they always feel that they have no time and can always find excuses for themselves.

Those who want to do it will find ways, while those who do not want to do it will find excuses. Each age group has corresponding troubles, and there are always trivial matters. But time is like water in a sponge. As long as you are willing to squeeze, there will always be time.

People who love to play games always have time, and people who love to play cards always have time. If you really love words and are determined to become a writer, you can find time to plan and enjoy writing. Creative work can bring the highest level of happiness.

Hemingway, Liang Shuming, Haruki Murakami and other writers

choose to concentrate on writing in the morning. Morning is the best time for memory and mental state, and the brain is more efficient after a night of rest. Scheduling important things like writing in the morning can make 1 feel relaxed and happy all day long.

Some people determine the direction of life very early and go on firmly. This kind of life is smoother, without detours or internal friction. However, most people's dreams have long been stranded due to the lack of environment and atmosphere in their early years.

Now, we have caught up with the golden age of mobile Internet. Since the media platform needs a large number of content creators, each platform also has a variety of incentive policies, such as guaranteed contract system, payment, sharing, bonus essay activities. As long as you have the ability to continuously output content, you don't have to worry about not having a chance.

Now is the era of information transparency, there is no lack of talent. Don't worry about age, education or writing level, the key is how long you can stick to it, one or two years? Can you write 500000 words or a million words?

Haruki Murakami said: "You can stick to things you like, but you can't stick to things you don't like." How to persist is a common problem. First of all to love the text, followed by self-discipline. It is best to have a few like-minded literary friends to encourage each other, or join the writing circle, and constantly stimulate potential.

Writing is ultimately not a contest of literary talent or literary proficiency, but a contest of thinking and insight, I .e., mental models. From my personal experience, writing is something that everyone can learn. As long as you have an idea, you can express it in words. When writing, imagine sitting opposite a person, chatting with him and saying what you think.

In life, many people are bound by traditional ideas, thinking that writing is unattainable, is a sacred existence, and is restricted by too many rules. They don't understand writing in the new media age. Since the popularity of 4G networks and smartphones, it has been an era of universal writing.

Whether you are an ordinary migrant worker or a cleaner, try to write a sentence or a paragraph with your mobile phone, and you can complete the whole article over time. As long as you are willing to register an account, you can become a writer. As the amount of writing increases and your ability to control words improves, you can become a writer in the eyes of others.

# Never remember, never forget

### 01

When reading the first 1 of books by peer writers, I noticed that they often wrote about their young and girlfriends, which gave me the urge to write and hope to include these stories in my books in the future.

My hair, Qi Xiaoyan, is one year older than me. We were classmates from preschool to junior high school. Even after being divided into classes in grade 3, we still go to and from school every day.

After graduating from junior high school, we worked together in the processing factory in the village, baking beer covers. But in the second half of that year, the small factory in the village closed. Xiaoyan went to Tongcheng to learn sewing, while I learned sewing in a shop near my home. Like our classmates who no longer study, we all chose to learn a craft. Elders often say, "craftsmen will not die of hunger in the famine year." Learning a craft is the long-term solution.

Xiaoyan is a simple and happy person, her optimistic personality and my pessimistic and sentimental contrast.

As far as I can remember, before I was in first grade, she always listened to me. We play together, dig mud, and sometimes even play to fight. But then I listened more to her.

In primary school, we used the nails of the notebook to make fishhooks, earthworms to make bait, bamboo sticks to make fishing rods, and fishing by the pond. On one occasion, I accidentally fell into the water, fortunately, Xiaoyan pulled me ashore in time.

We also went up the mountain to cut wood, dig loach in the fields, pick up peach kernels, dig pig vegetables, make wine with wild grapes, skip rope, jump house, kick shuttlecock, etc., and experienced many interesting rural things together.

In the last semester of the third year of junior high school, facing the tuition fee of 400 yuan, I decided not to go to school, but to work in a beer set factory, earning about 10 yuan a day. Xiaoyan has always advised me to continue to go to school, saying that in the last few months, we should stick to it and get a diploma, which is very useful for society in the future.

She instinctively persuaded me, perhaps hoping that we could go to school together and have a companion. I went back to school for a few months, but finally in the pre-examination, because of the examination fee of 180 yuan, I gave up my studies and bid farewell to the school examination-oriented education.

The village where our family is located is the farthest in the school. It takes more than 40 minutes to ride a bicycle one way. Every day before dawn, Xiaoyan would call me from behind the house to my door. We went to school together and were inseparable.

Xiaoyan makes breakfast by herself every day, while my mother told me to get up and eat it. Although my family's condition is not good, but the mother is the most dote on the child.

## 02

After studying sewing in our hometown for one and a half years, we all found different masters to take us to work in Fujian.

In the second year in Fujian, when my colleagues and I were shopping for clothes in the village market, Xiaoyan suddenly called me from a distance and waved to me like when I was a child. At that moment, I could hardly tell whether it was reality or a dream.

We came to work thousands of miles away from home, but we met in the same market. It turned out that her factory was in the town next door to us. I'm in Toshishi, she's in Ishinishi. Our factory produces beach pants and her factory produces jackets.

Occasionally, she and her colleagues will also come to our side of the market. She said that whenever she met fellow villagers from other factories, she would inquire about my news. At that time, everyone did not have a mobile phone, so it was difficult to connect. And now you finally see me.

The world is too small, Fujian is too small.

Since then, we know each other's factory location, every few months, we will ride a motorcycle to each other's factory to play. I also took several colleagues from the factory to her to play.

Every time, Xiaoyan will make good food for us. She will cook various dishes very early and buy many snacks. It seems normal now, but at that time we felt very happy, could rest and relax, and could get together to enjoy delicious food.

03

At the beginning of this year, my old colleague in Fujian sent WeChat to tell me that he had seen my hair somewhere in Tongcheng. She may not remember him much, but he remembers her. They passed each other in the street, but did not speak.

I asked, do you remember her? The old colleague said that I once took him to Xiaoyan's factory and saw our group photo. When I went to my house to play in the twelfth lunar month, Xiaoyan also came, so he was impressed.

Xiaoyan did well in the factory and did things quickly. That year, Quanzhou held activities, the factory celebration, selected 12 female colleagues to rehearse the program to participate, she and her cousin were selected.

Think of the soil and water in Tongcheng, Anhui, which is really nourishing! In such a big factory, they were both chosen.

A few days ago, when I was chatting with my daughter, I mentioned my hair. The daughter asked her how her life is now? I said it was quite good. She has a good character and works hard. After working in Fujian for a few years, she met a carpenter through the introduction of her uncle. After marriage, she stayed at home. Her home was very close to Tongcheng and worked in a nearby factory. Eight years ago, their family was demolished and divided into three suites, living an ordinary life of ordinary citizens, simple and comfortable. She has a son, the same age as you, who was admitted to Tongcheng No.1 Key Senior high school and may have a better result than you.

When I was young, I always wanted to leave Tongcheng, far away from my hometown, and felt that I didn't get enough love and respect in my hometown. It took many years to understand that the distance that everyone yearns for is not the hometown that others want to escape from?

If I hadn't left Tongcheng like Yanzi, I would have experienced a lot less displacement. After all, it takes only ten minutes to ride a motorcycle from our home to the center of Tongcheng City. Traffic became more convenient later.

Xiaoyan is an expert at housework. The life she chooses is very suitable for her. When I was young, I always wanted to go as far away as possible. I thought there would be a wonderful world in the distance. I didn't know how simple my idea was until I was middle-aged.

## 04

I envy Xiaoyan's character very much. People like her can live happily anywhere.

I often recall that when I was a child, we often clapped our hands and sang and danced: "little swallow, wearing a flower coat, come here every spring..."

About in the second grade, one day on my way home from school, I found a duck egg, which was light green. I took it and made up a jingle all the way, while Xiaoyan listened. I was born with divergent thinking, sensitive and pessimistic personality, she seems to have no, she has always lived happier than me.

In the fifth grade, we used to fantasize about going to town to do brushes or manes together after graduating from primary school, dreaming about what kind of beautiful bicycles to buy in the future, and imagining a beautiful work life. Every day on the way to school, we talk about these topics.

Who knows that the 1 paper policy popularized junior high school education. We had to go to junior high school 6 miles away from home. No one dared not go.

05

If I hadn't been able to catch up with the first nine-year compulsory education, I would definitely not have gone to junior high school. In that case, will I still write?

In fact, my junior high school Chinese scores are much better than those in primary school. Maybe I belong to a person who starts to understand very late. When I was in junior high school, I could easily get high marks in Chinese, English and history, and my Chinese scores were among the best in the whole grade many times.

Xiaoyan couldn't keep up with her studies in junior high school. Among the female classmates near my home, my junior high school results were the best.

If our 1 session still passed the quiz to select junior high school, neither of us passed the quiz, and more than 80% of the people also failed.

When we were in junior high school, we misread the time several times in the morning. The minutes and hours were reversed. We rode our bicycles to the school. Before dawn, we laughed helplessly.

On our way to school, we had to pass a hill early in the morning, surrounded by dark graves. It would be creepy to walk alone!

Xiaoyan is the person who accompanied me through my childhood, childhood and youth. The best years of my life were spent with her. She knew, participated and witnessed all my growth, misfortune, twists and turns, fatigue, happiness and progress.

Time flies, now our children are high school students, life is like a dream 1 a field.

Now we occasionally point out a compliment in the circle of friends. Sometimes we meet and talk in December. We usually don't have much communication, but this does not affect our important position in our respective lives.

Never deliberately remember, never forget.

## It took me 7 years to get up from the bottom of my life and become a content entrepreneur.

It took me 7 years to get up from the bottom of life. Content entrepreneurship is the most suitable way for ordinary people.

I'm the 1 Internet freelance worker with the moon in his left hand and sixpence in his right. In recent years, my monthly income has reached at least 50000 +, but this is inseparable from my accumulation and foreshadowing in previous years, as well as the great role of the Internet as an amplifier.

Internet content entrepreneurship is very suitable for those of us who have "no 3"-no background, no resources, no education.

I am the 1 80, junior high school did not graduate. As far as I know, my parents and the last three generations are illiterate and don't know a word. They can be said to be the bottom of the bottom.

I have studied sewing for two and a half years, worked as a garment factory assembly line worker for 6 years, worked as an electronics factory worker, worked as a salesperson, worked as a telemarketer, and opened a breakfast shop for several years...

How did I get out of life at the bottom?

1. Find your own inner love. Everyone has an ability more than 10000 people, that is your talent.

Since I was a child, people around me said that I have a good memory, sentimental and like words. I'm a super scumbag in science, but I'm doing well in liberal arts.

After the age of 2.30, I came into contact with the self-media, and the popularity of smart phones gave me the courage to write with mobile phones.

I began to write in the whole network under the pseudonym "Qi Fan Qi. It was very difficult to write 800 words in the first week, but now it is easy to write 3000 words + every day. I am not afraid of ridicule, not afraid of attack, insist on writing, optimistic about the trend of Internet self-media.

3. Text-centered, diversified development. I write copywriting, receive business manuscripts, write books, bring goods, distribute products, do community, live broadcast, etc.

4. Live a person as a team. I am a writer, editor, customer service operator, sales, bosom sister and blogger with goods. I am also a member of Anhui Writers Association and have signed a contract to publish several books. I am a typical compound worker.

I have been a freelance worker for 7 years. Only self-discipline can achieve true freedom.

It took me 7 years to drag myself out of the mire at the bottom. My life has undergone a qualitative leap, becoming what I like and affecting tens of thousands of netizens.

6. Learning ability is more important than academic qualifications, and growth is more important than success. Self-media content entrepreneurship mainly competes with perseverance, thinking and iteration ability, action ability and the ability to keep pace with the times.

7. To love as a career, to have a long-term thinking, and time to make friends, enjoy the benefits of time.

8. Appropriate to join some circles to learn, whether paid or free, their learning effect and energy absorption ability are completely different, and the degree of attention is also different.

# After middle age often hate past self

We Anhui Tongcheng City is a county-level city, under the jurisdiction of the prefecture-level city Anqing City. It is often said that Tongcheng City has the best economic development among the eight counties and one city under the jurisdiction of Anqing City, even surpassing the ancient city of Anqing. (In recent years, it has been changed and one county has been removed)

My hometown best friend once worked in Anqing for two months. What she heard most was: "Why do Tongcheng people come to work here? How nice Tongcheng is! Tongcheng people are smart or something..."(This may also be promoted by Tongcheng people themselves)

Brush factory can be seen everywhere in our hometown town, wool brush, wire brush, paint brush, roller brush factory... Everyone joked that the blind can encounter brush factory on the road. At the crossroads in the center of our town is a giant sign "Hometown of Chinese Brushes". Many people from mountainous areas will come to our town to work, and there are also a small number of people from other provinces.

Our next-door town-Tongcheng Xin'andu Town is the origin of plastic bags. It is said that 70% of China's plastic bags are produced in this town, and there are many packaging factories and printing factories.

Why did I spend two or three years studying sewing? And why did you go all the way to Fujian, 3000 miles away, to work as a working girl? In the first two or three years of working, it is common to work at 3 4 a.m. every night. I had to go to work at 8 o'clock in the morning until I was tired to vomit blood.

If I work locally, wouldn't I be the envy of others? Not to mention staying up so late to tire yourself out of trouble. In my hometown town or

Tongcheng City, I go to work early and come back late. I go to work by bike. Later, it is quite convenient to ride a motorcycle.

I can only say that when I was young, my brain was in water. If you are full of food and support, you have to find a sin. The more you think about it in middle age, the more you hate yourself. Don't go on the way, take the reverse road.

What is even more guilty is that my mother is a person with a very heavy heart for her children. Her illness later was mainly due to fatigue, and part of the reason was that she missed us too much and became ill. We can't be seen until the Chinese New Year in the first month. Every time I go out, she cries for a long time.

I had no idea that my mother's life was so short. If we hadn't gone to work in other places, I could have stayed with her for some more time, and maybe even she could have lived for some more years.

Young and ignorant! At that time, I heard that the salary in other places was high, several times higher than that in our family. My junior and a class of little sisters all go to other provinces to work, and very few people choose to work at home. This should be the ancients said "far fragrant near smelly!

When you really get to a foreign factory, the price of time is not much higher than the salary in our hometown. However, for the sake of so-called face, I was afraid that others would say that I would not be able to stay outside for fear of hardship. I did not return to my hometown in time to make a living and continued to suffer in other places.

Since I was dim and sensible, I have been eager to stay away from my hometown. I feel that I have not received respect and love in my hometown. When I grow up, I will stay as far away from my hometown as possible. But I didn't put myself in my mother's shoes.

Not only did I go out of town myself, I also took my second sister out. Originally, she worked in her hometown Tongcheng Printing Factory for more than two months. A few days ago, Second Sister also talked about when her mother sent her to work in Tongcheng. On this road in front of her house, her mother cried while walking. She felt sorry that she had to work in the factory every day when she was so young. Besides, I later took her to the Fujian garment factory...

People around you all say that learning a craft is a long-term solution. In the famine year, craftsmen will not die of hunger, and they have a skill that is stable. It is better to let your sister learn the craft with you. Sisters save money together quickly.

Years later, we were no longer in the sewing business. The sewing machine I used to cry and clamor for my mother to lend me money to buy was finally sold as scrap.

The essence of everything was that there was no insight, no Internet, no radio, TV, and extra-curricular books at home, and people were late and did not have their own opinions. What most people around me do, I will follow the crowd.

Inner cowardice, dare not bold to do self.

I am a person, just don't 1 a heart of my own!

After middle age, people hate themselves more and more.

# Literature is the last warmth of the world

There have been many netizens who were curious about my path to full-time writing. Looking back to 2014 and 2015, I was doing a small breakfast business in a village in Xi'an High-tech Zone. In fact, it is a temporary greenhouse with canvas on the iron frame and long rows of 1. The rent is collected by the village.

The street was crowded during the rush hour, surrounded by various snack bars, pots and pans clanging, full of human fireworks and the atmosphere of the market.

At that time, I inadvertently entered the QQ space with my mobile phone and indulged in it. After cutting and washing vegetables every afternoon and preparing the ingredients for the next day, I watched the shop and took out my cell phone to read the logs of friends in QQ space. From the space of one literary friend to the space of another 1, it is as if Columbus discovered the New World, allowing me to see another world away from the complicated world.

I remember that I also wrote a paragraph about the dynamics of demolition everywhere in Xi'an, lamenting how the demolished descendants found their spiritual home and where their soul habitat was. I often look at people in villages in the city in a daze and think, feeling the gap between people. It is often seen that migrant workers from construction sites wearing steel and glass caps and mud on their tooling come to buy steamed buns. They are reluctant to eat meat bags, mainly steamed bread, because steamed bread is more resistant to hunger. I sometimes look at those beautiful tall buildings and think, when can migrant workers who work so hard live in elevator houses?

I was born sentimental. In fact, I can't afford to live in that building.

I remember a friend of Anqing QQ space left me a message: "I can't see that you are still thinking deeply! Also for the demolition of people deeply touched, the somebody else compensation interest also can't eat..."

In the evening of the village in the city, the shouts of selling fruit, the ringing of tricycles, and the hurried footsteps of office workers are intertwined. What I like most is the old book stall next to it. The books are super cheap, which has become my favorite. The reading volume has greatly increased, and it is also my biggest nostalgia for the village. The four years in Xi'an, Shaanxi Province, a major literary province, have laid a good foundation for me to engage in writing later.

In April 2015, I transferred my stall back to my hometown and worked in the clothing factory in my hometown for several months. I put cloth on my skirt and made cuffs every day. The factory is dominated by middle-aged women nearby. They work more and get more according to piece work. They are suitable for taking care of families and children. They are better than being salespeople.

I am still busy, and I will look at QQ space text on my mobile phone and read the few books on hand.

The house in the town was also renovated. I had been doing this in the factory all the time, but the salary in the factory was lower than I expected. Go to the factory at 7:30 in the morning and come back at 10:30 in the evening. It is only 1600-2000 yuan a month. There is always a trace of heart is not reconciled.

In August 2015, my little sister called me to visit Shanghai. I want to try again! If there is nothing to do, I will still come back to work in my hometown at the end of the year. I began to prepare to work as a salesperson for a breakfast shop, including food and accommodation in 4000 yuan for January.

I helped in the hometown shop for a few days, and my little sister thought about it and said, "forget it! It is better for you to do this in your hometown!" She said she would find a chance to ask their company manager to see if she could introduce me.

My sister's company is an Internet company. 80% of its employees are mainly sales, with only a few programmers and designers.

My little sister's department manager is also our Anhui hometown, a post -85 woman. She asked little sister: "your sister computer office software can operate?" Little sister said: "no problem, I have taught the basic."

The manager thinks that the younger sister is excellent in her work and her sister should not be bad either. I bypassed the step of sending resumes and directly hired in the same department as my little sister. I became the person with the lowest academic qualifications in the company. I was older. Although there were people of the same age, they were old employees for many years.

Fortunately, there is nothing too profound in selling. At the beginning of a week of teacher training, about the company's development process, product introduction, phone calls and so on.

I have to make 200 or 300 calls every day. I can dial the phone without looking at the phone. If the customer is interested, he will extract the information from the notebook. Before leaving work every day, the number of email addresses of intended customers should be sent to the manager and copied to the director. The forms have ready-made templates and are not too complicated.

On both sides of my seat are college students who have just left school. They can't teach me computer knowledge.

It's just that my client writes some good words and sentences and paints every page of this book. For example: "Life is as gorgeous as summer flowers, death is as quiet as autumn leaves", "When you are old, you will feel sleepy...". Sometimes I will write a few words with emotion, but they are all broken.

This job is the first weekend job in my life. Although I often have to go to the company for training and meeting on Saturday, which is actually a single break, I am still very satisfied and happy for me.

At that time, I would read a lot of public articles on the weekend after work, and my heart was stirring. I felt that I wanted to burst out a lot of emotions and have a lot to say to the world.

I was in such an environment and mentality. With the help of my colleagues, I registered the WeChat public account "Qi Fan Qi Wei Journal" in 2016, which officially opened the road of writing and changed my destiny.

In the second half of 2017, my side business far exceeded my main business. I returned to my hometown and started writing full-time. In 2018, he signed the first 1 book "Let the Soul Shine on the Road to Dreams" and joined Anqing Writers Association, Anhui Writers Association and China Prose Association. Registered cultural media company, do MCN content matrix. In 2021, the "Everyone Can Learn to Write" and 4 collection books will be published.

I stumbled to become the 1 freelance writer and content entrepreneur. Through words as the fulcrum, I realized the great leap of spiritual material. Free control of time, financial freedom, to achieve the value of life and meaning.

My past life-studying sewing machine career, 8 years of running water work in coastal garment factories, working as a salesperson, an electronics factory worker and several years of breakfast shop experience-all these past life experiences are superimposed, so that I have no shortage of materials on my writing road. What's more important is that I have a deeper experience of the life of ordinary people at the bottom, feel the cold world and the warmth of human feelings, and let my words have a stronger empathy, because I am one of the 1 members.

Many readers and netizens said that my writing has a strong sense of substitution, which is very real and grounded, and has a sense of the times. Perhaps this is an encouragement to me, but I know that my article also has a lot of immature places, and I hope that the readers of this book can forgive me and correct me.

The book is only a summary of the past writing path and an encouragement to oneself. The work you are satisfied with should always be in the next one.

Much of this book is about my personal growth and my mental journey to life. Although I am a post-80s generation, my words can also resonate with many post-60s generation. I started the society very early, have a good memory, and at the same time I was in the torrent of online self-media, thus realizing the rise of individuals. I believe that people after 95 can also find some value in my words.

With regard to rural life, those long memories, childhood and adolescence, the text salvages and backs up our fading past and makes it eternal.

People who write words are happy. We can live our whole life into other people's two lives: one is the real world; the other is the spiritual world.

The Thanksgiving era gives ordinary people the opportunity to have so many writing platforms to place our writing dreams.

After "On the Road to Dream, Let the Soul Shine", "Just Be the Only Me, Not the Second Who", "Left Hand Moon, Right Hand Sixpence", I will continue to explore, think and record.

# Often feel loss

WeChat and WeChat communities have greatly facilitated the masses of the people and made social contact more convenient. Today, even rural people in their 70 s can use WeChat proficiently. In the early years, it was often said that young people were addicted to mobile phones, but now this group of old people seem to be even more addicted. They like to brush trembles and watch iQiyi videos.

In my hometown, there are many life service communities, such as recommend and working communities, carpooling groups, carpooling groups, etc. For example, from our hometown to Anqing, Hefei, Hangzhou and other places, there are people who provide relevant services. As long as someone posts travel information, mobile phone number and number of passengers, someone will be contacted soon. There are also people who make recommend introductions and are responsible for transportation. The price is very affordable, which is more convenient and cost-effective than driving or taking a bus.

Once when I was crossing the Anqing Yangtze River Bridge in a taxi, the driver made a 1 circle to get on the bridge. We asked him why he did this, and he said it would save bridge tolls. Ten minutes can save 21 yuan money, the driver thinks it is very cost-effective. Several elder sisters nearby also said that they would save some money by letting their families and relatives do the same next time. I laughed and said it was "the wool of the country".

Drivers talked about the hard work of their industry. Every sports car driver is an occupational disease. In order to 3 a business of 4 yuan, it sometimes takes an hour or two. Others have surgery on their backs and are no longer able to drive.

Every industry no longer has dividends at the later stage, only to earn some hard money. As a driver, this is not only a technical job, but also the consumption and maintenance of the vehicle, which requires a high degree of attention and consumes time and energy. At today's prices, if there is no monthly income of 10000 +, I really feel very worthless. Pay and harvest has been out of proportion.

Taxi drivers were a very prosperous industry before 2014, when operating licenses were very valuable and were hyped up. If a family had its own operating license and vehicle, the life at that time was very moist. There are also people who transfer their vehicle license plates to others to drive and earn the difference by lying down.

However, the emergence of the network about the taxi, sports car carpooling industry is 1 a major revolution.

What impressed me most was that when I was taking a taxi in Hefei, the driver talked about something that made him regret for life. His old watch bought a house in Hefei with money at the same time, and he also borrowed money for his old watch. At about the same time, he gritted his teeth and pooled his money to buy a taxi license.

Soon, the operating license fell sharply, and the house of his old watch appreciated rapidly a few years later. The money of the house appreciation was more than the money he earned from running a taxi for 6 years. The teacher said that he had borrowed money several times to buy a house for his relatives, but he didn't know he was going to buy it. When his own son grew up, he could only choose the insulation layer on the roof and the old building without elevator. He regrets that he missed the best golden period to buy a house.

I have to say that many times the choice is greater than the effort, but everyone's choice is the result of combining their own thoughts and cognition and weighing the pros and cons.

Sometimes, I think that it seems easy for some people to make money by doing community, IP, live broadcast and delivery, and workplace consultation on the Internet. Traditional offline and online are already two worlds.

On that day, a netizen in the Yimi group said that offline and online were already 100 times more shocking. I said that the traditional offline and online lines have formed a very clear separation, which is no longer the same.

I closely observe the online and offline two groups of people, often filled with emotion, but also very anxious, heart split. How long can the internet last? Artificial intelligence is so advanced that it may subvert and eliminate us in the near future. BAT may become a traditional company, no business is long-term, no model will not be reformed.

Where will the train of the times go?

Yesterday, I saw in a book that a post-90s girl was called "rich second generation". Her parents quit their jobs in the system in 1992 and went into business. They had 9-figure assets and were already one of the heads in Zhangjiajie.

She said her father had retired at the age of 60, fishing every day and was cheated of some money every year. Since the girl did the Internet, the probability of her father being cheated is much less, because his father will ask her anything.

When her mother recalled that year, she said that in the face of great wealth, people have a great impact on their hearts. Many successful people of the generation who started their own businesses under the reform and opening up cannot hold on to so much wealth. 1 is a more profound knowledge to be able to control wealth.

The girl thinks her mother is more gifted in business vision. In 2002, her mother bought a lot of land use rights, and her father thought it was boring to be a "landlord. He was born as a doctor and began to study traditional Chinese medicine since he was a child. He studied Confucianism first and then medicine. He always felt that he should do research and development to create greater value for the city. As a result, he basically lost everything. If it weren't for the fact that there was still some land in the city center when the company was bought, it would be absolutely insolvent now. Her mother's prediction came true.

Due to the different perspectives of her mother and father on social and economic development, they divorced and separated after 2002, which saved most of the achievements of starting a business in the sea.

This girl thinks that the family is also an organization, and it is also a primitive production organization of the smallest unit. When the organization does not have the ability to increase productivity, it is natural to consider the best partner to build momentum together.

The girl said that her father never met anyone as good as her mother.

Her parents have enjoyed the dividends of the times, and she believes that she cannot surpass her parents in any way in this life. But she wants to prove that she is no worse than her parents and can achieve financial freedom on her own.

She does the local US group business. When the company matures, she gets half of her income every year and the other half rewards the team. She went to Hangzhou to do some things related to the Internet, which was enough to realize financial freedom.

In the face of the torrent of the times, the choice of parents will affect the whole family, even the later generations. But when anyone faces a choice, no one knows whether it is right or wrong.

# My village, my dream

In 2002, my family has built a new building, but countless times in the dream is my old house, my father built 3 adobe house, rainy days, heavy rain outside, light rain inside. But the memory is still a lot of happy time, so that the new house, never appeared in my dream.

In my memory, my mother shouted at the top of her voice: sail, eat, come back to eat! Don't come back, like savages every day, crazy outside.

I understand very late and don't understand. I only care about playing. It seems that I don't understand anything else.

I like to play outside with my friends, fight, catch shrimps, play, run wildly and don't return home. I just don't like to stay quietly at home anyway. My mother used to call me like a "savage". The elders of the family joked that I had the wrong baby and was suitable for being a boy.

On the right side of my house is a hillside, where my family's land has planted peanuts and mung beans. I still remember a scene when my mother and I planted sweet potatoes there on a rainy day. There are also fragments of wheat and rapeseed that are often beaten on the dojo.

In our village, one person has eight fields, one family has several plots of land, and one plot of land usually 3 4 ridges. Belonging to small hilly areas, the fields are not fertile. If you don't plant it, you won't be able to bear it. The fields don't actually bring much real income.

When I was a child, I heard from my grandmother that she was not only a poor farmer, but also a poor farmer and a famous poor family in the village. When the system of dividing farmland into households was implemented, the village was really too bitter to see our family. We gave three more farmland to grandma as welfare to take care of the poor.

That's terrible. Several families in the team jumped their hands and feet to make trouble for a whole month. There are people in the Jianghu, since ancient times, any environment is the same.

When I was studying, grandma said to herself alone and sighed to me a little bit: in those days, the village had more fields to take care of my poor man. who made such a fuss and scolded so hard behind the house? now everyone in the fields doesn't like planting any more. for 30 years, hedong and 30 years, hexi!

Now I have sons who farm, and I have sons who eat commodity grain. No one in the field is too rare.

My uncle can eat commodity food, is entirely his own idea. My grandmother didn't have this vision and idea, and the family didn't have that ability.

My uncle was very smart in reading since he was a child. When he read that his grandparents in the second grade told him not to read, he had no money to read and came back to help his family. My uncle grew up sensible, diligent and filial.

When he had his own ideas on important events, his uncle was in his early 1.8 meters tall, and he secretly went to the village to sign up for the army. When everything became a foregone conclusion and the village came to inform him, my grandmother knew about it. 1 face was puzzled and then burst into tears.

It is said that my grandmother sat on the ground and cried all day that day. She cried because there was no one in the family to do anything. Grandpa has been in poor health and has a bad temper. It is good to hit people. The eldest son has left and there are no capable cadres. How can we live this day...

Good-hearted people around us persuaded that everyone would join in to help. Being a soldier is to exercise and learn. This is to contribute to the country and comfort everyone. My uncle took the initiative this 1 and directly changed his own destiny.

After two or three years as a soldier, he returned to his hometown and was told to become a full member to work in Anqing Chemical Fertilizer Factory with a city hukou. In those days, there was a shortage of workers in factories all over the country. It was a time when there was a shortage of talents. My cousins and cousins later became Anqing city dwellers.

There are only two people in our Qiwu team who eat commercial food, and my uncle is one of them. The other 1 is the principal of the middle school.

My grandparents were illiterate and my family was so poor. The uncle who has read only two years of books has become a regular worker, eating the country's food and getting a salary. Only in that era did he have a chance to realize it! This is also the magic of fate.

A few days ago, my aunt also told me that my uncle's earliest dormitory was also divided into housing funds, which was enough for her to provide for the aged. In 2000, they bought commercial housing in full. At that time, most people did not have the awareness of mortgage loans, so they could use the principal to make two sets. Later, my cousin settled down in Hefei.

Now, uncle is almost 80 years old. I think he is already in his time, so the starting point of the family has reached the ceiling. Already counted as a very lucky person.

A few years ago, uncle returned to his hometown to take care of his grandmother. They also planned to go back to the countryside to build a small hospital for the aged.

Uncle now walks and exercises every morning and evening. He is in a very good mental state and loves flowers and plants. He also grows fields and raises chickens and ducks so that his cousin can eat the crops from his hometown.

My village, my dream. This is the root of our life, but also the source of the writer's creation. Go back to the village where 1 was born and write at least ten articles...

# The path of self-healing

Once upon a time, every time I went back to my hometown of Qiwu, there was a lot of pessimism spreading. When I reached middle age, I gradually learned to heal myself and compromise with fate and everything around me.

We sisters stand chatting on the rice field at the gate of our hometown, or washing things by the pond. There will always be some old people who watch us grow up whispering. Their topic is mainly that these children are very neat, very motivated and capable, and do not lose to other boys. Unfortunately, their parents are not blessed. If they are still there, they can wake up laughing when they fall asleep.

There will also be old people who say that they did not expect that her parents, such good old people, raised several children, are more capable than our children, but it is a pity that good people suffer from bad karma.

When I go back to my hometown and look at my family and my childhood playmates, I will sigh in my heart, why other people's parents are healthy and healthy, why so many people live more than twice as old as my parents, and how can there be such a big gap? Why is everyone else so happy?

Why so many people can easily and naturally have the perfect in the world?

The day before yesterday, I asked my aunt, when I was a child, those playmates were young, what are they busy with now? Home or in the field? There are four of us who played well when we were young. They are one year, two years and 3 years older than me.

The little aunt said that one made a mold on the construction site in Tongcheng city, the kind of mold on the roof of the house. A foreign exhibition hall, set up exhibition shelves; There is also my good friend Yanzi making clothes in the street factory. Her son is very smart in reading. In the key class of our Tongcheng No. 1 Key Senior high school, their home is close to the city. Because of the expansion and demolition, there are also several houses.

The little aunt said you don't have to ask them, less than your career. I just ask habitually. I have never felt how good I am, and they are all very good!

In my mind, I recalled the past when I lost handkerchiefs with my friends, played with the police to catch thieves, went to the mountain to catch firewood, went to the river to catch fish, built pots together, caught stones together, played with raw dolls together, went to the ridge to catch pig grass, learned to ride bicycles, etc. That is the most happy life, the most worry-free time!

Xiaoyan and I were in the same class from preschool to grade 2 and sat at the same table. When we were learning calligraphy in the third grade, we were 1 unhappy. We took a brush and scribbled on each other's face and clothes. We were called to the office by the teacher.

At that time, she waited for me to go to school every day. After graduating from junior high school, we learned sewing skills together and followed different masters to work in Jinjiang factory in Fujian.

My aunt smiled and said, you are a better woman in Qiwu village. In fact, life only to the old time to know how life in the end.

Hearing some words from my elders, I am more 1 a kind of pressure and more 1 a kind of exclamation. Everyone is walking along the track of their own destiny and is trying to live seriously.

If fate can be chosen and changed, I certainly don't want such wealth as suffering. I definitely want to have a smooth and complete life.

Once in my father's article, I wrote that I would rather be a few centimeters shorter, darker and fatter in exchange for his longevity.

Seeing that many people's parents in their 50 s and 60 s are still alive, it is really a comparison between people and people! I only have the envy of the heart.

Now whenever I am pessimistic, I have learned to heal myself and think of what Anne Baby said to look at this world from the height of the universe.

Life in the world to complete his mission, and then go to the next cycle. Sick and dead, is a subject that everyone has to face. Past life cycle of cause and effect, and each person face the time is different sooner or later.

What kind of life will we experience in different time and space in the next life?

Last year, a literary friend told me that a special editor of a platform cried for 3 days after interviewing me in 2017. I was so surprised that I felt really guilty and let others cry for a few days. I didn't know before, I couldn't even remember the name of the special editor.

I just calmly narrate the experiences that I carry on my body 1 a kind of expression, as if I were telling someone else's story. I didn't feel much difficult except when I was in a bad mood occasionally. There are many people in the world who have experienced misfortune earlier than me, experienced more suffering and lived very tired. I have been lucky.

Man is always a contradiction of existence. No one is absolutely happy or unhappy, and happiness is only a short moment of feeling. More often, everyone in this world has to face the chicken feathers in life, the swords and swords in life, until the end, it is considered to have completed the life experience of this life.

When our thoughts enter a dead end, we must learn to self-regulate and self-heal.

Look, another bright day.

# Everyone is in their own fate.

Once upon a time, I always felt like this in my life. It is their business for others to be excellent. They have a good starting point, a happy family and excellent academic qualifications. As for me, I dropped out of school early in the third year of junior high school. My mother is a "good old man" commonly known in the countryside, and is the object of common contempt by people around me. My father died early. Such a family background is the arrangement of fate. I have no choice.

In those days, the old family often said, "craftsmen will not die of hunger in the year of great famine". My friends who dropped out of school and I all went to learn sewing, while the boys learned to be carpenters, bricklayers, etc. I also went along with the flow to join the ranks of learning sewing.

When I left school, my heart was full of joy.

After learning sewing for a year and a half, in 2000, I followed my fellow masters to a village factory in Dongshi Town, Jinjiang, Quanzhou, Fujian, thousands of miles away to do assembly line work. There, I continued to study motor for another year. In that factory, 1 stay is four or five years.

Later, I made clothes in Wenzhou and Hangzhou, and also made down jackets for others at the store in front of my home. Looking back now, I don't know how those years came.

When I was in that factory in Fujian, I worked until 2: 00 a.m. to 4: 00 a.m. every day, all year round. Ten o'clock every night is supper time, finish eating and then continue to work. Food taken late at night is nothing more than a dollar wonton, or crispy rice, or 1 bowls of noodles. This is the legendary "sweatshop" and the first half of China's industrialization, and I am just a small screw among tens of millions of people.

The big yard of the factory is like a cage. I used to fantasize about studying while working, improving my academic qualifications and changing my fate. But the reality is impossible. I fall asleep every day when I am too tired. I doze off at work and even fall asleep when I go to the toilet. The village is remote, surrounded by factories, where there is night school or vocational school? There is no time, environment or money to learn.

The outside world is not as good as imagined. Although it is prosperous and wonderful, it is also helpless. People can't fight fate, they have to learn to reconcile with themselves.

We often see large trucks in the factory, and the boxes of packed clothes are the fruits of our colleagues' labor. It is said that the clothes will be sent to Hong Kong and then to African countries. The boss of our factory is only a third-grade cultural person. Their brothers all run factories, but they used to sell cattle and vegetables. They later met the reform and opening up and the dividends of the region. He has a sister who specializes in receiving foreign trade lists in Hong Kong. The brothers quickly became rich and became more powerful figures in that village.

We migrant workers and migrant workers are all their tools to make money. At that time, the employees in my factory were mainly from Sichuan, Jiangxi, Guizhou, Hubei and Anhui.

Time is in a hurry, years have passed, and a new era has come. The popularity of mobile Internet, with a mobile phone can write and publish, I am one of the beneficiaries of this wave. From the beginning, only 600 words can be written to 1 thousand words, and then to 2000 or 3000 words, one word at a time, one book at a time, and redouble efforts to make up for the inherent deficiencies.

Thanks to God's love, after writing on my mobile phone for one and a half years, I realized full-time free writing, signing a contract platform, publishing books, joining the provincial writers' association and taking an examination of the university. After 5 full-time years, I have achieved all-round leapfrog growth.

In the mobile Internet is booming period, I also entered the 30 +. Through the network, I opened my eyes, enhanced my vision and realized my self-awakening. Once a woman awakens, she will be indestructible. For the rest of my life, I will strive to bloom and realize the meaning and value of life.

The Fujian factory where I was then has been going downhill since 2010. The added value of foreign trade itself is very low, and the treatment given to employees is limited. Many people would rather choose to work in their hometown than go so far away.

In that village in Fujian, many bosses moved their factories to Yunnan and Myanmar. The women's clothing factory I once worked in Wenzhou is a domestic brand. In recent years, the domestic environment and peer competition are fierce, and the probability is becoming more and more difficult.

I also made clothes for two custom down jacket shops in my hometown, but they didn't open them later. One transformed to open a hotel and the other to become an e-commerce company. They said that there are too many semi-finished down jackets now, and finished clothes are sold so cheaply and fashionable that hand-made down jackets have no market competitiveness at all.

There is a wife of shop-owner, little bing elder sister, I once wrote her growth story. In the first month of the year before last, I went to her house to play. She was surprised that I took the road of writing. She now opens a shop in Tmall. Her brother-in-law does customer service for her. There are several people in the family who make clothes. Small ice elder sister don't have to rely on the flow of people in the street in the past, just make clothes in her living room.

Xiao Bing Jie is 4 years older than me. Her life is another version of inspirational story. She grew up reading first grade each year. One day at the end of the fourth grade, she came home happily with a certificate of merit, but her mother ran away from home and never came back. She stood at the intersection countless times and looked out, hoping that her mother's shadow would appear.

Her mother once said that Xiao Bing was so good at studying that she would have to pay for her to study in the future, but she finally left. Her father was one of the few fathers who would never read to her again. It was all small ice elder sister who begged relatives to intercede and tried her best to barely read the second day of the junior high school.

When Sister Xiaobing was 12 years old, her father tailored her with hoes, poles, and baskets. They went out to work together. As long as she walked slowly, her father yelled at her from behind, kicking and beating her. Her father thought it was useless for girls to study, to do farm work at home, and to marry someone in their village at the age of 30. Later, Sister Xiao Bing learned sewing technology by borrowing a sewing machine from her cousin. She relied on herself and her father to fight and negotiate many times.

She once said that when she was a child, she hated her mother very much. Why did she run away from home. When she grows up, she understands that such a father is really difficult to get along with. No wonder her mother can't get along.

When I helped make clothes for Xiaobing's shop, she also told me that when she was a child, her mother took her away from home and begging while walking. She was given a piece of meat to her mother, and she picked it up and stuffed it 1 her mouth. From then on, she was nicknamed "delicious guy". Her mother had several experiences of taking her away for a short time. Perhaps she wanted to try to take Xiao Bing with her, but she was powerless and left her at home.

Sister Xiao Bing works in Shanghai, doing chores in a clothing factory, cutting thread ends, doing small scalding, making running water, making whole pieces, and then making sample clothes and board design. She also likes reading literature books, know a lot of knowledge.

The 1 thing that touched me most about Sister Xiaobing was that she asked a fellow villager to borrow a clothing model book, which was difficult to buy in Shanghai. She used her off-duty time to copy down all the thick sample books. What kind of 1 spirit is this! In the years she has been making sample clothes, she has been teaching herself in her spare time.

She opened a shop in our town, designed clothes, and learned all by herself. Many people in this world are so serious and hard to live, these are the silent majority.

I often think that if Sister Xiaobing's mother had not left, if she had been born in a slightly better family, if she had met a better platform, with her intelligence and enthusiasm, her life would have been hundreds of times better than it is now!

Being born as the bottom of the bottom, meeting that kind of family, that kind of father. Now Xiaobing elder sister in the same background, is also a complete life, career small success, completed self-transcendence.

She ended her working years after the age of 30 and went back to her hometown to open a shop. A few years later, we turned to online store operation. We all woke up after the age of 30 and realized our self-growth.

Looking back on the time when I used to make down jackets for several months in winter at Sister Xiao Bing's house, I was very happy every day. She is cheerful, humorous and funny. She is a person who loves life and is full of energy. No matter how bitter the past is, she can say it with a smile.

Once, a customer came to ask which is the "wife of shop-owner". I was burying my head in making clothes. Sister Xiao Bing was sweeping the floor. She said, "Look, it must be the wife of shop-owner who is sweeping the floor! That's me." Another time, I asked her to zipper accessories accessories, she pointed to the floor tiles on the ground with a long ruler, body a turn, laughed and said: "one two three, sail qi, please look at the big screen..." I laughed so much that my stomach hurt.

Sister Xiaobing also talked about her husband working as a decoration bricklayer near her factory. When he was free on rainy days, he GG1 her to hang out together. In order to sit in the front of the car, he gave off the back seat of the bicycle. This is another funny story.

She just started to learn sewing machines. The 3 month training course required 150 yuan for tuition. Her father did not support it, and she did not have any money. Her cousin promised to borrow the sewing machine. She came up with an idea and went to the owner of the training class to mortgage her tuition with the sewing machine. I went to the mill many times to talk about it, and finally the boss was kind enough.

The past is like smoke. It has been more than ten years since I made down jackets in Xiao Bing Jie's store. She said a lot of things, very interesting and interesting, some people think, some people feel heavy. There are laughter in tears, tears in laughter. This is life! This is all beings!

People like Sister Xiao Bing can live well in any situation, be happy and contented, and be good at creating happiness and happiness. Such mentality and spirit are worthy of admiration and learning.

The rolling tide of society, the wheel of time flies, the continuous iteration of various industries, enterprises, factories, individual stores and individuals are all exploring the ups and downs in their own destiny trajectory. We are all passers-by in this vast world and have our own destiny.

## impermanence is life, good attitude is the most important

I heard today that civil servants in a county next door to our hometown will be paid once every two months from April this year. This is how many years will happen once!

It is said that 20 million yuan is not enough to pay all civil servants in the county. There is also a public kindergarten in the county seat. In the past, teachers were paid monthly whether they had a holiday or not. Now the teachers take turns on duty, one person works for a month, and the teachers who don't work have no money that month.

Suddenly sighed, our generation is witnessing history! We have witnessed the rapid development of real estate for 20 years, like a wild horse running fast. People who catch real estate dividends in time make a lot of money. Housing prices have become the best "weapon" to erase young people's dreams ".

For those who did not keep up with the real estate train in the past, wealth has also been harvested invisibly, and the currency is devalued massively.

I have also personally experienced the squeezing of coastal sweatshops. The workers in the factory work every day and night. They are really people like machines. I don't get off work until early morning every day, and it gets light when I take a bath after work in summer. There are no holidays all the year round. Only on the nights of Mid-Autumn Festival, Dragon Boat Festival and National Day do not work overtime. That is the "holiday" in the eyes of the boss ".

What is even more absurd is that garment factories, including all the factories nearby, do not pay their employees together until the end of the year. Every year, I go to the factory after the Lantern Festival in the first month and go home in the twelfth month, as if I have sold it to others all the year round.

Usually only the 10th, 20th and 30th of each month borrow living expenses. Some colleagues borrowed 50 yuan, some 100 yuan, some 70 yuan and most 100 yuan.

With this amount of living expenses, we will save and save, deduct a little and send it back in an envelope. I am still confused. It is clearly the hard-earned money earned by our workers, and the word "borrow" is still used.

I still remember that on the evening of the 10th of each month, the boss's daughter came to the workshop with a bag on her back, and the colleagues were in a commotion. They were very excited and could borrow money! Some colleagues whistled, some snapped their fingers, a rare moment of joy.

Each of our workers took the yellow account book with his own clothes to queue up. The boss's daughter wrote someone's number to borrow 100 yuan on the account book. Then our employees signed and got the 100 yuan she sent. She humbly said, "Thank you, thank you." It seems that the boss gave it to us, grateful.

At that time, we used our own sewing thread to make clothes. Of course, everyone liked to rob the S-size clothes to make them, which could save thread and time. There is a big difference between S and XXL, and occasionally there are disputes over small size clothes.

Now it seems that none of the factory regulations in that factory are in line with the labor law. Why does everyone take it for granted? The factories in the surrounding villages all look like this.

Why did I stay in this factory for four or five years? Later, he also made clothes in Wenzhou, Hangzhou and his hometown. Why didn't you dare to jump out of that circle, even if you were a salesperson or salesperson, it would be better to be closed in the factory, and your thinking and vision would be opened earlier.

Why didn't I go to Guangdong? Later, I heard that there are single holidays and libraries in some factories.

Why don't I know how to find someone, get a Secondary specialized school certificate to apply for a sales front desk or something? Last time I saw a woman in a video who also dropped out of school early, but she spent money to get a Secondary specialized school certificate, applied for a 4S store sales, and later became a luxury salesperson. She was open-minded and confident.

A few days ago, I saw another woman in the community sharing. She also dropped out of school very early, but she was more courageous and courageous than me. After working in the factory for half a year, she decided to learn computer and later applied for a merchandiser.

Looking at their stories, I feel that they are so flexible and smart. Why were they so stupid and became tool people in their best years.

At that time, people seemed to be numb. Teachers and villagers could do whatever they said. My mind only thinks about how to save money, how to try to improve my work speed, how to repay my family's debts earlier, and when to build a building for my family. In case you change your job, change your environment and 1, you will have no money, so you don't even dare to change your industry, even if you change your factory.

Salespeople and other jobs, no matter whether they eat or live, can't save money. After all, they are still poor and short-minded!

Anyway, I didn't have a choice back then. If the years can go back to that year, I will definitely have to stay in the garment factory for so many years.

After 2013, the emergence and popularity of smartphones marked the end of one era and the beginning of another. The major self-media platforms were born, and you sang and I appeared on the stage, just like the princes of all parties in ancient times. Each platform has different tonality characteristics, bustling and bustling.

Microblog, WeChat Public Number, Today's Headline, Jianshu, Baijia Number, Netease and other platforms have given ordinary grassroots a chance to speak out, and as a result, countless people have been achieved.

The popularity of mobile Internet enables everyone to get information quickly. Even if big things happen in distant countries and distant provinces, after a minute or two, the entire network will be overwhelming, and anyone can see it by turning on their mobile phones. The Internet makes the world flat.

The Douyin video platform has reached hundreds of millions of users in more than two years, which is simply miraculous. Both 4-year-old children and 80-year-old people like to play with tremolo. TikTok (Douyin Overseas Edition) is also very popular abroad and is said to have a tendency to surpass Twitter.

Where there is a market, there is demand. On the US takeout, a little on the phone, the food you want will be delivered to you. If you need to go out, make an appointment for a car on your mobile phone in advance, and a professional will be your driver. Don't worry about driving, don't worry about finding a parking lot, and take a nap in the car.

WeChat transfer and remittance, bank APP transfer on mobile phones are seconds...

Our generation also experienced the familiar postal green logo of the past post office filling in money orders to send money. When I was a child, I also saw telegrams, wrote countless hand letters, used magnetic card phones, and had high telephone bills. Now as long as there is a wireless network, even if separated by thousands of mountains and rivers, can see each other.

Live delivery, artificial intelligence, driverless...

Someone once said: "Taobao is not dead, China is not rich." Now the live broadcast of various platforms with goods is booming, which is the trend of the times.

The rise of an industry, there will be another industry in decline. Every great change is the redistribution of social wealth resources.

Over the years, society has undergone earth-shaking changes. We are all experienced and participants. We are all witnessing history!

In the future, where will our social "big ship" eventually go? Under the raging waves of the times, what kind of life trajectory will we have as individuals?

# Do you have such a landlord aunt?

Whether you are in Beijing, Shanghai, Guangzhou, Shenzhen, or in any other city, in our memory, in our wandering years, there will be an unforgettable landlord aunt.

I have seen many famous artists write about their landlords, and I still remember that Chi Zijian's landlord is the 1 Jewish descendant of nearly 80-year-old exiled Harbin-Jilena. She loves clean, tidy, elegant, and loves music. And art...

I also want to record my landlord in clear and shallow words. I have been in Shanghai for two years. The rented house is located in a relatively high-end community near Century Avenue in Pudong. I am quite satisfied with its greening, safety and geographical location, and it is adjacent to Metro Line 6 and Line 7.

The landlord's aunt is 1 50-year-old Shanghai native. She seems to have a smile on her face at any time and speaks softly and slowly. Her skin was very smooth up close, without the wrinkles she should have at her age. She said she was in a good mood and didn't like to worry about it. Even the house I rented was bought by her friends in this community more than ten years ago (it was noble people who persuaded people to buy a house more than ten years ago). At present, she has two houses in Pudong and Puxi, and her only daughter is studying in the United States.

She said that she rented a house first to see people, is to see people talk about rent. Because my sister also rented a house with her for four years before. At the beginning of last year, she went back to her hometown Hefei to develop. I moved here when there was a vacancy. The landlord himself only comes when he signs the contract once a year. Sometimes he comes by and has a look. Usually we only transfer money to her on WeChat every quarter.

She is not as difficult to speak and stingy as other people say that Shanghai people are. On the contrary, she is very generous, straightforward and very humane. In such a good community as ours, she rented us a house of nearly 120 square meters for only 3000 yuan.

There are colleagues who live in our same neighborhood. They also need 2500 yuan to 1 a room, and they share the rent. They often have to queue up for bathrooms. Coupled with second-hand landlords, their monthly electricity and internet charges are more than twice as expensive as those of first-hand tenants. They all expressed envy, jealousy and hatred for the price I rented, and some even couldn't believe it, saying that our landlord had too much money...

Who has too much money? Think about it, oneself is really a great blessing. I also asked the landlord aunt why we are so good. She said: Her house is also for people to live in. If you meet someone who is close to you, you will receive some rent symbolically. You sisters are very likable, and I'd be happy to rent it to you at a lower price. When you live in it, you must pay attention to the safety of water and electricity, and help me watch the house. The total number of people should not exceed four.

She also said to us every time: "thank you, thank you!" When collecting rent, we will bring some fresh food from abroad for us to taste.

The landlord's aunt also shared with me a photo of the winter countryside she had just taken in Chicago, USA. Before, she always liked to take photos in her spare time. She has been studying photography for more than a year. She often goes to various places to take photos. She is the 1 aunt with feelings and pursuits.

She often goes to the United States to visit her daughter, and she has always paid attention to my public number. Later, I learned that I love writing articles and said that I can use her photos when I need them in future articles.

Seeing the pictures she sent, I only had the words "picturesque, dreamy, beautiful to cry" in my mind.

I backed up and saved all the pictures she sent. There has always been a saying in my heart: meeting such a landlord and aunt is really a blessing from my previous life, and it is the 1 blessing and blessing in my life! Only cherish, Thanksgiving!

I think everyone who has gone out to make a living must be familiar with the word "landlord. In fact, it is not only the relationship between interests, but also 1 a kind of feelings. It's not like a hotel, a guesthouse, there's not much contact.

Many years later, we recall the time when we worked hard and drifted, the city where we stayed, and we will certainly recall all kinds of things about the landlord.

# About the train road in front of the door

In my childhood memory, a railway has been built not far from my door. After school, we often walk along the railway. This route is straighter and can be regarded as a shortcut.

On one occasion, I heard adults say not to walk by the railway, because there is a big river in front of me, and a 1 railway bridge will be erected so that the train can pass smoothly. We small fart children mischievously asked, "isn't it just a bridge? Let's just walk carefully from the side."

Adults say that bridge repair is a big project, and the smooth completion of large bridges is often accompanied by the saying of "collecting the soul. To this day, I still don't know whether this is superstition or people's imagination. Legend has it that when a bridge in a certain place cannot be successfully completed several times, it will take spiritualism and use the souls of cattle or people to support the bridge.

These legends are described as lifelike, saying that a Taoist priest used a crock tied with red cloth. When someone passed by and responded, the soul would be recruited and tied with red cloth. And the person who is evaded will disappear.

During that time, the adults warned us never to walk near the railway again, and if strangers shouted, they would never agree. Although we are dubious about these claims, we dare not violate them for fear of the authority of adults. I often hear how many old cows have been sacrificed on a railway bridge in a certain place to put the bridge together.

There are also rumors that an old woman in a certain place led her grandson past the bridge and heard the Taoist who repaired the bridge shouting. The little boy simply answered, and died within a few days of returning. There are various opinions about the cause of the little boy's death.

Some say that he was taken to Eyrium to help carry the bridge because he promised the Taoist priest's evocation, while others say that he died by eating steamed bread.

People have the mentality of believing what they have rather than believing what they don't have. After discussing with the parents of other small partners, my parents decided to take turns to send us to school every day until the bridge was completed.

We can only look at the railway from a distance every day and follow our parents around until the railway bridge is completed and the Hejiu Railway is opened to traffic smoothly. I have not personally seen or heard of anyone in this village being conjure up and killed for building a bridge.

The vivid protagonists of those legends often refer to someone in a certain place, but they are the result of word of mouth and embellishment.

At the moment, I was lying in bed, tapping on my cell phone, hearing the clang of the train from far to near, thinking of the legends of my childhood, and always laughing unconsciously...

# Childhood with Grandma

I spent most of my childhood with my grandmother, and the summers always make me miss more.

There was a big willow tree behind Grandma's house that neither of them could embrace. In the hot summer, it has become the most natural place to escape the heat, especially in the early 1990 s when the material was poor.

After dinner, the neighbors moved out of the cold beds and brought cattail leaf fans to talk about the south wind or the size of the wind tonight. There were also voices saying that it was cool tonight and I could have a good sleep. At this time, I am running happily with fireflies on the side.

Grandma was busy scrubbing the cold bed at home with well water and called me to come and sit down quietly. Don't run all sweaty. I said with a poor mouth, I used to sit and you told me a story. Grandma said yes.

I lay on the cool bed, looking up at the stars and moon in the sky, listening to my grandmother tell the story of "goddess of the moon. Grandma didn't forget to shake the cattail leaf fan back and forth on me. The edge of the cattail leaf fan was wrapped 1 circles with cloth strips, and the handle was extremely smooth due to its long use, with traces of time. Grandma gave me a fan of the wind amplitude is not big, the movement is gentle, cool wind slowly floating, not a mosquito dare to bite me.

Sometimes grandma will tell "seven fairies" "Cowherd and weaver" and other stories. Listen, listen, I went to sleep. Sometimes it was too hot to wake up in the middle of the night. Grandma seemed to have telepathy. She woke up from her sleep immediately and continued to shake the cattail leaf fan for me until I fell asleep again.

After dinner the next day, grandma will continue yesterday's story, shaking the cattail leaf fan, and sometimes juggling out apricots and peaches to me. Later, as I grew up, I realized that she was reluctant to eat fruit snacks and saved her meager pocket money to buy books for our sisters to go to school.

Grandma is like an omnipotent person in my heart, with endless stories. Therefore, I became the envy of the small partners in the village, known as the "story king".

Grandma sometimes uses stories to extend the truth of life, such as "stealing needles when you are young, stealing gold when you are old" and other simple and philosophical words, teaching us to be supercilious and strive for what we want by ourselves. She hopes that when people mention us, it is a thumbs up instead of shaking her head and not wanting to mention it.

Grandma would also take me to the nearby mountains to cut wood. I would drag the corner of her dress, and I would follow her wherever she went, bouncing along the way, very happy. Later, she lost her sight, and there was no such time anymore. She became someone we needed to hold.

Although grandma has been away from us for many years, her voice, appearance and smile, the scene of shaking the cattail fan to tell stories to me on a summer night, are fixed in my mind like a movie lens, and become the most warm and unforgettable picture in my heart. Those days without mobile phones, computers and air conditioners became enriched by her company.

Perhaps, it is the influence of this old man I love deeply that makes me a story writer.

# In the memory of steamed pork

Each region has its own specialties. In my hometown Anqing, Anhui Province, steamed pork with flour is an essential dish for hospitality. We also call it fried meat powder locally. Do you have any in your hometown?

I remember the first time I ate steamed pork with flour was at my classmate Xiaomei's house. One weekend, I went to her house to play. Their house was having lunch. There was a bowl of green vegetables and a bowl of steamed pork with vermicelli on the table. Her mother enthusiastically filled me with rice and several pieces of steamed pork with flour. I was particularly touched by the delicious smell.

The meat is wrapped in a layer of powder, which is not greasy and delicious. I envy the living conditions of the little beauty. We haven't had meat in our family in months. It is estimated that Xiaomei's mother has long seen it and wants me to try her craft and mend her body. She smiled and said, there is still in the bowl, you and Xiaomei eat the meat clean. That was the first time I ate steamed pork with flour. I ate two large bowls of rice and ate all the steamed pork powder in the bowl.

Later, a factory was set up in the village, and my mother led us to work overtime to supplement the family. The living environment is getting better and better. My mother always remembers that I want to eat steamed pork with flour again.

So she began to prepare, with rice, glutinous rice, star anise, fennel, cinnamon, etc., soaked and washed the rice, let me light a hot pot, she put the rice into a small fire and stir-fry. The color of the rice changes. After it feels hot, add pepper and broken star anise and fry it together. Stir-fry until the rice grains swell and smell delicious, then you can stop. Then my mother mashed the fried rice and seasoning with her hands.

Then, she mixed the chopped pork slices with steamed meat powder, sprinkled with salt and monosodium glutamate, and steamed over high fire. After one hour of steaming, the aroma of steamed pork with flour is fragrant.

When my mother wants to lift the lid of the pot, I always ignore the hot hands and pick up a piece of meat as soon as possible. The meat will become fat but not greasy, and the taste will be smooth. My mother looked at me and smiled happily, but she ate very little. She said that she would cook for me every day when the family was well off.

The delicious of steamed meat with flour depends mainly on how the steamed meat powder is done. Steamed meat powder tastes well adjusted, and steamed meat with flour is naturally delicious.

These years in the field, rarely eat the hometown of steamed pork. The steamed meat powder in the supermarket, although beautifully packaged, can't make the taste of hometown. The steamed pork in memory is the taste of hometown, the taste of mother, where there is the warmth of family, the love of mother, and our childhood.

# Reading and Wise Men Talk about to, Dance with Soul

"There is poetry and calligraphy in the belly", "reading a hundred times, its righteousness", "the book has its own golden house, the book has its own Yan Ruyu", "I am afraid of reading", "love reading children, will not go bad", "books are the ladder of human progress" ... These classic sentences are all about the importance of reading to people. Reading can reshape our spiritual character, it allows us to have a strong inner strength, calmly deal with this rapidly changing society.

In the barren years of material life, access to books is extremely limited. As long as I catch the opportunity to see the words I like, I can't wait to extract them, hoping to melt every word into the bone marrow.

After a little more time, every afternoon and evening, I will take time to go back to read books in old book stalls. The cycle goes on and on, and the books I have read, 1 of them, have influenced me imperceptibly and are stored in my blood. Every time I read a book, I talk to the wise, talk to the master, and dance with my soul. It is my own happy flow time.

When I was doing breakfast business in Xi'an, I got up at 4 3 every morning and put a radio on the corner of the panel. While doing things, I listened to famous classic books such as Lu Yao's "Ordinary World" and "White Deer Plain. Race against time to absorb spiritual nutrition, let me in the busy and tedious reality of secular life, see another spiritual world.

These nutrients allow me to face the blows of life and physical problems, because my heart has a broader time and space. As Maugham said: "Reading is the 1 place to carry a refuge". A person who loves to read is not easily defeated.

The early habit of loving words made me want to express, want to talk, and want to be "seen" under the tide of mobile Internet ". It seems that I must have become the 1 freelance writer by accident, signed and published 5 books, and realized time freedom and economic independence.

Without my previous reading and accumulation, I would not have been able to seize the current opportunity to write from the media.

I have read a sentence: there are successful people with low academic qualifications in any industry, but this person must be a person who loves reading and learning and thinking. I dare not say that I am a winner, but the habit of reading did change my fate.

The year before last, I was invited to do the 1 sharing meeting of "reading and writing" in the report hall of a school. I told these students: everyone must keep the habit of reading. When you read more books, you will have deeper thinking and a wider world in your heart. You can know earlier what kind of life and life you want, and you may also have the opportunity to become a 1 famous writer. Ancient and modern, Chinese and foreign, which celebrity does not love to read?

If you feel that everything in your life is going well, you should also read it, experience the sorrows and misfortunes of others in the book, and increase the thickness of your life; if you encounter ups and downs in your life, you should also read it, because you only know that there are people in this world who are more miserable than you, and see how they face those hardships and how they get out of the dark moments of life.

Reading is the investment with the lowest threshold. Reading is the best spiritual salvation and the best spiritual practice.

# The years are like songs, and everyone's life is a book.

01

When I dropped out of school, I learned sewing in an acquaintance's shop in the village. I carved "Where there is a will, there is a way" on the left side of the sewing machine and "Where there is a will, there is a way" on the right side ". At that time, I actually did not know what the dream was.

At that time, I had a heavy notebook dedicated to expressing my feelings and keeping a diary. I named it "The World". I imitated the book and divided the content into chapters 1, 2, and 3. I recorded the personnel of the surrounding villages I heard in the master's house. Every 1 pages were densely recorded. What I saw and heard.

Many years later, when I saw the TV series "The World" written by Teacher Liang Xiaosheng, I couldn't help feeling that I had boldly taken such a grand topic.

At that time, when I was a little over 14 years old, my understanding of the world was only a little bit.

Due to the scarcity of sewing work in the village, the following year, I moved to the town to continue to learn sewing skills. It takes more than 40 minutes to get to the town by bike. I often wonder if my long legs were trained by cycling at that time?

At the master's house in the town, I read the works of Liang Xiaosheng and Bi Shumin. At that time, Bi Shumin was still a rising star in the literary world.

The two books seem to have been given away when the master attended the event. The master's home also subscribes to the half-year "Reader" magazine. Whenever she goes to Anqing to wholesale cloth, I also secretly read it.

When I was studying in town, I loved to hear stories about the garment factory making money. 1 I hear this, I listen to it. At that time, I knew nothing about dreams, life planning, reading to change fate and other concepts. The only idea in my heart was to make money to improve my life.

My senior sister went to Tianjin in the second half of the year to make clothes. In December, she went back to the shop to play and told us that she could earn more than 600 yuan a month, which made us apprentices envious.

At that time, we had seven teachers and sisters. Another girl and I were the last to join. Naturally, we took on the chores of cleaning, cleaning and taking care of children.

The master occasionally asked me to iron my clothes, roll my trousers and sew buttonholes, but when I made a mistake in sewing the waist of my trousers, I was severely criticized by the master, and then I returned to my chores. I must admit that I learn things slowly and my brain is not as bright as others.

The costume master in the town is a woman in her early 30 s. She is 1.7 meters tall and has an extraordinary temperament. She is known as one of the four beauties in the town. She was the first person in town to think of a combination of cloth and curtain sales, and one who liked to design new styles of clothing. In modern terms, she has a forward thinking, forward-looking vision and business acumen.

To this day, I still remember her beautiful face and the beautiful handwriting on her size notebook.

On one occasion, the master went to Anqing to attend a Taiwanese fraternity (she has an uncle and grandfather in Taiwan). After returning from the meeting, I brought a little gift to each of our teachers and sisters. Although it was only a disposable soap, shampoo and some snacks in the hotel, it was a novelty to us.

I was given a small box of soap, which I cherish as a treasure and use only a little at a time. The teacher said that she took home all the things others didn't want and gave them to us. I remember the small brown box of soap. I used it for a long time until I used it up. I also treasured the small box like a cultural relic.

When I was an apprentice in the village, I had too little work; when I went to school sewing in the town, because there were too many people and my ability to accept it was poor, I felt that I had not learned any skills and could not cut and make 1 complete clothes independently. In retrospect, there are always some regrets.

## 02

After studying sewing in the town for a year, my family helped me find a 1 master to take me to a factory in Fujian through the introduction of acquaintances. Due to the limitations of information and cognition, I worked as an apprentice in Fujian for another year. My sewing skills are not superb, but before and after the worship of three masters.

When I was in junior high school, people nearby said that clothing factories in other places could earn more than 10,000 yuan a year, which made me and my younger generation extremely excited. I had planned to work in a factory outside for 3 years and build a beautiful building for my family. However, when I really entered this industry, I found that the income was not as much as others said. Perhaps the dividend period of the industry had gradually receded, and the wages of foreign trade clothing 1 dropped and then dropped.

I am located in Fujian Quanzhou Jinjiang Dongshi Town Panjing Village, almost every household is a garment factory. Even if I have studied sewing machines for two or three years in my hometown, I still have to learn electric sewing machines (flat cars) for one year in other places. In fact, the electric sewing machine can be familiar with it after stepping on it for three or 4 days, and then you can slowly grope for money.

But at that time, it was generally agreed that the first year should be for nothing, and the masters earned the difference. The main role of the master is to lead the way. They paid for the round-trip fare, which saved a lot of expenses for my family and was very attractive. Before going out, my mother was worried that I had no money to use outside, so she sold her hair and gave me 20 yuan. The neighbor's old lady and my grandmother also gave me 5 yuan's money respectively, which they saved by frugality.

The master in the factory usually gives the apprentice 15 yuan every 10 days to buy pocket money and daily necessities. The meal was eaten with the master and 1000 yuan was given to take home at the end of the year. My monthly pocket money is 45 yuan, I even 50 cents of steamed stuffed bun are reluctant to eat, often hungry. I will use the 1 bag of 5 dime Rejoice Shampoo in three times. After using it, I will wrap it in a plastic bag for another use. The money I save will be sent home in an envelope when I write a letter, usually 5 yuan, sometimes 10 yuan, and 50 yuan at most.

At that time, there were about 15 fellow-townsman girls who were apprentices like me, and one of them was a master couple with 12 apprentices. It is said that the couple's net income for the year was more than 30000, which was in 2000.

When I first arrived in Fujian for half a year, my feet were not adapted to the alkaline water along the coast, and my right instep had a hole in the back of my right foot, which was festering and itchy. I can only step on the electric sewing machine with my left foot and wear school uniform every day (school uniform is the best dress for me). I remember that the red school uniform in junior high school cost 60 yuan a set, and the school stipulated that every student must buy it.

School uniform is really a good thing, it protects my dignity and decency. I thought that if I step on the electric sewing machine with my left foot, my right foot will get better. I didn't expect the situation to get worse and worse. I have to limp when I walk, accompanied by pain. Jiangxi colleagues in the factory gave me a nickname "left foot warrior", which is unique in the whole factory.

When I was young, I was unaware of everything. The teacher did not mention taking me to the clinic, and I did not dare to speak. Every day I only know how to eat and work, eat and work, like a tool man. I am even worried that the money for watching my feet will be deducted from the 1000 yuan. I dream that my feet can heal themselves.

Until a fellow villager reminded the master that my feet might be disabled if I don't look at them. The teacher's reply at that time was: "disabled on disabled chant ..." However, she still took me to the clinic to hang the salt water. After more than half a month of treatment, the wound gradually healed. Now, I still have a fuzzy scar on the back of my right foot, and it still hurts in rainy days.

During the treatment, I didn't delay much work except to hang water. I reminded myself to speed up and even work harder than before to compensate for the time spent in the clinic. My master is much gentler than other masters.

I have seen other masters punish their apprentices standing by the pillars of the workshop, reprimanding loudly, even kicking her electric sewing machine and clothes frame with their feet, which can be seen by the whole workshop. Just because the girl dozed off while making clothes.

In the factory where I worked in my first year, I worked until 3 4 a.m. every night, and I had to go to work at 9 a.m. The apprentice arrives earlier in the morning than the master, so how can he not doze off? You can sleep on the toilet. It may seem inconceivable now, but then it was the norm.

In fact, when my master went out from his hometown, he also brought another girl apprentice. We took the green train together and lived in a dormitory (the dormitory has 6 upper and lower bunks). She hadn't learned a day about the sewing machine at home. After arriving in Fujian, she felt dizzy when stepping on the machine every day, saying that she was in poor health and wanted to go home. She was always sad and homesick.

She stayed for about a month. The teacher took her to the station and her family picked her up. Then the master and fellow villagers often said that the girl was afraid of hardship. From their point of view, it is estimated that they will say so! They are also at the bottom of the food chain.

I don't want to be told that I'm afraid of suffering. In fact, I am also very homesick, want to go back. But I didn't even have the fare, so I didn't dare to think about it again. Three thousand miles away from home, working more than 17 hours a day, only 1000 yuan at the end of the year. And my fifth grade weekend odd jobs, almost 10 dollars a day. This hourly salary is not as good as my treatment in my hometown, but I am struggling outside in order not to be told that I am afraid of hardship, and in order not to be laughed at by my old family.

At that time, the public opinion environment believed that people who came back after staying outside for a period of time were very humiliated. I hate that I don't have my own opinion. Now that I think about it, I really gnash my teeth. I was stupid that year. Why don't you want to go home with that girl? Come back to work in the town by bike, do brushes, go to packaging factories, plastic bag factories, you can also go to work in Tongcheng City, you can also take care of your family and help your family work during the busy farming season.

When I was studying sewing machines in the town, my classmate Chen Jin saw that he was making wire brushes across the street. He had 3000 or 4000 yuan a year. We often meet in the morning and evening by bike, and we don't have to stay up late in the factory in front of our house.

When I reached middle age, I realized that during the two and a half years as an apprentice, choosing to work in other provinces was simply reversing my life and going backwards. Is it just to provide material for my writing today? The price is too high. People can't use later cognition to measure their former self, everything is life.

The deep reason is that I have always disliked my hometown. I have been coldly treated since I was a child, and I have not felt much love and respect. I am always eager to grow up quickly, far away from my hometown, the farther the better. Really to the outside, found not as good as imagined, also unwilling to go home.

In fact, the distance we long for is not the hometown that others are tired of staying?

## 03

At that time, people from mountainous areas often came to work in our town, and our town was known as "the hometown of Chinese brushes". Tongcheng is the main producing area of plastic bags, which is said to occupy more than 60% of the national market share.

If I had known that my mother's life was so short, I would never have chosen to work so far away. Every year, I start in the first month and go home in the twelfth month. I feel like I sold it to someone else. Even if I earn less at home, at least my body will not be tired to fall ill in my beautiful youth.

At that time, in the factory in Fujian, we only went home once a year. Anhui people attach great importance to going home for the New Year. Some colleagues in Sichuan and Guizhou only go home once every three or four years. 1 of my Sichuan colleagues in the workshop next door, her daughter didn't even recognize her when she came home.

In retrospect, how sad it was. Those who experienced all this or witnessed all this did not have so many regrets. People who do not have so many regrets in their thoughts and hearts naturally have much less sadness.

In 2002, the closing time in our factory was changed to 2 a.m.

That year, I worked as a clothing inspector for several months. The clothes from the processing factory are sent to the warehouse of our general factory. Sometimes it needs manual inspection, so we will find old employees to be inspectors. Check where the clothes are dropped, needle skipped and asymmetrical. If they fail, stick them with yellow adhesive tape and let others take them back for rework. The inspector's daily salary is 30 yuan (40 yuan a day in 2004). They all live in the factory and eat their own food.

If you make your own clothes, you will get more for more. On average, a pair of beach pants costs 1 a dollar, and I can make 3 40 a day on average. Because of my quick work, I am one of the higher paid workers in the factory.

The beach pants worn by African refugees are produced in the factory. The design is complicated. The big pocket is pasted with small pockets, the side of the big pocket is zippered, the surface is also covered with three-dimensional pockets, oblique pockets, pockets at the knees, patch pockets at the back of the buttocks, and hook and loop stickers at the mouth of the pockets. There are a dozen pockets in a pair of shorts.

When working in the factory is tired and tired, I often face a lot of repairs. Sometimes I really want to throw my clothes into the sea. I often wonder, who invented clothes?

In those days, we made clothes and listened to the radio. I remember listening to some radio dramas such as "Passion Burning Years" and some emotional interactive columns of questions and answers.

True Garden is our favorite show. The opening line of the program is: "not far away on the sea, there is a white sailing boat, quietly sailing to the other side of the soul."

The host of that show is called Bai Fan. So much so that when I was writing in 2016, I also brought the word "sail" when I took my pen name. The program mainly reads letters written by some migrant workers and can also order songs and send songs to others.

The host's voice was kind and beautiful, and the reading letter was interspersed with some songs, such as Wu Bai, Zhang Xinzhe, Ren Xianqi, Andy Lau, Adu and others.

Whenever a colleague buys back a tape, I always borrow the piece of paper with the lyrics first and ask her to extract the lyrics. I want to extract them and copy the lyrics on the pocket cloth.

...

Past such as smoke, years such as song!

Rolling red dust, times change!

Everyone's life is a thick book, a book with unique charm.

## 04

According to the news, after 00, when I am not happy at work, I will lift my leg and leave. I will fire my boss. Our group of post -85 people have suffered so much. It is said that 1 Jiangxi colleague who entered the factory two years earlier than me was beaten by his boss and burned the back of his hand with a cigarette...

Some of my colleagues who entered the factory a few years later than me did not learn sewing machines for a day. They did not need a master. They could make money by entering the factory and being led by the team leader to make assembly lines.

Later, no matter you learn any craft such as carpenter, bricklayer, paint, etc., you don't have to learn for a few years. You can earn money while learning and doing it, not to mention relying on the breath of the master and anyone.

Due to the popularity of industrialization, the folk practice of mentoring and mentoring has become history. In recent years, the working hours of working in coastal areas have been shortened year by year.

You see, a few years earlier or a few years later, everything is very different.

People are just the product of the times. In such a big environment (small environment), they are weak and weak, and they are really unable to change.

Remembering that the predecessor writer Lu Tianming once wrote: "Everyone, of course, including you and me, is actually a passive actor on the historical stage. The chief screenwriter and director can only be the times and society."

# Those far away craftsmen

Once upon a time, someone hung a camera around his neck and wandered around the villages, shouting, "Take a picture, take a picture, who wants to take a picture?" At that time, those who could own a camera and engage in this profession must be those who have a flexible mind and a bit of a doorway.

In my memory, I only have a black-and-white photo when I was 5 years old. In the photo, I was standing next to the children's car with a small bald head and wearing a bib. So far, my family and relatives have said that I have been like a boy since I was a child, and my character is even more so.

After I was in junior high school, this kind of person who hung a camera to take pictures at home has disappeared. With the development of the times, they have been eliminated.

Later, it was popular to go to the photo studio to take pictures. There are a lot of clothes to choose from, you can match several sets of clothes when taking photos, and then choose a few lenses, how much is a lens, how many pieces are washed, and there are many kinds.

In recent years, the photo studio has also been affected by the new development trend. When I was doing a small business in Xi'an, the next door was a photo studio, and the owner was a Henan woman of my age. She said that there are few people taking ID photos, and fewer people come to take life photos, because many people already have digital cameras, and the camera function of mobile phones is becoming more and more powerful.

She recalled the scenery time. In 2003, there were two months, and she earned nearly 10,000 yuan a month just by taking ID photos. At that time, it was the SARS period, many places needed to check certificates, and smart phones were not yet popular.

She said with emotion that it was more and more difficult to cherish money when it was easy to earn. Only by transforming into a large-scale studio to take wedding photos can we survive, and to make a brand, but that requires a lot of investment, not every ordinary photo studio can successfully transform.

Every period of development of society can achieve many careers and eliminate some.

Recalling those disappearing occupation, when I was a child, I often saw cobbler, he was a thin middle-aged man. As long as he 1, every family in the village will take out the shoes with holes, including handmade cloth shoes made by his mother and military-style yellow sneakers. The children will also join in the fun, twittering around the shoe repair stall, just like the New Year.

The cobbler often carries a burden when he enters the village, with a shoe mending machine on one side and a basket filled with accessories for shoe mending. Shoes torn, toes kicked, can be mended by the cobbler's skillful hands, be joyfully worn as new shoes. At that time, people did not feel that life was hard, but it was easy to be satisfied.

In my memory, there was a blacksmith's shop not far from my home. The two brothers were busy by the fire all day and their business was booming. The two often have a towel on their shoulders, bare arms, and the whole person is black. Now that I think about it, how do they work in high temperatures every day in summer without air conditioning?

They made the wood cutters, rice sickles and shovels used by the people in the village. As a child, I felt that this blacksmith was simply a masterful craftsman and full of admiration.

As I grew up, passing by their door, I found their business more and more deserted. Until one day, the village was talking about the blacksmith brothers working in other places and the shop was closed. Outside to make more money than this, their family three generations of iron craft is so abandoned. Everyone a sigh!

My brother-in-law used to be a bamboo craftsman, who was good at weaving sleeping mats, washing vegetable baskets and picking seedlings. When he went to his brother-in-law's house, he always cut open the bamboo around a piece of rag, cut it into thin slices, and woven it into objects that people needed by his magical hand.

We get hand-woven items, repeatedly touch, look, there is a kind of joy and happiness.

Uncle used to be a tinker, carrying the burden to the villages like a cobbler. In those days, pots and pans would not be thrown away easily if they were broken. When the pot was mended, they would not be used until they were mended.

I once followed my uncle through the streets. his long voice shouted, "mend the pot, mend the pot". Every time you go to a village, it will cause a stir of excitement. I saw uncle picked up the pot, shined on the light, determined the location of the broken pot, scalded it with tin, and changed the bottom of the pot for the big hole. One by one, the craftsmen knocked and beat, which produced the effect of reunifying the mirror. In addition to a small part of the patched pot with obvious traces, it was more as good as new.

In the late 1990 s, the cooking industry suddenly disappeared, and people like uncle San went out to work.

Once upon a time there were door-to-door shavers, not now called barbers and hairdressers. At that time, the shaver carried a small wooden box to each village to shave men's heads, and settled the bill together at the end of the year, which was economical and practical.

My brother-in-law, a bamboo craftsman, later went to Wuhan to do plastic bag business. Like a shaver, blacksmith and cobbler, he changed his career to make a living.

Those craftsmen are a special group of people in a particular era, a product of the times. Before the market economy was officially developed, they were people who traveled north and south and had a broad vision. They were proud and confident because they had a craft. "In the year of the Great Wilderness, craftsmen will not die of hunger."

However, with the development of society, the division of labor of products is becoming more and more detailed, and the rapid development of mechanization and technology has made those older generations of craftsmen disappear from people's field of vision, withdraw from the stage of history, and become a symbol of a certain period.

I came from the years when there were craftsmen, witnessed the production process of those old crafts, and witnessed their prosperity and withering. Can understand the story behind each item: enjoyment, perfection, temperature, joy, and a love that is hard to give up on life and life.

What will happen to our hot career or technology in the next 20 years? Only time will give the answer!

# Old house and earth hearth

In fact, the new house has been built for some years, but it is strange that when I dream back at midnight, I always dream of the old house I lived in when I was a child, not the building I built later.

The old house carries most of my childhood memories, whether it is carefree happiness or inferiority of poverty.

The 3 old house made of adobe was built by my father in the year I was born. According to grandma, in order to build these 3 tiled houses, my father gets up early and greedily every day. all the adobe used to build the house was made by himself in the field with wooden molds, and could be used only after a few days in the sun. The wooden beams on the roof were also carried back step by step on foot to his grandmother's Shucheng mountain area by himself.

In that era of extreme shortage of materials, especially for poor families, even the most ordinary 3 adobe houses consumed all the painstaking efforts of the family. Grandma mentioned these bitterness will keep wiping tears.

The left side of the old house is the kitchen, and the door is a big stove. Listen to the old man said, build stove is a technical work, high chimney ventilation is better, otherwise very expensive firewood. Some poorly built houses will be full of smoke, and the pot and hearth should fit together.

Most people will have two pots on the pot table, one for cooking and the other for cooking. There will be two water well tanks in the middle to simmer hot water. When the meal is ready, the hot water is used to wash the face and the dishes. Later, with the aluminum well tank, hot water will be put in a water bottle when it is opened, which can save firewood and time.

Above the hearth are hanging shovels, copper spoons, chopsticks cages and other objects, pasted with the four words written during the Spring

Festival: "Fire and water are safe". There will be a large water tank under one end of the pot table, in which there is a water ladle made of half dry gourd to scoop water.

At that time, wooden pot covers were used. When cooking, the edge of the pot was often surrounded 1 a dish cloth to avoid air leakage. I often sit on the mat at the door of the stove to help plug firewood, with straw, rape straw, pine hair and branches, etc. Sometimes it is always easy to put out the burning fire when using sticks and branches. Even if I blow hard with my cheeks, my eyes will often choke to tears and the fire will never start.

My mother would tell me, "people should be solid and fire should be hollow". It is necessary to put up the branches and leave a gap in the middle so that the fire will flourish. There are also people who will install a bellows. When firewood is not good, they will pull the bellows 1, which is conducive to the ventilation of firewood.

The hearth, the wooden lid, the firewood, and the rice cooked in the cauldron are very fragrant. After the rice soup, add a few small fires, and the rice will slowly overflow with aroma. You can smell the aroma from a distance, which makes you salivate. After each meal, I will soak the fragrant and crisp rice crust under the rice soup to eat, not to mention how beautiful it is.

The first thing I did when I came home from school in the afternoon was to run into the kitchen to find the rice crust left at noon to soak in boiling water and eat pickles with relish.

Autumn is the season for sweet potato harvest. Our sisters often put sweet potatoes in the stove hole to cover the Mars kindling together. After smelling the fragrance for more than an hour, we can't control the dark skin outside or how hot our hands are. We change our left hand for our right hand, our right hand for our left hand, and we eat when we break it. The golden flesh bite, wow, delicious! Don't mention how cool it is. To this day, the fragrant, hot roasted sweet potato is still one of the most beautiful delicacies in my heart.

With the popularity of liquefied gas, rice cookers, induction cookers and other electrical kitchenware, it is now rare to see the earth stove in memory, the wooden lid, the big pot, the smell of sweet potato... All this will be submerged in the depths of time.

In the future, we will only have to spend a high price to experience the farmhouse, right?

The hearth, the fire, the mother, that is the eternal warm existence in our hearts!

# Everything has its limitations

More than 10 years ago, CCTV hosted a large-scale publicity campaign of "Brand China" to select a list of consumers' favorite local brands. At that time, there were 40 local brands on the list: Dabao, Little Nurse, Waveguide, Bubugao, Wanlida, Tongfang, Oaks, Boston, Hengyuanxiang, Youngor, Seven Wolves, Li Ning, Senma, Sugiyama, etc.

Among these brands, I am familiar with Semir, Metersbonwe, Li Ning and Little Nurse. Senma is a local brand in Wenzhou. At that time, Wenzhou also had a Metersbonwe that was quite popular. In 2008, there were stores in Sema and Metersbonwe on the street where I did business. Semir means "what" in Wenzhou dialect, and its slogan "what you wear is what you wear". These two brands are moderately priced, suitable for mass consumption, and were very popular at the time.

My second sister used to work as a shopping guide for Senma Store in Shanghai. I remember Second Sister once said that the store she was in could sell more than 10000 a day and have more holidays. However, the shopping guide gets a commission according to her own turnover. The second sister said that her personality is not very suitable. She is scrambling for time every day, eating a few mouthes casually, and her colleagues are robbing customers and fighting over and over. She has only been doing it for more than 3 months.

Times surging, these brands seem to have gradually disappeared. In 2007, I worked in a brand women's clothing factory near the university town in Chashan District, Wenzhou, Zhejiang Province. The trademark was "Xuefanni". The boss's sister's factory has been more successful. It has specialty stores in more than 100 countries around the world. Her brand is called "Snow Song". At that time, several famous avenues in Wenzhou had billboards of the "Snow Song" brand.

It is said that the boss's sister is a very legendary figure. She took her family to make clothes at the age of 17. She learned to design from the small store and became bigger step by step. She also took the lead in realizing the importance of the brand. Before she got married, she also fought a lawsuit for the factory and her mother's family. In the end, she only took away the trademark of "Snow Song. All the equipment in the factory was left to her brother, the factory I stayed in, "snow fan Ni".

When I worked there, the boss and his sister were probably not much older than I was then. Some colleagues praised her for looking young, beautiful and elegant when they saw the founder of "Snow Song" going back to her mother's family to do business. Although she only took away the trademark when she got married, she still far exceeded his brother's development in only a few years.

Due to the opportunities in Zhejiang and the large environment, as well as their own hard work, they have established their own brands. We outsiders work for them and make a living there. It is said that earlier, in the 5 s and 1960 s, almost all Zhejiang people came to Anhui to make a living. They can't grow crops in the saline-alkali land, and they will be hungry if they don't make a living. At that time, they envied the "Central Plains" people! It's really thirty years of Hedong, thirty years of Hexi.

Before 2015, the growth mode of traditional brands is to register a trademark first and then publicize it with all resources. Just as "Snow Song" has giant advertising lights displayed at high-speed intersections, Wenzhou Radio has their publicity and promotion. Then use brand fame to attract franchisees around, open stores. Brand, processing, production, sales one-stop, belong to the domestic trade.

I just walked out of the big factory in Fujian where I worked. What they did was foreign trade. They used large trucks and containers to send them from Hong Kong and transport them to all parts of Africa. In those years, foreign trade was very prosperous. Later, the US dollar depreciated, labor costs in the mainland increased, and foreign trade factories became less and less profitable. Many of our villagers would rather work in their hometown factories than go to the coast. After 2012, many garment factories along the coast have moved to Yunnan, Vietnam and Myanmar.

In the twelfth month of last year, I happened to meet a fellow colleague from Wenzhou women's clothing factory. I also asked her, what happened to our "snow fan Ni" and his sister's "snow song? She said she didn't know either. This fellow-townsman sister used to lead the team leader in that factory. When she invited me to eat hot pot years ago, she said the most about how I became a "writer".

I said, according to the development trend of this network era, if the women's clothing factory we stayed in that year did not transform in time and attach importance to network marketing, there is a high probability that it has declined. My third uncle is a mending pot, and my brother-in-law is a bamboo craftsman, weaving baskets for picking seedlings, washing vegetables, picking rice baskets, etc.

I still remember my brother-in-law sitting on the ground playing the mat. I also followed my third uncle to see the mending pot and used the tin to mend the small hole in the bottom of the pot. It was really a job without gold content and was eliminated by the times in a few years. How much is a pot worth? In a few years, brother-in-law's business has also been eliminated by the times. Machine-based mass output, this kind of manual work is not comparable. Now to buy a mat, buy ready-made finished fast and cheap. At that time, it took my brother-in-law several days and nights to make 1 bed and mat, which was too expensive.

Brother-in-law once sighed behind his back that he thought my grandmother had no foresight. His peers learned carpenters and bricklayers at home, and my grandmother taught them pot menkers and bamboo craftsmen. My brother-in-law did very well when he was studying and won the certificate every year. The poor family and the lack of awareness of reading, let him come back early to work for the family, and then find a master to learn bamboo craftsman. It can only be said that every person and family has its own limitations.

When I dropped out of school, none of my family relatives could give me a way out, let alone a direct relative. Seven turns and eight turns, I found a teacher introduced by a distant relative to take me to Fujian. It was a woman a year older than me. I am also lucky. Among all the masters in the factory at that time, she was the most gentle. She did not speak loudly and swear, let alone hit people.

When I became stable in Fujian factory, I introduced my brother-in-law to my factory for ironing clothes and my aunt to the flow workshop for making clothes. Two years later, with the encouragement of my fellow villagers and I, my brother-in-law contracted the entire ironing table in the back workshop of the factory. After working for a few years, their family income has been greatly improved, and now their beautiful house is still built with the money they earned in Fujian.

Later, I left the factory in Fujian and heard from my hometown that the boss invited a big meal every year and called several representatives. My brother-in-law must be one of them. He is an old employee and a contractor of hot Taiwan. Those years were also the years when my brother-in-law had the strongest sense of existence. Later, the Fujian foreign trade factory went downhill, and the villagers left almost. Brother-in-law has been working on the construction site in recent years, working hard, often following various construction sites around.

Back then, he had his own independent dormitory in the factory, which was clean and bright, and there was a special place for cooking. Anhui school was respected in the factory, which was much better than the environment and situation on the construction site now. Now, every time we go back to our hometown, we will bring some milk or red envelopes to our aunt. She refuses to accept the money anyway, leaving at most 1 boxes of milk.

Every time I ask my brother-in-law how, my aunt always says that no one takes him. What else can I do in my life? My brother-in-law didn't go home all the year round, and he didn't care much about his children. His only son, my cousin, didn't finish the second day of the junior high school. As the cousin of the only child, he dropped out of school earlier than we did. Now I am also on the construction site, fishing for three days and drying the net for two days.

Every time I hear such words, there is always a deep sense of powerlessness. My little sister was looking for a job on the street when she was a teenager. One by one, she asked and printed her own information to find a job. From the beginning to Shanghai's 100-dollar bed for a month, to the supermarket's shopping guide, to the Japanese restaurant's job of covering food and housing, to becoming a company's administrative worker, I shared a single room with my cousin and fellow villagers in Shanghai's Zhangjiang Gaoke community, replacing a slightly better living environment step by step.

She later paid her tuition fees by mortgage in installments, took her own undergraduate course, took her own Japanese level 2, and took her own judicial examination. Everyone, every profession, every family, every company, has its time environment and various limitations of personal character.

I think that in 2000 years, there were many motorcycle workers in various places, and I have sat many times. Later, it was eliminated by sharing bicycles. I have used that kind of universal charge before, flashing, but now I don't need it at all. I used to have a neighbor who opened a photo studio, a Henan girl, who was already aware of the crisis. She said that if she did not transform into a wedding photo studio, she would be eliminated. I remember she also told me that SARS in 2003 required photos to be checked. Only by printing a single photo, she could earn more than 8000 a month.

Fortunately, their family's consciousness is quite advanced, and they have already bought two suites when the house price in Xi 'an is 3000 or 4000. This Henan girl is still my QQ friend. The train of the times passed by, did not keep up in time, did not complete the basic wealth preservation, slowly easy to slip to the bottom, forming a vicious circle, more and more difficult.

Either some future generations have ultra-high IQ in reading and change the fate of the class through the college entrance examination, but the "cost performance" of the college entrance examination is not as high as that of 30 years ago. Or to see the trend dividend and seize the opportunity to achieve a breakthrough, this requires vision, luck, action and other comprehensive ability. Today, when I was reading "Top of the Times: The Internet Builds a New Economy", I felt too much. Those industries that have disappeared, those companies that have failed to transform, those people who have not kept pace with the times, and then live more and more tired.

When Nokia was acquired that year, senior leaders told reporters sadly, "I don't think we did anything wrong, but I don't know why, but we just failed". The wheels of history roll forward, and it will not be stopped by anyone's negative slowness.

I have so many living materials to write, but I have always failed to write the words I want. I have been tepid for so many years, which is also my limitation. Everything in the world has its limitations.

# Can you seize a tuyere and fight for 10 years less?

## 01

The tuyere always becomes the past before we realize its existence, and it is always chased as an important opportunity after the fact. When in the wind, we often can not identify, more do not know how to grasp.

In fact, people who can grasp the tuyere usually begin to accumulate in related fields before the tuyere comes. If you wait until the wind to come to start from scratch, it will not be able to seize the opportunity, because everything is too late.

Therefore, you have to be at the edge of the information source, otherwise you can't see the information level you are in, which will determine who we are. We need to try to get close to the important sources of information, which is very critical.

Since 2017, every year, some people have said that WeChat's public number is not good, and the media has no chance. However, there are still people who successfully operate the public number every year, relying on the public number to live a moist life and enjoy freedom.

My old student, Miss Deng, started to be a public number in 2019. In just one and a half years, she attracted more than 100,000 fans and realized freelance.

Even in 2023, there are still people who successfully operate the public number, have no worries about their basic life, and can support themselves through the public number.

If you always fall behind because of insufficient information channels and backward information sources, you will continue to miss the best opportunities of this era. Sometimes a wrong step, you will miss all the way.

For example, for several Internet opportunities in the past two decades, most people born before 1970 can hardly grasp them. They are not sensitive to the Internet and have poor acceptance ability. For example, Taobao in the early 2000 s created countless people, the micro-business in 2013, and the self-media explosion period from 2015 to 2016, but most people missed it perfectly.

Most of the people who started Taobao were born in the 80 s, and most of the successful micro-merchants were born in the 90 s, while those who were born in the 90 s and 95 s were mainly born in Xiaohongshu, B station and Douyin platform. This is determined by their sensitivity, adaptability and platform tonality.

Some of the post-60s generation find it difficult to accept some of the trendy vocabulary of these platforms for a while.

If you are optimistic about a certain field, you should try to work in this direction, read more relevant books, get close to the circle of this field, from physics to psychology, even if you start late now, as long as you continue to work correctly and firmly, you will always seize the next outlet and complete the ability transfer quickly.

Many people ask me, is it still too late to write and do self-media?

I always say that it is never too late to wake up and want to act. When you think it's too late, it's the best time.

This year, many people get a good sideline income through the public number, as well as people who get attention through the video number. A network colleague gave the public a 30000 + through a video on the video number. On Little Red Riding Book, Fast Hands and Shake Tone, there are still people coming out every month.

## 02

I have a former colleague Xiao Liang, born in 1987. We used to work in a garment factory in Fujian. However, not long after he came to the factory,

I went back to my hometown for physical reasons. But I still have some impressions of this fellow colleague.

Later, he changed to work in a garment factory in Zhejiang. When listening to the radio, he learned about the development trend of e-commerce, as if he saw hope, and began to study this field in his spare time, starting from the basic operation of Taobao. However, due to the pressure of purchasing goods and the difficulty of capital turnover, he had to return to work in the clothing factory for a few months, and then continue to do Taobao, which has been tossing for more than 3 years.

Until 2012, he began to work full-time Taobao. In 2014 and 2015, his career had a small explosion, earning 500000 + in a month at the highest. By 2018, he had seized the bonus of Pinduoduo, and the sales of 1 pants exceeded 9 million last month. Although it is not much for those successful Daniel, his starting point is just a 3 with no education, no background and no contacts.

With a good income, he bought three apartments in Zhejiang and invested in shops in his hometown of Tongcheng City, all of which were started before the skyrocketing house prices. Over the years, he also led many Tongcheng villagers through the network to increase a lot of income, changed the fate.

This year, he began to try to shake the sound of e-commerce. In the current environment, although it is not as good as it used to be, he also cooperates with other anchors and participates in some other projects. Fortunately, this old colleague has completed the original accumulation. Even if he stops doing anything, he can exceed 80% of the people.

He also said with regret that during the golden period when he first arrived in Zhejiang, he took many detours because there was no one to take and no principal in his hand. All rely on their own step by step to explore, cash flow difficulties, and then back to the factory to work, step by step to adhere to so far.

Everyone's life will encounter tuyere opportunities, as long as you can seize once, you can achieve transformation. My former colleague, although Taobao did not catch up with the best bonus period, let him come into contact with e-commerce and saw the infinite possibilities of e-commerce. With a little savings, he devoted himself to e-commerce full-time and ran to Yiwu with a bag alone.

These are the important basis for his later take-off. If there is no Taobao operation experience, did not go deep into the e-commerce circle, then later will not seize the spell more tuyere.

If he has only been in the clothing factory, and every day he comes into contact with colleagues who make clothes, and does not communicate with people in the e-commerce circle, then his thinking will naturally have great limitations.

Fortunately, he decisively ran from Fujian to Shengzhou, Zhejiang to find a factory and explore other possibilities. The working hours in the factory in Shengzhou, Zhejiang are a few hours shorter than those in Fujian, and the salary is slightly higher. Sometimes in the off-season, he doesn't have to go to work at night, which gives him time to think and study.

At that time, most of our fellow villagers and colleagues in Fujian factories did not dare to change factories easily, let alone change factories across provinces.

At that time, everyone felt that the crows in the world were as dark as black, and only in a factory could they save money. Everyone is afraid of the cost of trial and error. The main thing is that people are poor and short-minded! How many people in our real society may have greater achievements and prospects, but because of their own limitations and necessity.

### 03

After tasting the benefits of Taobao, my fellow colleague once again went to Yiwu, Zhejiang Province alone to find out the circle of e-commerce. Everyone he met when he went out was an e-commerce merchant.

He rented one of the basements where they lived. When he saw that Yiwu was full of high-quality and inexpensive products, his eyes lit up and he thought, this time is really the right one.

These decisions are based on his own opinion, but also the fate of the favor. The summer before last, he sold a house in Yiwu in time, and after deducting various costs and taxes, he also made a net profit of 1 million. It was a wise decision. If you only sell that house now, the result will be too bad.

Before, I saw him make a dynamic statement in the circle of friends, saying that when he met the tuyere, pigs could fly, saying that he was lucky and stepped on the e-commerce bonus. I want to say that the wind is not blowing only to one person or 1 group of people, but to all people in the whole society.

Although my former colleague Xiaoliang is not engaged in the field of self-media, he is also a person who has made achievements due to the Internet and is a beneficiary of this mobile Internet era. Some of his growth decisions are the same at the bottom of the self-media field.

I have also heard that many people opened Taobao stores before 2010, that is, they entered the game during the best bonus period, but they did not stick to it and finally went back to work. There are also many such groups, and they have not been able to make a 1 career in e-commerce and support several employees like my old colleague in Yiwu.

Therefore, you don't have to worry about being a self-media late and writing late. As long as you improve your cognition, find the right method and stick to deep cultivation, you will always get your own bonus. We just need to improve ourselves from yesterday.

## Are people strong enough to live? In the face of fate, stop talking about justice...

I am a person who can remember things very late. I can remember very limited things before the age of 10, only a few fragments.

When I was in the second grade of 1., one day on my way home with my children after school, I suddenly saw my grandmother coming face to face with a bamboo stick from a distance and called me, "Faner, you accompany me to see Dr. Xiao Wu (the village barefoot doctor). My eyes suddenly seemed to be blindfolded and I couldn't see clearly."

I am young, ignorant and playful. I said I would go home with my little partner. If I don't accompany you, you can go by yourself.

Grandma went to the village alone to see the barefoot doctor. Maybe from that day on, grandma's eyes slowly went blind.

I remember once, the aunt in Anqing went back to her hometown and took her grandmother to our county hospital with her uncle. The doctor said that the operation could be done or not. A female doctor also said, "What kind of knife do you open when you are old..."

Later, I heard grandma nagging countless times, blaming the female doctor's words, and regretted that I was not firm at that time and did not insist on surgery. Mainly because she herself did not expect to live a few more decades of life. There are old people in the same village who can see their eyes after surgery. Grandma is envious.

Grandma is a person with strong self-esteem. Even if she can't see her eyes completely later, she will insist on living alone. In her words, "if you want to eat earlier, you should eat earlier, and if you want to eat later, you should be later. You can end up at ease!"

Every day she groped her way through the 3 adobe house alone, living in the dark.

People in the village say that grandma's eyes are blind and crying. She is a person with extremely low tear glands. Whether she is happy or unhappy, she will cry.

My dad's death hit my grandma particularly hard. When grandma was carrying water in the well beside the pond at the door, she put the water on the side and sat on the mound to rest. when she thought about it, she would cry. she thought about her son in hard karma and cried out about the injustice of fate. why did she send black hair in white? she was also worried about the growth of our sisters. at that time, my little sister was only 1 years old.

Sometimes when working in the vegetable garden, grandma would cry for a long time when sitting in the ditch, as if only crying was what she wanted to express to the world most.

When I was young, I often heard her crying. Sometimes at night, the neighbor next to her house called us again: "Your grandmother is crying at home again. I'm afraid she will not be able to think about it, so I go to comfort her."

Several times when she cried badly in the middle of the night, the woman at the door said, "Do you want to send a telegram to let your Dongxiang (my uncle) come back." Grandma would always say, "I'll be fine in a minute, but I can't bother him. It's not easy for him to work in Anqing."

She really cried day and night for two months. Grandma paid a heavy price for blindness.

It turns out that there are people in this world who can make 1 eyes cry blind. This is a painful double tragedy.

I understand late, my mind seems to be missing a track-minded person, for grandma's grief at that time can not empathate. When I saw her crying in front of me, I never cried with her, even if I shed 1 tears, as if I were looking at an irrelevant old man coldly.

Now, in my middle age, I have become a professional writer. When writing such memories, I will cry like rain. In some sleepless nights, when I think of my grandmother, I will cry. The tears that I did not flow once are doubled.

Grandma is really a very bad karma person, her life is full of suffering and sadness of the life.

She had prayed to heaven many times that she would die soon. She said it was a blessing for others to live one more day, that was longevity. For her, every extra day she lives is not full, and God refuses to accept her easily, which is punishing her.

In those turbulent, hungry and extremely poor times, my grandmother lost her parents and grandparents in her childhood and followed her only relative (her old lady) to beg for life. The old lady continued in her old age. When my grandmother was 8 years old, she was promised to my grandfather, and the old man took her with him to continue begging.

About those years of beggars, she said the most in front of me. What she feared most was the big German shepherd of the landlord's family. Some dogs were taller than people and barked. She was so scared that she hid in the corner and shivered that she would rather starve than come out.

When Grandma was a little older, she went to the landlord's house to work long-term. Although there is no penny at the end of a year's busy work, you can control your mouth, that is, the most basic survival, which is better than begging for stability and dignity.

As a child, she knocked ice, washed clothes, washed quilts, tidied up and did all kinds of housework in the landlord's house in winter. She started working before dawn every day until evening.

She said that the old woman of this landlord saw me when I was in my teens. The landlord's family had moved to the city long ago, and their descendants were developing very well. The old man came to our village specially when he went back to his hometown to kiss. He 1 his feet and looked very expensive in his clothes.

She wanted to find out how my grandmother was doing, and when she heard that my father had died so young, she sat and lamented for a while. When he left, the old landlord gave my grandmother 20 yuan money, very enthusiastic.

I heard my grandmother say to another old man in the village at the door, "It's really someone's life! When she (the landlord) was young, her family had so many fields, many poor people worked for her family, and now all her children and grandchildren are so successful, and the family is prosperous. People are cruel but not dead!"

The landlord is also an elite class of a specific age. The excellent genes of the ancestors are there, and the family is usually not bad. And my grandmother is still the poorest family in the whole big village, or a very unfortunate family, her own eyes are still blind.

At the moment, I am thinking, grandma doesn't want to be a person who can help others. after all, she is happier than she is. however, her fate is not as good as her wish. when she was a child, she worked long-term for others. when she was old, she still had to be favored by others.

Grandma often said in front of our sisters: "Pity your father for leaving early, otherwise you will not be worse than your children of the same age in food and clothing. Your father is more diligent and works day and night. The days are getting better and better. Other people have some, and our family also has some. Unfortunately, people are not strong enough!"

Every time I listen to grandma rambling on about the past countless times, as long as I don't respond for a while, she will touch 1 hand: "are you still listening to me? Fan'er, are you there?"

Grandma is also a strong person, life is not strong!

Grandma said to us countless times before her death: "My blind grandmother has nothing. She can't see her fingers. She can't help you a little. She also needs you to take care of me. Only after I die, I must bless you..."

Most of the time, grandma groped alone by the pond to carry water in a small iron bucket, wash clothes and cook, and grow vegetables in the vegetable field at the door. I can't imagine how my blind grandmother can do this!

Sometimes on weekends, grandma asked me to help carry dung to the vegetable field and water the vegetables, giving me 20 cents each time.

Her money is her uncle's pocket money to buy her oil. She dug it out of her teeth and pasted it to our family in disguise. Most of them encourage us to work.

Our sister's firewood on the mountain is 100kg at the market price of 10 yuan. She will weigh her, take her to the vegetable field, carry water and dung. She will give us 1.0 money. We will get the treasure.

Grandma said that buying firewood from others is also money, which is not as good as earning money for her granddaughter. It is also good to buy books and pens, which also improves their enthusiasm for doing things.

In retrospect, the first object of my life was to work for my own grandmother.

I still remember the kind smile of grandma and I carrying the firewood scale. We can get dozens of catties of loose wood a day on Sunday. As a child, I can exchange my labor for money. I am very happy and have a sense of accomplishment.

When my grandmother was young, she should have been a person with sharp and angular features, double eyelids and big eyes, and a very kind-hearted person.

I have seen many times that the beggars she gave were all half full of rice poured into their bags, while others only grabbed a little rice with their hands to send the beggars away.

Grandma said that I am a bad karma person, and I love bitter people.

Grandma is tall, beautiful, capable and strong, but her era and family failed to give her a little chance, let alone a smooth fate. She doesn't know a single character, nor does my father.

My grandfather died when my grandmother was middle-aged. It was a hard life and a miserable life.

Under the fate of motionless, what power is in control of the fate of people, the strong is fate after all!

In winter, grandma said it was 1 torture. The emaciated grandmother is most afraid of the cold. She said that she has no blood on her body and is more afraid of the cold when she is old.

In the twelfth month of the first year she left, I went back to my hometown to see her. At night, I packed thermos bottles for her and put them in her bed. Grandma was very excited and satisfied.

In 2012, Grandma passed away on the second day of the winter solstice. It is said that she was dead when her uncle delivered the meal in the morning.

In the southern countryside without air conditioning, electric blankets and heating, she did not go through that winter, and I wandered outside to make a living. I don't know what I thought back then. I didn't go back to grandma's funeral. Was I doing early business in Xi 'an that year, reluctant to go out of business, or reluctant to pay the fare? Anyway, I didn't go back, which became a pity in my life. If it is now, it will fly back anyway.

In another parallel world, I hope my dear grandmother will no longer have misery, poverty and grief. Have health and happiness, ears and eyes, can read and read, can have a good everything.

Because of grandma, every old man I see is like her; because of grandma, I become a good person.

# The power of the fate god

Some readers and friends once said that most of the bloggers on the Internet came from ordinary families, but you really came from the grass-roots family at the bottom. You are extremely resilient and it is not easy.

There are countless people in society who may have similar backgrounds or unfortunate experiences, and most of them may get stuck in the quagmire, unable to climb out, and no longer have the courage to pursue their dreams...

In fact, who does not want to have a smooth life, a smooth fate? All of them are cause and effect in previous lives. In reincarnation, there will always be misfortune befall someone or a family.

A person's birth area and family environment, early everything, how can an individual choose? It's all fate!

People all say that suffering is wealth. If I could choose, I wouldn't want such wealth! I have no choice!

## 01

Anhui Shucheng and Tongcheng this hot land together gave birth to us.

My mother was born in 1963, and she was the only one of the seven siblings who did not attend a day of school. My aunt also read 1. second grade.

She is from Shucheng, Lu'an, Anhui, and her grandmother's house is the kind of big ravine that opens doors and rings around the mountains.

My father was the only one of the four brothers who didn't go to school. Uncle also read the second grade. My father was born in the countryside on the outskirts of Tongcheng, Anqing, Anhui.

The 15-year-old mother and 32-year-old father were introduced to each other. A family hopes to marry outside the mountain, find a breakthrough for poor families, and at least exchange some food to supplement the family, even if it is good to have two loads of rice a year.

A family is poor, illiterate, old and difficult to find. I look forward to visiting a simple, honest and obedient girl from a poor family in a mountainous area to complete the mission of carrying on the family line.

It can be said that my mother and father were victims of their respective extended families. In those years when it was a luxury to eat well, how many people could have the right to choose their own destiny?

My father and mother got married a few years later and completed their life events.

So this they combined together, with our sisters 3 one.

When I was a child, the middle distance from Tongcheng to Shucheng was to take a tricycle, which was dusty and dusty. I had to walk for a long time at both ends. The road to the other end of Shucheng is really called the eighteen bends of the mountain road. It turns around and can't always see the head. Therefore, it takes a year or two for my mother to go back to her mother's family.

Sometimes, in order to save money on traveling expenses, her mother walked all the way and started to set off before dawn.

In the early years, the traffic was not developed, and everyone lived a very difficult life. Relatives seldom met. I had never seen my aunt's cousin look like before I was 15.

Due to the long distance and inconvenient transportation, my sister-in-law used to be in poor health and suffered from carsickness. It was not until my mother died in 2002 that she came to my house for the first time.

Later, the road to Shucheng was improved. At the junction of Shucheng and Tongcheng, there was a stone tablet saying: The asphalt road here is Tongcheng, and the dirt road over there is Shucheng, which is obviously divided. That is the talk that Tongcheng people are proud. In those years, Tongcheng was much superior to Shucheng in terms of economic development.

After all, there are many private enterprises in Tongcheng. We can meet brush factories and plastic bag factories in the wrong way in our town, which is called "the hometown of Chinese brushes". 60% of the brushes come from our place.

A few years later, the roads on both sides of Shucheng and Tongcheng are already cement roads, and there are also many direct vehicles.

Shucheng is now known as "the back garden of Hefei". Tongcheng is already neck and neck, both cities with beautiful scenery and profound cultural heritage, and both are important talent production places in Anhui.

Under the introduction of my sister-in-law, my second sister started a family and lived in Shucheng. Shucheng is now the place where I go more frequently than when I was a child.

Time passed quickly, and we were also middle-aged. I became a self-media person and a full-time writer. Second sister is a white-collar worker in the company, and her sideline is a photographer and a food blogger. We are all self-taught the day after tomorrow.

## 02

In 2004, I went home to recuperate due to massive hemoptysis.

In the second half of the year, I bought a mobile phone, Nokia blue screen mobile phone 1200 yuan, which was my savings when I worked in Fujian the previous year. At that time, I was recuperating at home and my colleagues were making money outside, but I was spending money. My heart was infinitely sad. I also had a time of grief and indignation over the injustice of heaven and the stinginess of fate.

When I was in a garment factory, I always wanted to get a high salary, always wanted to get the first place or the first few places. Due to physical reasons, I had to stop. When I went to my hometown, I spent a long time doing psychological construction. I had to accept the fact that my body could not match the overloaded labor intensity in the factory.

I read in a magazine that sometimes, God makes you 1 a minor illness because you are too tired and want you to have a rest...

I will take a step back to think about this matter and treat the unfortunate things in front of me from a positive angle.

When Fujian was diagnosed with tuberculosis, the doctor said that there are now relevant hospitals everywhere, which can be treated free of charge. There are exclusive institutions everywhere, which are funded by Japan, and the global treatment of such diseases is free. Before I returned to my hometown, my third uncle had already helped me find out the specific location of our exclusive treatment facility in Tongcheng.

I think that in the past years, many celebrities had such a good family history and had the same disease, which could not be cured for many years. In the past, it was called "consumption". In the early decades, many people in rural areas died of this disease.

I was just lucky to be born decades later than them, and in my time, this kind of disease was just a bad cold, and it was completely cured in half a year to a year.

People in rural areas are also called "rich and noble diseases". It is only when they eat well and drink well that they do not do things quickly.

Those six months were indeed the most leisure time since I was an adult. I ate, played and slept. The few magazines at hand are all written and painted by me, and the diary is also full of sentences, with no chapters. At that time, it was too boring.

Later, I simply did not think that so many of my fellow colleagues were working hard outside, and I was sitting at home, and I no longer compared with anyone to save money, make money, and save money. All the new colleagues I know in my hometown have mobile phones, so I l gritted my teeth and bought one.

The new colleagues I know in my hometown and the colleagues in Fujian factory have completely different consumption views.

03

When I handed my cell phone to my grandmother, she touched it in her hand, stroked it repeatedly, took it back and forth, and shook it with her hand, smiling.

Grandma said, "This thing has no wires. How can you make a phone call? Can you hear the words? Where did the voice come from? Telephone and cable are understandable. What treasure is this?"

My grandmother began to sigh again: "You people are really good. You have enjoyed the blessings of the times and the light of the party."

It is said that the descendants of poor families have a deep love for teachers, which is certainly reasonable.

In 2007, I made an assembly line in a women's clothing factory on the edge of Wenzhou Chashan University Town. The colleague sitting in front of me and another colleague did not know how to talk about the teacher, saying that they could not figure out why his head was on the RMB, and that he was not a teacher. He had already driven a BMW...

I sat in the back while making clothes and listening to their conversation. I was so angry that I wrangle with them.

Although reading is limited and knowledge of history is limited, this love for teachers is already 1 belief from the soul, from the seeds planted by my grandmother when I was very small. That is God's existence!

Grandma said that we were weaving cloth at that time and got up at 3 4 o'clock every morning to weave cloth. She pointed to the textile cart on the wooden building: "Rice is eaten by beating and forged by hand every day (in our local dialect, rice is ground by hand). Everywhere you go, you 1 measure one, two, one with your feet. Firewood is chopped and burned up the mountain. At that time, there were many people who needed firewood, and only deeper mountains could get firewood..."

Grandma had someone to send a telegram and someone to write a letter for her to contact her uncle. For the new communication tool-mobile phone, the old man can't accept it for a while.

In 1996, Tongcheng County, Anhui Province, where I was located, was changed to a county-level city. In those years, there were 8 counties and 1 city under the jurisdiction of Anqing, and that city was our Tongcheng city. People chatted and said that Tongcheng's economic growth rate was faster than that of Anqing ancient city.

On the night when the county was changed into a city, fireworks and movies were set off everywhere, which made it feel lively and prosperous. Individuals and families seem to be getting better as well.

My village partner and I also went to the gate of the village branch to watch a movie together with our classmates from the village. It seemed that we were all proud of the change of our hometown from "county" to "city". In fact, we were just joining in the fun.

The other day, when we were watching an open-air movie, people didn't know how to talk about the 1 topic of "fairness. I concluded with the 1 sentence: "Only death is fair to everyone."

In 1998, there was a bus directly to Tongcheng Square not far from our door. At that time, the fare was one yuan and it took nearly 20 minutes by car. In other words, it takes 5 six minutes to walk from our village to the bus station and there is a direct bus to the city.

In 1998, the year of severe floods, crop production was greatly reduced. A lot of relief clothes have been distributed in the village. We are like a treasure. They are much better than our usual clothes. They are fashionable and fashionable. That is not without the help of good people in the city.

We often have to go to the street to sell vegetables to live, the family never buy vegetables, let alone eat meat dishes. The vegetables in the vegetable plot have to be saved and sold to subsidize their lives. (Unless pigs go into the water when killing pigs, chicken fever or ploughs come to work, the food is better)

In the 3 year of junior high school, I ate pickles brought from home in the morning at noon every day. The family members of the school teachers sell the prepared dishes and sell them beside the canteen. They still remember that the vegetable leaves and bean curd soup are 1 for 30 cents, which is 1 iron ladle. If there is a little minced meat in the dish, it is 1 5 dime. For 3 years, I only envy others for having the money to buy fresh dishes.

Especially the students in the town, there is actually one person who will bring two dishes and spend money to buy fresh vegetables to eat. I think they are all lucky people outside the sky. They are really from a different world from me.

In 1998, the rice fell to a share in 35 yuan, and the people in the village sighed. It is said that the sharp drop in rice was due to the impact of the Asian financial crisis, which made farmers bear most of the burden.

Since ancient times, if there is a tragedy of the times in any period, the bottom people must be the most bitter, life is certainly worse. This has always been the case, this is an indisputable fact.

Grandma said she used to pick firewood to sell on Tongcheng Street, all on foot. She said: "You are really good now. You go to the street to buy something, there are buses, bicycles or motorcycles. Your generation is really lucky."

Your grandfather's biggest dream was when he could eat enough rice. He said, "How delicious the rice is! It was a dream he had never dreamed. Your grandfather only needs to live 10 more years to realize it. He only needs to live 10 more years!"

Grandma also often mentioned that she could pick firewood faster than men in those days, and she could not lose any farm work to anyone in the whole village.

At the moment, I am thinking that if grandma lived in our present age, she would certainly live a much better life and perhaps achieve a small career. Even if a person has the ability again, also must have the big environment to support. A person is very small and powerless in front of the times. Individual destiny and the times are closely related.

Even now, if some big people in our society or around us were born in some countries in the Middle East, they may not be able to have everything they have now.

Looking back now, when I was recuperating at home, I didn't tell my grandmother that I was ill, and I don't know if anyone in the village mentioned it. Grandma didn't ask me why I suddenly came back.

In 2004, I had the most time with my grandmother since I dropped out of school. Later, every year only a few days at home during the Chinese New Year, visiting her and listening to her chat.

If I knew that I could become a professional writer in the future, I should have taken a small notebook and recorded every word my grandmother said.

Be thankful for all the grace of fate, good or bad.

# That year in the town school tailor time

In 1999, because there was not much sewing work at home, my family introduced me through acquaintances and asked me to go to the town's master to learn sewing technology. I ride my weighted bike to town every day, which takes about 40-odd minutes one way.

Shifu is the 1 tall 32-year-old beauty, known as one of the four beauties in town. At that time, there were already six senior sisters in her store, and I was the last one to join. Shifu was the first tailor in the town to operate cloth and the first tailor shop to carry out curtain business.

On the other side of the main road opposite the tailor shop, there is a wire brush processing factory, where my primary school and junior high school classmate Chen Jindi works. It is said that she can earn nearly 4000 yuan a year, which is a relatively prosperous brush industry in our town, attracting many outsiders to work in the town.

Later, I didn't know which year, I heard that Chen Jindi froze to death under the bridge one winter due to mental disorder, which made me sigh and silent for a long time. Recall that in 1999, when we were young girls, we met on the road, talking and laughing while riding bicycles, full of fantasies about the future. Things change, life changes.

When I was an apprentice, I paid a deposit of 100 yuan and brought my own sewing machine. Because there are already several senior sisters in front of me, my new apprentice, my daily work is mainly to do odd jobs: unpacking and washing, mending, locking holes, picking feet and ironing clothes. What I do most is to help the master with housework, such as sweeping the floor, mopping the floor, wiping the floor, taking care of the children and washing clothes. At that time, the master's family had two daughters, the oldest was 8 years old and the youngest was over 2 years old.

The master's little daughter is very cute and her skin is white and tender. I often hold her hand in the street, sometimes holding her in the back street around. I remember once, the teacher asked me to take my baby out to play and buy some wangwang snow cakes. I tasted the snow cake a little bit and found it very crisp and fragrant. At that time, I sighed that there were such delicious snacks in the world, which made me long aftertaste. At that time, I secretly thought that if I had money in the future, I must eat enough.

At that time, this idea was sincere, but now, even if the snow cake is in front of me, I have no desire to eat it.

On another occasion, the teacher asked me to take the baby out to play and buy a few catties of fruit. I specially took the master's baby to my aunt near the station to buy fruit. When she saw it, she was frightened and worried that it was too dangerous for me to take such a lovely child across the road. She told me not to bring my baby to buy fruit from her next time.

My aunt is a compassionate person and is very kind to everyone. She will not treat my grandmother differently because she is a weak family in the village, nor will she treat her badly because she is blind. Instead, she will take care of my grandmother in all aspects. Now I finally understand why she cared so much.

There is a master sister named Hai Xia in the master's family. She has been following the master for many years and has been able to make clothes independently. At that time, the master gave her 250 yuan a month to help her with her work, which was equivalent to our "little master". The master often goes to Anqing to purchase goods. When he is not at home, senior sister Haixia is responsible for many things.

That year, I didn't learn much about making clothes. On one occasion, I put on a waistband. As a result, the waistband of my clothes was twisted and very uneven. The teacher asked me to tear it down. She put it back on the waistband and let me watch. Since then, the master has never done any technical work for me. I continue to do odd jobs and take care of children.

In addition to having no money, I have a very simple and relaxed life every day. See seniors buy instant noodles to do snacks, I can only envy. If I go back and ask for money, my mother will keep saying, I don't study now, why do I need money? I also don't think I can open my mouth, besides, my family really has no money.

There is also a little elder sister Qiuxiang, her home is not too far from the town. I have been to her home, her sister is very good, is our school at the beginning of that year top-notch students, the whole school famous. At that time, her sister was already studying for a master's degree at Anshi University and received a scholarship every year. This little elder sister has many books bought by her sister, including "How Steel Is Made" and several thread-binding books, such as "Selected Works of Mao Zedong". That was the first time I really read a masterpiece, a rough reading of "how the steel is tempered".

A few years later, in a clothing factory in Fujian, Xiao Qiu, who was sitting beside my station, was also from the village of the little senior sister. I asked her about the little elder sister. She said that her sister later studied for a doctor's degree and developed very well. She also brought her sister up. Said my little senior sister also developed well later.

At the master's house, I also saw the "Reader" magazine for the first time. There are single books and annual collections. When the master is not at home, I sometimes look through. There are also essays by Bi Shumin and Liang Xiaosheng in the desk drawer where the master cut the clothes. I have seen some of them.

One December a few years ago, when I passed the town again, where I had learned tailoring skills, I instinctively looked around, only to find that everything had changed. I didn't see my master. Even if I met her by chance, she might not recognize me. Maybe I can still vaguely recognize her figure.

In the past 20 years or so, I have never met those six senior sisters again. Life is long and hasty, like passers-by, we each hurried forward. In the course of the years, the beautiful people and things that I met when I was young have gradually become blurred, but I hope to record them in words. Let these memories be perpetuated in my words.

# The past is like smoke-stepfather

Many things do not want to recall too much, memory also automatically blocked many details.

I can't remember when my stepfather came to my house. During his years in my family, he didn't spend much time at home every year. He worked outside all the year round, mainly doing coolies on the construction site, so his memory was not deep.

I only remember the day when my stepfather officially moved to my house from the village next door, a simple ceremony was held. At that time, I was still young and played with my sisters in the village. I said I also wanted to make a bride, holding adobe in my hand. One side of the village sister laughed: "Do you know which one is watching tonight?"

I was puzzled. They said, "That's your mother!"

I only remember that piece. In fact, I should not be too young at that time. I don't know why, I don't remember many things clearly when I was a child.

After my father died, many people suggested giving my little sister away so that the family could be more relaxed and even contacted, but my mother could not bear it.

Later, from time to time, someone introduced someone to my mother. I remember one of them was a pig killer in his 40 s and 50 s. He looked uncomfortable and his hair was very greasy, which made people afraid. Fortunately, my mother did not agree.

Grandma and brother-in-law both advised their mother not to remarry and stay in Laoqi House Village, where there are acquaintances. People in a village are all named Qi, and everyone can take care of each other. Although there are also some bad places, it is better than going to the outer village by my mother alone.

At that time, our family had 3 adobe houses, with yards, fields, windmills, electric fans, and our sisters were all around. If the mother remarries, it is impossible for others to accept so many children at once, not to mention that the mother is a person who attaches great importance to the family.

She followed her grandmother's advice and was wise to stay in the old house of Qi.

In the past years, women often choose to marry when they have no way out, while men may passively divorce when they have no way out.

In this context, my stepfather came to my house. He is from the village next door. I heard that he was introduced by his stepfather's cousin. He believes that although there are 3 children in our family, it is better than one person. At least there is a home and hope.

My stepfather's surname is Xie. He is a man who has never been married. He is tall and handsome. He is 6 years older than my mother. He looks younger than my mother. He is also illiterate, but he is very nice, especially clean and diligent.

In my impression, he would tidy himself up every day, and the towels at home, even if they were very old, were always flat.

In retrospect, there may have been real feelings between mother and stepfather. After all, when my father was introduced to my mother, she was only 15 years old. She didn't understand anything. She was completely at the disposal of my grandmother and family.

When my father was alive, he worked in a ceramic factory and would do farm work sooner or later. His monthly salary would be paid to his mother. My father is 17 years older than my mother. I heard that he loves his mother very much.

My mother also told me that when she was undergoing sterilization in the village branch, her father was watching out the window and cried with heartache.

The stepfather and mother have a small age gap and they seem very loving. The stepfather is too honest. He does the heaviest work on the construction site, but he has the lowest salary. He is not at home all year round and will only come back when the farm is busy. Even more frustrating, he was often not paid, which was common at the time.

When I worked on weekends and summer vacations in the fifth grade, my daily income was close to my stepfather's, and my money would not be less. It was a small processing factory run by my neighbor's brother, and the salary was very reliable.

Sometimes, the second and younger sisters go to help count beer cones after school in the afternoon and work for two or 3 hours. Those adults will advance cash to us in advance.

They also said with a smile that a few children working for a few hours in the evening would be enough money to buy a notebook for a week.

My mother and stepfather see that we can read and do things flexibly, so we can make money when we are young, and we are no less than adults. The neighbors often praise our sisters in front of them.

They seem to think that we will be more promising than them in the future and are very tolerant of us. I am the one who likes to talk back and be naughty. They have to let me go and even be a little afraid of me.

The one where I worked at the weekend was the first one in the village to have a telephone. I remember that it cost 2500 yuan to install it. The telephones of the surrounding neighbors were all transferred from his home. Their family is warm-hearted and very nice.

My stepfather seldom took to the streets with his colleagues to make phone calls. My cousin called me and my mother to pick it up. My stepfather's first sentence was: "How are the pigs at home?"

It became a long-running joke among his colleagues.

His colleagues are all migrant workers, carrying large bags and small bags to various construction sites in the first month of each year. Lucky people can bring back some wages, and good old people like stepfathers often work for nothing.

Grandma also praised her stepfather, and her stepfather was also good to grandma. If he can get paid on the construction site, he will bring 1 small gifts to everyone, and give them to grandma if there is something delicious, and he will rush to do it when he sees work.

I don't know why, I'm not very impressed with him, and I don't spend much time with him. He stayed in my house for about seven or eight years.

Later, I fell off the cart on the construction site. I heard that my brains fell out and died. My mother was sad for a long time.

At that time, I was working as an apprentice in Fujian. After receiving a letter from my second sister, I learned that my stepfather had passed away for several months.

I still remember the second sister said in the letter: "Uncle has left this beautiful world, and my sister must work harder to make money..."

After the death of his stepfather, the village cadres and brother-in-law took his mother to the construction site where the accident occurred. My mother was illiterate and her expression ability was not very good. They let her cry when she saw the contractor. Finally, the construction site gave more than 30,000 yuan for burial.

A few years later, my mother fell ill. Some fortune tellers said they missed her stepfather too much, while others said that both her father and stepfather were pestering her.

Do not know in another world, whether they met again?

# I am a contradictory person.

There seems to be a lot of contradictions in me. Many people praise me for my good memory. My sister, my friends, and many former colleagues all say so, but I have never felt that I have a good memory.

During adolescence, in the clothing factory, I was working as an inspector with some fellow villagers for a while. Our factory has many branch factories, and the clothes from the sub-processing factories have to be inspected by the old employees when they get to our general factory. The inspector's job is to sit on the inspection table in the warehouse workshop, see what's wrong with the finished clothes, and stick yellow gummed paper as a mark to make people rework, such as unevenness, jumper needle leakage, asymmetry, etc.

I still remember that at that time, it was 30 yuan a day to be an inspector, and then it rose to 40 yuan a day. It was fixed and did not follow the piece rate. Naturally, it was much easier than making clothes. Talking with colleagues while working does not affect income. At that time, a fellow named Xiaoqiu sat next to me. She was from a town in our hometown. Her skin was very fair and tender, and she looked very charming and lovely.

She once received the 1 letter and put it on my side after reading it. I asked, "Can I see it?" She said, "Yes." I looked at it roughly. A few days later, when we talked about the letter again, I repeated the main contents 1 times from beginning to end. She was greatly surprised: "How can you remember so well? Xiao Qi, he has the ability to never forget anything!" I don't remember at all.

In fact, I am only selective memory. For abstract things, the sense of direction is very poor, super road crazy, and digital blindness, how to remember attentively, always can't remember. There's 3 a fork in the door and I get lost. Not modesty, but never really think you have a good memory.

I don't remember much before the age of 15. Some people say that people who can embark on the road of writing have a sensitive and delicate heart, but I am extremely insensitive to many times. My parents never shed tears when they died. When my mother died, it was still my second sister who cried at the edge, and my sister who cried at the edge of her bad karma. There was a short 1, tearing my heart and lungs. I was brought to cry by them.

Because my mother was married across regions and counties, her family was far apart. My sister was carsick and in poor health. It was not until my mother died that my sister came to my house for the first time. I don't know if her heart has ever regretted that she had not overcome difficulties to see her sister who was honest and hard-working married far away.

I am a person who feels extremely blunt about pain and misfortune, which is also beneficial invisibly. For others, it seems to be suffering and cannot be crossed, but for me, it is completely numb, as if it has nothing to do with my individual life.

Many years later, I became the 1 full-time writer, I still have a lot of tangled contradictions. Sometimes I want to be a writer with peace of mind, without live broadcast, video, community, etc., but under the cruel social environment, I can't have income to support it. If you want to bury yourself in writing well, there is a way out. In fact, there are many people who write better than us. Even if you are excellent, there are also a lot of excellent people in the society. This is the essence of the inner volume.

I can only combine literary and artistic behavior with commercial thinking to make money to feed my dream, just like the title of my book "Moon on the Left Hand, Sixpence on the Right Hand: Life in the Way I Like". Hopefully, in the near future, I'll be able to support myself on the royalty income from books. I just need to read and write quietly every day. It will be my supreme glory and the best dream.

# She was born with a disability and was born in the countryside. In her third year of online entrepreneurship, she achieved an annual income of one million.

She was born with a disability and was born in a rural area. In her third year of online entrepreneurship, she achieved an annual income of one million. This is a very magical story, as I once said that sentence: the legend is not in the sky, the legend is around.

Knowing the story of Enron's growth, you will feel that movies are not even dare to be made like this. It is true that art comes from life, but sometimes it is not as wonderful as real life.

She is 4 one meter tall, her spine is naturally curved and her body is deformed. Since she was a child, she spent her childhood and adolescence in loneliness without playmates or peers.

She said her dream was to be a teacher. The students all laughed at her: "You are not as tall as the podium, and you still want to be a teacher?" Some boys stopped her after school and laughed: "How did you grow up like this? You are a dwarf..."

When people in the village are talking about her and pointing fingers at her, some villagers will also suggest: "It is better to throw away such a child..."

But Enron's grandmother planted the seeds of love and faith for her. Every time someone looked at her with a strange look, grandma would say to her: "child, you must be the Buddha sent to the world, don't care what others think of you, study hard, you will become a very powerful person..." Every time Enron with tears, hard nodded.

When I was a child, when Enron was playing alone outside, as long as she saw her mother's figure, she hurried back because her mother would scold her. Her mother always said, "It's a shame to have such a monster daughter. "If it weren't for grandma's love, her mother would want to throw her away.

When Enron went to college, he envied others to fall in love. Seeing that others are all in pairs, she is alone, but she also knows her actual situation.

Her classmates have also introduced her to the object, others see, without saying a few words, will say: "I have something to go first. "

She has also registered a number of dating sites, are similar results. She was ready for a lifetime of celibacy.

When she no longer had any hope, she began to study at ease and worked part-time as a tutor on weekends, one day she met a man who was now her husband when she handed out leaflets outside. At that time, he opened a training institution outside school, and Enron was a graduate 2 student. The boy took good care of her. The next day, he set up an office class for her. From the day he met Enron, this man regarded her as the person who would take care of his company in his future life.

Her classmates, in turn, came to envy Enron. Some classmates and boyfriends have changed several times, some are still single, saying that Enron has reached the top match at one time, that is, they are rushing to get married, and they are such handsome people, small business owners, and so kind to Enron.

When Enron was about to get married, her 20-year-old brother died in a traffic accident, and the family was plunged into great grief. Enron and her husband to discuss, they married to live in Enron's family.

The patriarchal atmosphere on their side is very serious. In fact, her husband is an only child. We admire the big pattern of her husband and her parents, tolerance, and support all the ideas and decisions of her son.

Enron's parents drove buses and later also went into the coal business. Her husband thinks it's too bad to waste shredded powder. He wants to use these to sell honeycomb briquettes. He plans to do activities first and then sell them. The leaflets had already been sent out. When the people from the village came to collect them, Enron's mother stopped others outside, saying that it was not a gift and could only be bought with money. Enron's husband was very helpless and felt that he was thinking about them everywhere, but he could not get any affirmation.

Because Enron's husband's business sales philosophy is different from Enron's parents, there have been some minor disputes. Enron was on her parents' side every time. At that time, their husband and wife also fell into confrontation and confusion.

It was not until after Enron taught herself psychology that she slowly realized her husband's difficulty and saw his many efforts.

While they were still dating, Enron's mother asked her to borrow money from her current husband. At that time, her husband was still a young man living in the basement. After hearing Enron's request, he swiped 10 credit cards and collected 30,000 yuan to change 1 new buses for Enron's family.

Enron recalled her husband's support for her along the way. She proposed not to live at her mother's home and to live with her husband in the city to avoid the unhappiness caused by the age generation gap and thinking habits.

A group of 1 of us listened to Mr. Enron's story on the spot, and we always felt that real movies were afraid to be made like this. We didn't know whether the novel was illuminated into reality or whether reality was written into the novel?

Enron has also been studying psychology and energetics since then. The psychology she is doing now has extremely strong energy, which has made many small partners realize through sideline. Under Enron's powerful energy blessing, many people changed their fate. They all called Enron teacher their noble.

It is not simple for people who can do a good job in the network sideline. What is tested is people's empathy, transformation, content, marketing, etc., and the ultimate sales is personal energy.

In her third year as a sideline on the Internet, Enron realized a million-dollar annual income. How did she do it?

Enron teacher in the case of a monthly salary of 5000 yuan, with two months' salary to sign up line class study. Every time she participates in a community, she earns 10 times her tuition. This courage and courage is not available to everyone.

She uses every penny with ROI thinking, realizes self-appreciation, constantly breaks the circle, dares to think and do, and can learn and sell now, and sell very well.

In itself, Enron teacher is a 10-year educator and a secondary psychological consultant. She has learned all kinds of online knowledge, such as copywriting, circle of friends transactions, marketing systems, etc. She has integrated these knowledge points to form her own unique Enron education system, which has helped many people increase their income by 10 to 40 times.

She understands psychology, has strong energy, is very good at oral expression, is also good at providing emotional value, and has strong empathy. In fact, most of the time, online education sells its own energy and future expectations.

Last month, a Zhejiang customer, who was also the 1 teacher in school, paid Enron teacher 150000 yuan in one lump sum to learn from Enron teacher. This is also the personality charm of Enron teacher. After all, no one's money came from the strong wind. Money is also an exchange of value and energy.

Enron teacher has only been working as a sideline on the internet for 3 years, and has achieved a million-dollar annual income. The line she ran was over, and many people flew to Shandong on purpose just to see Mr. Enron with their own eyes.

She said that in the future, she would consider setting up an Enron Education Foundation to help out-of-school children return to school. She would travel seven continents and give speeches around the world. Like Nick Huzhe, she would make more people stand up again and ignite more dreams.

Enron teacher always emphasizes that people should be grateful. Grateful people are easy to meet noble people. Noble people not only bring opportunities, but also bring more important resources, bringing new horizons.

That's what she said and did. Get along with her, like a spring breeze, warm and enthusiastic, she is also very willing to people, really practice the concept of giving up to get.

She said that if you continue to give value to others and continue to give, you will naturally gain good popularity, fans, noble people and opportunities. From a marketing perspective, altruistic is the top sales strategy.

When her peers, that is, most teachers, were standing still, Enron teachers had been studying and improving for so many years. When she integrates this new knowledge into the classroom, she can give students more inspiration and become a more special teacher. She let a lot of tired teenagers back to school, many later read a doctor.

Teacher Enron said, don't let your future life be sorry for the suffering you have endured! Empower with love and drive life energy with life energy! Influence more people upward to good, to achieve personal value amplification of 100 times.

I very much believe that on the day when teacher Enron can give a speech at a global university, countless listeners will be shocked by her wonderful speech, and many people will use her light to walk out of the darkest moments of life, find their own mission, and then live a warm bloom.

(ps: teacher Enron did not have good congenital qualifications. when she was studying, the class representative helped her to talk about math problems. after three times, she was still confused and still could not solve the problems. The representative of the class shook his head helplessly and said, "You seem to have lost a muscle. "Enron teacher could not accept it for countless times because of her poor study. She believed that her physical disability was congenital and could not be changed, but her poor school performance was her own reason. She struggled to take the college entrance examination twice before barely going to college, but Enron teacher may be a late person who passed the postgraduate entrance examination once. In 2012, he was admitted to the establishment teacher of the local key middle school with the first result. It is not too late to dream in life. God will treat people with strong tenacity.)

www.ingramcontent.com/pod-product-compliance
Lightning Source LLC
Chambersburg PA
CBHW080321080526
44585CB00021B/2431